ACTS
...AND THEY CONTINUED

A COMMENTARY BY
CARROLL ROBERSON

Published by Innovo Publishing, LLC
www.innovopublishing.com
1-888-546-2111

Providing Full-Service Publishing Services for Christian Authors, Artists & Ministries: Books, eBooks, Audiobooks, Music, Screenplays, Film & Curricula

ACTS
. . . And They Continued

Copyright © 2022 by Carroll Roberson
All rights reserved.

No part of this publication may be reproduced, stored in a retrieval system, or transmitted in any form or by any means electronic, mechanical, photocopying, recording, or otherwise, without the prior written permission of the Author. All scripture is taken from the King James Version (KJV) of the Bible. Public domain.

ISBN: 978-1-61314-817-4

Cover Design & Interior Layout: Innovo Publishing, LLC

Printed in the United States of America
U.S. Printing History
First Edition: 2022

Has God called you to create a Christian book, eBook, audiobook, music album, screenplay, film, or curricula? If so, visit the ChristianPublishingPortal.com to learn how to accomplish your calling with excellence. Learn to do everything yourself, or hire trusted Christian Experts from our Marketplace to help.

CONTENTS

Introduction vii

Chapter One 1
Chapter Two 19
Chapter Three 44
Chapter Four 55
Chapter Five 70
Chapter Six 91
Chapter Seven 101
Chapter Eight 123
Chapter Nine 141
Chapter Ten 161
Chapter Eleven 181
Chapter Twelve 190
Chapter Thirteen 203
Chapter Fourteen 222
Chapter Fifteen 232
Chapter Sixteen 249
Chapter Seventeen 268

Chapter Eighteen 286
Chapter Nineteen 301
Chapter Twenty 318
Chapter Twenty-One 334
Chapter Twenty-Two 354
Chapter Twenty-Three 366
Chapter Twenty-Four 379
Chapter Twenty-Five 389
Chapter Twenty-Six 400
Chapter Twenty-Seven 412
Chapter Twenty-Eight 426

Extra Biblical Resources of Paul & Peter 439
A Note from the Editors 442

INTRODUCTION

The book of Acts is an exciting journey of the first followers of Jesus the Messiah. It is extremely valuable as we see the works of Jesus throughout the four gospels *continued* through the work of the Holy Spirit, or the *Ruach HaKodesh*. It serves as a bridge between the four Gospels and the Epistles. Acts covers a period of over 30 years between the mid-30's AD to the mid-60's AD. The Jewish Community who knew and believed that Jesus was the Messiah was unstoppable. They persevered even though they were persecuted and scattered throughout the known world. The Holy Spirit, the third person of the Triune Godhead, is mentioned more than 50 times. After the nation of Israel committed the unpardonable sin in **Matthew 12**, the *Kingdom Parables* of **Matthew 13** come to fruition in a more precise way as we journey through the 28 chapters of the book of Acts. Because it is a *transitional* book containing both Jewish believers and later Gentile believers, there have been many false doctrines that have divided the body of Christ over the years. We will mention these as we go through the verses and explain them within their context. Doctrine must *not* be developed from the historical incidents in the book of Acts.

Author & Date

There is overwhelming evidence that the book of Acts was written by Luke who also wrote the gospel of Luke, one of the four gospels. There are over 700 Greek words used in Luke's gospel and in the book of Acts that do not appear elsewhere in the New Testament. Luke is believed to have been a Hellenized Jew who had perfect understanding of the events that occurred during the life of the first Church and was a traveling companion of the Apostle Paul and was also imprisoned with Paul.

"Luke, the beloved physician" **- Colossians 4:14**

"Only Luke is with me" **- 2 Timothy 4:11**

There are three times in the book of Acts that Luke changes the first-person pronoun to *"we."* **(Acts 16:10-17, 20:5-21:18, and 27:1-28:16)** The author Luke knew first hand many of the other workers, such as Timothy, **(16:1)** Silas, **(16:9)** Sopater, **(20:4)** Aristarchus, **(20:4, 27:2)** Secundas, **(20:4)** Gaius, **(20:4)** Tychichus, **(20:4)** and Trophimus **(20:4)**. It is commonly believed that Luke was the pastor of the church in Philippi for six years.

The early leaders and historians *after* the book of Acts was written confirmed that Luke was the author. These included: Irenaeus, (130-200AD) Clement of Alexandria, (150-215AD) Origen, (185-254AD) and Tertullian (160-200AD).

Luke was a careful historian who included biographical and geographical details. There are around 80 references to the geography in the Roman world, and he mentions over 100 people by name. While Luke was writing in Koine Greek, which was the common language in the Roman world, he was thinking in Hebrew. **(Acts 21:2, 26:14)** Luke may have received the accounts in Hebrew, either written or oral, and translated them to Greek. His knowledge of Jewish holidays and Temple traditions go beyond that of a mere historian. Luke weaves quotations from the Old Testament to show his familiarity of the Torah, the Prophets, the Psalms, and historical writings. It proves that he was a longtime student of the sacred scriptures. The physician Luke also used unique medical terms in several places throughout the book. **(Acts 1:3, 3:7-9, 9:18, 33, 13:11, 28:1-10)**

There are no illusions to four important events that occurred after Paul's imprisonment, such as:

* *The burning of Rome and the persecution of the believers by Nero in 64AD*
* *The martyrdom of Peter and Paul in 67AD*
* *The destruction of the Temple in Jerusalem in 70AD*
* *Jewish Christians fleeing to Pella in the Transjordan*

This leads us to the conclusion that the book of Acts was written sometime around 62AD.

VALUE

The book of Acts gives us the spread of the gospel of the Lord Jesus Christ to the Jews and officially to the Gentiles with a transition from law to grace. The good news is leaving Israel and going into the non-Jewish world. When Paul was called to take the message of Christ to the Gentiles, he was commanded to share the gospel with the Jews first. **(Acts 13:5, 14, 16:11-13, 17;1-2, 10, 16-**

17, 18:1-4, 19:1-8, and 28:17) Jesus the Son of God was present in the four gospels, but now the Holy Spirit is present. **(John 16:7-8)** There is the transition of the Holy Spirit being *with* all believers to the Spirit being *in* all believers by faith.

> *"For the law was given by Moses, but grace and truth came by Jesus Christ."* **- John 1:17**

Thousands of the Jews who lived under the Mosaic Law heard the gospel of the death, burial, and resurrection of Christ who were saved and eventually died. The transition was then made to the Gentile believers. God always had the Gentiles in mind, and we see His promises come true. **(Isaiah 42:6)** While the Gentiles would hear the gospel of the Jewish Messiah, they were never to forget the Jewish roots of their faith. However, they were no longer under the bondage of the Jewish traditions. God mysteriously used the unbelief of the generation who saw the Messiah to fulfill His plan for the Gentiles. Here is a good outline to follow:

Acts 1-7 - (Jerusalem & Jewish)

Acts 8-12 - (Judea and Samaria & Transition)

Acts 13-28 - (Uttermost parts of the world and Gentiles)

There are many issues and topics that will be addressed as we make our journey through this powerful book, but we must never lose sight of the most important subject, the person of Christ himself. Here are some of the titles that are mentioned:

Jesus the Christ – *(4:10, 9:34, 10:36)*

Jesus Christ – *(5:42)*

Lord Jesus – *(4:33, 7:59, 11:20, 15;11, 16:31)*

Lord Jesus Christ – *(11:17, 20:21, 28:31)*

Lord of all – *(10:36)*

Savior – *(13:23)*

Deliverer – *(10:43, 13:38-39, 20:28)*

The One raised from the dead – *(2;32, 4:10, 17:31)*

The Righteous One – *(3:14, 7:52, 22:14)*

The Exalted One – *(2:33)*

The Rejected Stone – *(4:11)*

The Judge of mankind – *(17:31)*

The Returning One – *(1:11, 3:20)*

Son Jesus – *(3:13, 26)*

Holy Child Jesus – *(4:27, 30)*

The Holy One – *(3:14)*

The Prince of Life – *(3:15)*

Son of God – *(9:20)*

The writer has titled this commentary, **"Acts, And they continued….."** How can we see the *acts* lived out in our own lives? We don't have the power to heal a lame man as the apostles did. The author can honestly say that he has never touched someone who has died and he/she was able to live again. And even if we could, that person would only be here for a short time because that person would die again. How is the ministry of the Lord Jesus Christ *continuing* through us?

Miracles aren't necessary to be a faithful disciple of Christ. If that were the case, then all of us would be failures. While miracles still happen, they have a different place today than when the apostles who walked with Jesus were alive. What about preaching and teaching God's holy Word? We all have been commissioned to speak to others about the precious Lord Jesus who can save their souls. We all have a sword of the Lord in our possession, so what is keeping us from being serious students? What about our own personal families? Have we shared the life-changing message of Jesus with them? What about the people in our communities, our churches, and Christian friends who need encouragement? We can continue the work of Christ by how we conduct our business and how we react to adversity in our own lives. We *continue* the work of our Lord as we disciple others. Our deeds may seem mundane, but with the presence of the Holy Spirit within our own lives, there is a great abiding miracle in each one of us. We can *continue* the works of Jesus by showing the world around us a lifetime of faith and being faithful to the end of our journey. This is why it is so crucial that we, as professing followers of Jesus, stay filled with the same power that filled those early followers of the Son of God- **The Blessed Holy Spirit!**

CHAPTER ONE

THE MINISTRY OF CHRIST ON EARTH

Acts 1:1-2 - *The former treatise have I made, O Theophilus, of all that Jesus began both to do and teach, Until the day in which he was taken up, after that he through the Holy Ghost had given commandments unto the apostles whom he had chosen.*

The very first verse connects us to the gospel of Luke:

It seemed good to me also, having had perfect understanding of all things from the very first, to write unto thee in order, most excellent Theophilus, That thou mightest know the certainty of those things, wherein thou hast been instructed. **(Luke 1:3-4)**

Who is Theophilus? *Theophilus* means *"lover of God,"* and was most likely a high-ranking Roman official, who also was a man of honor. The phrase *"most excellent"* was also used by Luke to address Felix **(Acts 23:26)** and Festus **(Acts 26:25)**. Luke may have been using his personal friend Theophilus for the publication of this book to show him that the ministry of Jesus that began in his gospel continued to spread throughout the Roman world through His apostles.

"Jesus began both to do and teach" - Notice that Jesus proved the validity of His teachings by performing His deeds first. Jesus didn't come to this earth to give Israel new ideas or some new lesson on ethics, but to show what God's love was really all about. Jesus started His kingdom with the outcasts of Israel and then called the most unlikely men to be His apostles.

"Until the day in which he was taken up" - This connects us to the Ascension of Christ in the gospel of Luke:

> ***And he led them out as far as to Bethany, and he lifted up his hands, and blessed them. And it came to pass, while he blessed them, he was parted from them, and carried up into heaven. (Luke 24:50-51)***

After Jesus died on the cross and arose, He still taught His disciples through the power of the *Holy Ghost, until* the day that He went with them to the Mount of Olives *(Bethany lies on the eastern side of the top of the Mount of Olives)* and ascended back to heaven. The same *Holy Ghost* that was upon the Son of God would continue His work in the book of Acts.

THE POST-RESURRECTION MINISTRY OF CHRIST

> **Acts 1:3** - *To whom also he shewed himself alive after his passion by many infallible proofs, being seen of them forty days, and speaking of the things pertaining to the kingdom of God.*

The *passion of Jesus* was His death on the cross. The remaining 11 disciples, who were chosen by Christ, saw *convincing proofs* of His resurrection throughout the 40 days He remained on the earth. The resurrection of Jesus was not just mere imagination of some mystical assertion. During the 40 days of His post resurrection appearances, Jesus taught His disciples about the *kingdom of God.* He took the Old Testament and taught them about the coming *Messianic Kingdom,* as well as the *Mystery Kingdom* that would include the Church-Age that began in the book of Acts, when the Holy Spirit would dwell inside the believers, both Jew and Gentile. Jesus was the long-awaited Jewish Messiah, so he would need to explain to His disciples why the physical kingdom did not come when He walked in Jerusalem. God has always been the sovereign ruler of the universe, and He would rule in the hearts of those who embraced Jesus His Son. There will come a day when He will burst through the curtains of human history and reign on the earth.

THE PROMISE OF THE HOLY SPIRIT

> **Acts 1:4-5 -** *And, being assembled together with them, commanded them that they should not depart from Jerusalem, but wait for the promise of the Father, which, saith he, ye have heard of me. For John truly baptized with water; but ye shall be baptized with the Holy Ghost not many days hence.*

Three commands that came straight from the lips of Jesus:

* *They should not depart from Jerusalem*
* *They should wait for the promise of the Father*
* *They would be baptized with the Holy Ghost*

Notice the connection of what Jesus told the 11 disciples to the words of John the Baptist:

John answered, saying unto them all, I indeed baptize you with water; but one mightier than I cometh, the latchet of whose shoes I am not worthy to unloose: he shall baptize you with the Holy Ghost and with fire. **(Luke 3:16)**

The expressions *"with," "in,"* and *"by"* the Holy Ghost always mean the same thing. This prophecy of our Lord would be fulfilled in just ten days.

Jesus makes it clear that the *water baptism* of John was in contrast to the *Spirit baptism*. Biblical salvation is a supernatural work of God of heaven, when someone truly believes that Jesus is the Son of God, turns away from sin, and then is filled with the Holy Spirit. The Spirit baptism is what makes an individual a member of the body of Christ.

For by one Spirit are we all baptized into one body, whether we be Jews or Gentiles, whether we be bond or free; and have been all made to drink into one Spirit. **(I Corinthians 12:13)**

Jesus' Answer About the Messianic Kingdom

Acts 1:6-7 - *When they therefore were come together, they asked of him, saying, Lord, wilt thou at this time restore again the kingdom to Israel? And he said unto them, It is not for you to know the times or the seasons, which the Father hath put in his own power.*

Why did the disciples ask Jesus *when* the *Messianic Kingdom* would come? It was because the Old Testament prophets taught that Israel's national restoration would be the results of the pouring out of the Holy Spirit. **(Study verses in Isaiah 32:15-20, 44:3-5, Joel 2:28-3:1, and Zechariah 12:10-13:1.)**

Then shall they know that I am the Lord their God, which caused them to be led into captivity among the heathen: but I have gathered them unto their own land, and have left none of them any more there. Neither will I hide my face any more from them: for I have poured out my spirit upon the house of Israel, saith the Lord God. **(Ezekiel 39:28-29)**

The apostles did not understand that the baptism of the Holy Spirit that was coming to individual believers in Christ was not the same as the outpouring of the Holy Spirit upon national Israel that the prophets foretold. Jesus had told the apostles earlier that they would sit upon thrones and judge the 12 tribes of Israel:

> *And Jesus said unto them, Verily I say unto you, That ye which have followed me, in the regeneration when the Son of man shall sit in the throne of his glory, ye also shall sit upon twelve thrones, judging the twelve tribes of Israel.* **(Matthew 19:28)**

"*Wilt thou at this time restore again the kingdom to Israel?*" – Their question was not *"if,"* but *"when?"* It was the expectation of all of the religious Jewish people that when the Messiah came, He would restore Israel to the glorious days of David and Solomon. It is a sad day when many of our Christian churches teach replacement theology, meaning that the Church has replaced Israel. There are literally hundreds and hundreds of verses in the Bible that directly refer to the reign of Christ on the earth.

We must understand that it was a sub-group within Israel that rejected Jesus as its Messiah. It was the majority of the Pharisees, the Scribes, the Sadducees, and the religious Sanhedrin during the time that Jesus walked this earth. If *all* of the Jews rejected Christ, there would be no need for the book of Acts. The first Gentile to officially accept Jesus is not mentioned until **Acts 10**. There were thousands of Jews who received Christ on the Day of Pentecost. Early estimates run into several hundred thousand Jewish Christians in the first century. There were enough to change the course of history. Sometimes we forget that because the Jewish Christians were a sect within Judaism, they received a certain amount of protection from the government of the Roman Empire. God was orchestrating and using Rome to help spread the gospel, and they didn't even know it. A small mustard seed started to grow in the Galilee, and it grew into a tree so the birds of the air could lodge in the branches. **(Matthew 13:31-32)**

"It is not for you to know the times or the seasons, which the Father hath put in his own power." - Jesus is saying that the divine, appointed time for Israel to be restored should not worry them. They must be concerned about preaching the gospel and being faithful to what He has called them to do. There are ages to come with many signs to the lost world that the disciples could not understand. God will be longsuffering and draw out multitudes of Gentiles to be in the fold before Israel will be restored.

And other sheep I have, which are not of this fold: them also I must bring, and they shall hear my voice; and there shall be one fold, and one shepherd. **(John 10:16)**

THE APOSTOLIC COMMISSION

Acts 1:8 - *But ye shall receive power, after that the Holy Ghost is come upon you: and ye shall be witnesses unto me both in Jerusalem, and in all Judaea, and in Samaria, and unto the uttermost part of the earth.*

Notice that the words of Jesus changes the subject from the restoration of Israel to their commission by using the word *"But."* Jesus was sending them out, but not in their own strength. The *Holy Ghost* would give them the power to do what *Jesus* had commissioned them to do, not just to do what *they* wanted to do. Jesus is now reiterating to the disciples that they will be *witnesses*. Again, they cannot be powerful witnesses without the Holy Spirit:

> **But when the Comforter is come, whom I will send unto you from the Father, even the Spirit of truth, which proceedeth from the Father, he shall testify of me: And ye also shall bear witness, because ye have been with me from the beginning. (John 15:26-27)**

The apostles would be given the power of the Holy Spirit to tell the world about JESUS. The Holy Spirit's job is to equip them to witness about what they had seen and heard from JESUS.

"Jerusalem, and in all Judaea, and in Samaria, and unto the uttermost part of the earth." – The words coming from Jesus would give them the geographical outline of their commission, and would give us the outline of the book of Acts. Jerusalem is where Jesus shed His blood and rose again. The first chapters would be dedicated to telling the good news in Jerusalem from **Acts 2:1-8:4.** Then *all Judea and Samaria* would be the regions from **Acts 8:5-12:25**, and *the uttermost part of the earth* would be from **Acts 13:1-28:31**. We are reminded of this powerful verse in the writings of Isaiah:

> **And he said, It is a light thing that thou shouldest be my servant to raise up the tribes of Jacob, and to restore the preserved of Israel: I will also give thee for a light to the Gentiles, that thou mayest be my salvation unto the end of the earth. (Isaiah 49:6)**

The Ascension of Jesus and the Promise of His Return

Acts 1:9-11 - *And when he had spoken these things, while they beheld, he was taken up; and a cloud received him out of their sight. And while they looked stedfastly toward heaven as he went up, behold, two men stood by them in white apparel; Which also said, Ye men of Galilee, why stand ye gazing up into heaven? this same Jesus, which is taken up from you into heaven, shall so come in like manner as ye have seen him go into heaven.*

"he was taken up" - Jesus was lifted up
"a cloud received him" - Jesus was enveloped in a cloud
"he went up" - Jesus went into heaven

We need to connect the verses where Jesus predicted His own ascension:

And no man hath ascended up to heaven, but he that came down from heaven, even the Son of man which is in heaven. **(John 3:13)**

What and if ye shall see the Son of man ascend up where he was before? **(John 6:62)**

Jesus saith unto her, Touch me not; for I am not yet ascended to my Father: but go to my brethren, and say unto them, I ascend unto my Father, and your Father; and to my God, and your God. **(John 20:17)**

The ascension of Christ has three vitally important meanings:

* *Jesus' earthly ministry was completed*
* *Jesus' work will continue through the apostles*
* *Jesus is exalted at the right hand of the Father*

The greatest works of the Messiah are: *His incarnation, His baptism, His transfiguration, His crucifixion, His descension, His resurrection,* and *His ascension.* Each one of these works should be studied deeply by every professing follower of Jesus.

"two men stood by them in white apparel" - When angels appear in the life and ministry of Christ, they usually are in the form of *young men*. The *white apparel* shows that they were from heaven, where righteousness dwells:

His countenance was like lightning, and his raiment white as snow. **(Matthew 28:3)**

And entering into the sepulchre, they saw a young man sitting on the right side, clothed in a long white garment; and they were affrighted. **(Mark 16:5)**

And it came to pass, as they were much perplexed thereabout, behold, two men stood by them in shining garments. **(Luke 24:4)**

And seeth two angels in white sitting, the one at the head, and the other at the feet, where the body of Jesus had lain. **(John 20:12)**

To personalize the visit of the angels, they call the disciples *Ye men of Galilee*. The angels were sent from heaven to let the disciples know that God not only knew them, but He even knew the geographical location where they were from. Jesus came from heaven and started His ministry in the Galilee, and called His closest followers from there. They lived some 80 miles north of Jerusalem, but while they are standing on the Mount of Olives, the angels did not forgot where they lived. Interesting!

The angels gave them a special promise, *this same Jesus, which is taken up from you into heaven, shall so come in like manner as ye have seen him go into heaven.* The crucified and risen Lord left this earth in a cloud, and He will return in clouds of heaven. Clouds have become very special to this author over the years because they have been seen as symbols of God's power, glory, mercy, and truth.

> *And then shall appear the sign of the Son of man in heaven: and then shall all the tribes of the earth mourn, and they shall see the Son of man coming in the clouds of heaven with power and great glory.* **(Matthew 24:30)**
>
> *And then shall they see the Son of man coming in the clouds with great power and glory.* **(Mark 13:26)**
>
> *Behold, he cometh with clouds; and every eye shall see him, and they also which pierced him: and all kindreds of the earth shall wail because of him. Even so, Amen.* **(Rev 1:7)**

THE APOSTLES BACK IN JERUSALEM

> **Acts 1:12-14 -** *Then returned they unto Jerusalem from the mount called Olivet, which is from Jerusalem a sabbath day's journey. And when they were come in,*

> *they went up into an upper room, where abode both Peter, and James, and John, and Andrew, Philip, and Thomas, Bartholomew, and Matthew, James the son of Alphaeus, and Simon Zelotes, and Judas the brother of James. These all continued with one accord in prayer and supplication, with the women, and Mary the mother of Jesus, and with his brethren.*

The fact that the apostles went back into Jerusalem shows their *obedience* to Jesus and their *courage* because Jerusalem was not a safe place to be. *A sabbath's day journey* was 2,000 cubits, or about three-fourths of a mile from the Mount of Olives into Jerusalem.

"an upper room" – The definite article shows this as not just any *upper room*, but *the upper room*, the place of the Passover and where Jesus appeared to them after His resurrection. There is a strong tradition that it was located in the home of Mary, the mother of John Mark. Notice these two verses:

> *And he shall shew you a large upper room furnished: there make ready.* **(Luke 22:12)**

> *And after eight days again his disciples were within, and Thomas with them: then came Jesus, the doors being shut, and stood in the midst, and said, Peace be unto you.* **(John 20:26)**

> *"Peter, and James, and John, and Andrew, Philip, and Thomas, Bartholomew, and Matthew, James the son of Alphaeus, and Simon Zelotes, and Judas*

the brother of James." – We find these disciples listed previously in **Matthew 10:2-4, Mark 3:16-19,** and **Luke 6:14-16.**

"with the women, and Mary the mother of Jesus, and with his brethren." – The women who had followed Jesus from Galilee included *Mary Magdalene, Joanna, Susanna, Salome, some others, and* the wives of some of the disciples. *Mary, the mother of Jesus* was there, and this is the last time she is mentioned in the Bible. The half-brothers and half-sisters of Jesus were also there. **(Mark 6:3)**

"one accord in prayer and supplication" – They all were in intense prayer, all *in one accord*. Often we find the phrase *in one accord* in the book of Acts. The Holy Spirit brings unity among the believers. **(Acts 1:14, 2:46, 4:24, 5:12, 7:57, 8:6, 12:20, 15:25, 18:12, 19:29)**

The Old Testament tells us how beautiful it is when believers are joined together in unity:

Behold, how good and how pleasant it is for brethren to dwell together in unity! It is like the precious ointment upon the head, that ran down upon the beard, even Aaron's beard: that went down to the skirts of his garments; As the dew of Hermon, and as the dew that descended upon the mountains of Zion: for there the LORD **commanded the blessing, even life for evermore. (Psalm 133:1-3)**

Peter Speaking About Judas Iscariot

Acts 1:15-20- *And in those days Peter stood up in the midst of the disciples, and said, (the number of names together were about <u>an hundred and twenty</u>,) Men and brethren, this scripture must needs have been fulfilled, which the Holy Ghost by the mouth of David spake before concerning Judas, which was guide to them that took Jesus. For he was numbered with us, and had obtained part of this ministry. Now this man purchased a field with the reward of iniquity; and falling headlong, he burst asunder in the midst, and all his bowels gushed out. And it was known unto all the dwellers at Jerusalem; insomuch as that field is called in their proper tongue, Aceldama, that is to say, The field of blood. For it is written in the book of Psalms, Let his habitation be desolate, and let no man dwell therein: and his bishoprick let another take.*

To show the size of the upper room, there were about *120 people* present. Who were included in this group? Could it possibly have been some of the people whom Jesus healed? Perhaps Mary, Martha, and Lazarus? What about the mothers and fathers of the apostles and relatives such as Cleopas? Peter was the leader of the disciples, but that did not mean that he alone would choose the replacement for Judas Iscariot. It was a very serious matter that had to be addressed. As Jesus had taught them, it was needful for Peter to set things in proper order to those present, and to connect the betrayal of Judas to the Old Testament and to say that *this scripture must needs to have been fulfilled.*

"which the Holy Ghost by the mouth of David spake" – This showed the dual authorship of God's Word. The Divine author was the *Holy Ghost,* and the human author was *David.* While David may not have understood what he was writing, he wrote down exactly what the Holy Ghost inspired him to write.

"For he was numbered with us and had obtained part of this ministry" – Jesus chose Judas Iscariot! He was able to travel with Jesus and the other apostles and even perform miracles.

> *Then he called his twelve disciples together, and gave them power and authority over all devils, and to cure diseases.* **(Luke 9:1)**

Greed has destroyed many Church leaders and many followers of the Lord Jesus. It destroyed Judas!

> *Then saith one of his disciples, Judas Iscariot, Simon's son, which should betray him, Why was not this ointment sold for three hundred pence, and given to the poor? This he said, not that he cared for the poor; but because he was <u>a thief</u>, and had the bag, and bare what was put therein.* **(John 12:4-6)**

"Now this man purchased a field with the reward of iniquity; and falling headlong, he burst asunder in the midst, and all his bowels gushed out." – In **Matthew 27:3-10**, there seems to be a contradiction, but Matthew recorded that Judas hanged himself while Luke records what happened to his body after it was thrown over the city walls. The city of Jerusalem was ceremonially unclean until Judas' body was thrown over the city walls into the *Valley of Hinnom*. Judas purchased the field indirectly through the priests using the betrayal money to buy it.

"*Aceldama, that is to say, The field of blood*" – This place became *known unto all the dwellers at Jerusalem*. In 1892 the Greek orthodox built a monastery in the place where many burial tombs were found.

"*For it is written in the book of Psalms, Let his habitation be desolate, and let no man dwell therein: and his bishoprick let another take.*" – In the Hebrew style of *stringing the pearls together*, Peter used these two passages from the Psalms:

> *Let their habitation be desolate; and let none dwell in their tents.* **(Psalm 69:25)**
>
> *Let his days be few; and let another take his office.* **(Psalm 109:8)**

The betrayal of Judas Iscariot should be a warning to the body of Christ today. Just because someone has charisma and is able to draw huge crowds and even perform miracles, it does not mean that they truly belong to the Lord. **(Matthew 7:21-23)**

QUALIFICATIONS OF THE TWELFTH APOSTLE

> **Acts 1:21-22 –** *Wherefore of these men which have companied with us all the time that the Lord Jesus went in and out among us, Beginning from the*

baptism of John, unto that same day that he was taken up from us, must one be ordained to be a witness with us of his resurrection.

To qualify, he must be a Jew who had been with Jesus from the baptism of John the Baptist through His earthly ministry, and seen Him gloriously resurrected, and then His ascension. This disqualifies Paul to be the twelfth apostle as some have proposed.

THE SELECTION OF THE TWELFTH APOSTLE

Acts 1:23-26 - *And they appointed two, Joseph called Barsabas, who was surnamed Justus, and Matthias. And they prayed, and said, Thou, Lord, which knowest the hearts of all men, shew whether of these two thou hast chosen, That he may take part of this ministry and apostleship, from which Judas by transgression fell, that he might go to his own place. And they gave forth their lots; and the lot fell upon Matthias; and he was numbered with the eleven apostles.*

Barsabbas, (Aramaic) – *"son of the Sabbath"* and **Justus**, (Roman) name for *"upright or just."*

Matthias – Comes from the Hebrew name, *"Mattityahu,"* and it means *"gift of Yehovah."*

It is commonly taught that the disciples chose *Matthias* and his selection was not of God. This cannot be true because they prayed and asked the Lord to show them which man has the best heart for this all-important position. This man would not be *voted on* in the typical democratic way of most churches today. God chooses the twelfth apostle! This has caused major problems in the modern church. Many people go into the ministry just as a vocation or they are selected by a group of people. Having the ability to speak well, dress well, and have a formal college degree does not qualify anyone to be a pastor or evangelist. They must be ordained by God!

Casting lots was a valid method in Bible times for determining God's will. **(Lev. 16;8, Josh. 14:2, Neh.10:34, 11:1)** The names of the two men were probably written on stones and placed into some type of vessel. The vessel was shaken until one of the stones fell out. The stone that fell out had the name of *Matthias*. After the coming of the Holy Spirit, this method would no longer be needed.

Two other places where *Matthias* would be included are:

Then the twelve called the multitude of the disciples unto them, and said, It is not reason that we should leave the word of God, and serve tables. (Acts 6:2)

And the wall of the city had twelve foundations, and in them the names of the twelve apostles of the Lamb. (Revelation 21:14)

CHAPTER TWO

THE INITIAL COMING OF THE HOLY SPIRIT

Acts 2:1-4 - *And when the day of Pentecost was fully come, they were all with one accord in one place. And suddenly there came a sound from heaven as of a rushing mighty wind, and it filled all the house where they were sitting. And there appeared unto them cloven tongues like as of fire, and it sat upon each of them. And they were all filled with the Holy Ghost, and began to speak with other tongues, as the Spirit gave them utterance.*

Before we begin trying to unravel one of the most important passages in the book of Acts, it is needful to be reminded that this passage is one of the most debated and misinterpreted in the entire Bible. The body of Christ has been sharply divided for decades, in part, because of the different interpretations of this one section of scripture. We must approach this transitional passage in the New Testament *carefully* within its original context, contrast, and connections to the Old Testament.

"And when the day of Pentecost was fully come" - *The Day of Pentecost* (50) is also called *the Feast of Weeks*. It was celebrated 50 days after the Feast of Passover. The first sheaf of the *barley* harvest was presented to God at Passover, and the first sheaf of *wheat* harvest was presented to God on the Day of Pentecost.

It is strongly believed by religious Jews that the Feast of Pentecost was when God gave the Torah to Moses. As the Law was given on this day, the fulfillment would be the giving of the Holy Spirit. The Law was on tablets of stone while the Spirit was written on the hearts of the people. **(Please read Jeremiah 31:31-34)**

When it says <u>the</u> *Day of Pentecost had fully come*, this means that this particular feast was ready to be fulfilled, and it was ten days after Jesus had ascended back to heaven. The disciples were in the upper room waiting but did not know exactly when the Holy Spirit would come. Would it be four days? Seven days? No, it would be ten days to fulfill the feast. Four Jewish feasts are fulfilled in the New Testament:

* ***Feast of Passover*** - *Jesus was crucified*

* ***Feast of Unleavened Bread*** - *The Sinless Jesus was buried*

* ***Feast of Firstfruits*** - *Jesus the Messiah arose from the grave*

* ***Feast of Pentecost*** - *The coming of the Holy Spirit*

"And suddenly there came a sound from heaven as of a rushing mighty wind" – It was a whooshing sound *like* the wind. It's interesting that the words *wind* and *spirit* are the same in both Hebrew and Greek- *Ruach* or *Pneuma*. This author thinks it is necessary to stop and reflect on a few passages here, since the *wind* is the symbol of the Holy Spirit:

> **Genesis 1:2** - *And the earth was without form, and void; and darkness was upon the face of the deep. And the Spirit of God moved upon the face of the waters.*

> **Genesis 2:7** - *And the Lord God formed man of the dust of the ground, and breathed into his nostrils the breath of life; and man became a living soul.*

> **2 Samuel 5:24** - *And let it be, when thou hearest the sound of a going in the tops of the mulberry trees, that then thou shalt bestir thyself: for then shall the Lord go out before thee, to smite the host of the Philistines.*

> **Ezekiel 37:9-10** - *Then said he unto me, Prophesy unto the wind, prophesy, son of man, and say to the wind, Thus saith the Lord God; Come from the four winds, O breath, and breathe upon these slain, that they may live. So I prophesied as he commanded me, and the breath came into them, and they lived, and stood up upon their feet, an exceeding great army.*

> **John 3:8** - *The wind bloweth where it listeth, and thou hearest the sound thereof, but canst not tell whence it cometh, and whither it goeth: so is every one that is born of the Spirit.*

"and it filled all the house where they were sitting" - While the apostles would be the ones God would use as the leaders, the Holy Ghost came upon *all* that were in the house. Here the word *house* is strongly debated between Hebrew and Greek scholars. The Greek word is *ho oikos*, and means *residence*. The Hebrew word for house in the Old Testament is *habayit*, and it is used for the *Temple* in many places. Did the Holy Spirit initially come into the world in the *upper room*, or somewhere in the *Temple* precincts? After much thought, this author believes that the Holy Spirit came to the disciples in the *upper room* because the Spirit had departed the Temple in the book of Ezekiel. **(Ezekiel 11:23)** The Temple, during the time of Jesus and the apostles, was built by the wicked king Herod and was not the habitation of God as in the days of Solomon.

"And there appeared unto them cloven tongues like as of fire, and it sat upon each of them" - God was not only sending the Holy Spirit down through the sound like the *wind*, but the sight as of *fire*. A cluster that looked like fire was divided and distributed into individual flame-like tongues. The *Shechinah* glory of God was resting upon each one of them and purifying them *as gold tried in the fire*, preparing them for their proclamation of the gospel to the huge audience that had gathered in Jerusalem for the feast. Under the Old Covenant, the Spirit rested upon the nation of Israel, but in the New Covenant, the Spirit would rest upon individuals. The coming of the Holy Spirit had to startle and alarm them, as well as equip them. The appointed time, or the Hebrew *mo edim,* had come!

What was the *gift of tongues*, or the Greek ★*glossais*? It meant that they would be gifted to speak in other *languages* that the apostles had never been taught before. It was a real language with all of the grammar that the languages of the known world used in that day. It was not some ecstatic, repetitious, gibberish that we hear today by many religious preachers. Without casting doubt on anyone's personal experiences, this gift of languages in **Acts 2** was given *as the Spirit gave them utterance.*

★ (Much damage has been done in religious circles by trying to make people think by speaking in a repetitive three of four syllables that it is passed off as unknown tongues and they have the gift of the Holy Spirit. After studying the life and ministry of Christ for many years, this author has not found anywhere where Jesus or his apostles did that. The Charismatic and Pentecostal movement teaches that a person must have a post-salvation experience of Spirit baptism, and the sign is speaking in an unknown tongue. This is biblically incorrect. It was a tri-lingual society in Israel in those days. The religious Jews spoke Hebrew, the Galilean Jews spoke Aramaic, (A dialect of Hebrew), the pagan Romans spoke Latin, and the common language on the streets of the known world was Greek, brought into the world by Alexander the Great. **(Luke 23:38)** *The supernatural gift of languages was needful for the spreading of the gospel of Christ in the early first century.)*

THE EFFECT OF THE COMING OF THE HOLY SPIRIT

Acts 2:5-11 - *And there were dwelling at Jerusalem Jews, devout men, out of every nation under heaven. Now when this was noised abroad, the multitude came together, and were confounded, because that every man heard them speak in his own language. And they were all amazed and marvelled, saying one to another, Behold, are not all these which speak Galilaeans? And how hear we every man in our own*

> *tongue, wherein we were born? Parthians, and Medes, and Elamites, and the dwellers in Mesopotamia, and in Judaea, and Cappadocia, in Pontus, and Asia, Phrygia, and Pamphylia, in Egypt, and in the parts of Libya about Cyrene, and strangers of Rome, Jews and proselytes, Cretes and Arabians, we do hear them speak in our tongues the wonderful works of God.*

It seems clear that the experience in the upper room has resulted in the apostles going out into a public area somewhere in the Temple precincts or at the top of the southern steps in Jerusalem. Although the text does not say, a *multitude* could not fit inside the upper room. The Day of Pentecost opened the gospel of the Lord Jesus Christ to *Jews, strangers of Rome, and proselytes. (Gentiles who had converted to Judaism)*

Notice that these were *devout men* from every nation. It was the custom that the people who came to the Feast of Passover *stayed* until the Feast of Pentecost. These were men who were saints like in the Old Testament who believed that the Messiah was coming. Since they lived away from Jerusalem, they needed to hear that the crucified Jesus was their Messiah. It had to be more than just words. It had to be in the power of the Holy Spirit.

"that every man heard them speak in his own language. And they were all amazed and marvelled, saying one to another, Behold, are not all these which speak Galilaeans?" - The people were astonished and the more they heard, the more astonished they became. Why? They could tell by the dialect that the apostles were from *Galilee*. The *Galileans* were not known to be highly educated people, and they had a distinct guttural sound. Because of the Holy Spirit, they had been given different languages. This also showed how God receives the glory by using the *foolish things to confound the wise.* **(I Cor.1:27)** Jesus chose the simple fishermen from Galilee to prove to the people that it was a real, supernatural miracle from the God of heaven. This pattern is still being used by the Lord today.

In contrast, in **Genesis 11:1-9**, at the *Tower of Babel*, languages were given to confound the people. Here the gift of languages was given to *communicate* the message to other nations.

"Parthians, and Medes, and Elamites, and the dwellers in Mesopotamia, (Aramaic) *and in Judaea,* (Hebrew) *and Cappadocia, in Pontus, and Asia, Phrygia, and Pamphylia,* (Greek) *in Egypt, and in the parts of Libya about Cyrene,* (Greek) *and strangers of Rome,* (Latin) *Jews and proselytes,* (Hellenized Jews and Gentiles, Greek) *Cretes* (Greek) *and Arabians,* (Nabataean, an Aramaic dialect) *we do hear them speak in our tongues the wonderful works of God."* - When the multitude heard these Galileans speak about *God's wonderful works,* they felt God's compassion for them and the rest of the whole world. Hallelujah!

The Day of Pentecost was the time when *two loaves* of *leavened bread* were to be waved before the Lord. *Two loaves* would symbolize the Jews and the Gentiles, and the *leaven* symbolized that both were sinners who needed salvation.

> **Leviticus 23:15-17** - *And ye shall count unto you from the morrow after the sabbath, from the day that ye brought the sheaf of the wave offering; seven sabbaths shall be complete: Even unto the morrow*

> *after the seventh sabbath shall ye number fifty days; and ye shall offer a new meat offering unto the* Lord. *Ye shall bring out of your habitations <u>two wave loaves</u> of two tenth deals; they shall be of fine flour; they shall be baken with <u>leaven</u>; they are the firstfruits unto the* Lord.

They were also commanded to take care of the *strangers* during the Feast of Pentecost, but this time they were giving the stranger something more important than physical bread:

> **Leviticus 23:22** - *And when ye reap the harvest of your land, thou shalt not make clean riddance of the corners of thy field when thou reapest, neither shalt thou gather any gleaning of thy harvest: thou shalt leave them unto the poor, and to the stranger: I am the Lord your God.*

We need to also connect what Jesus said to fully understand the pouring out of the Holy Spirit upon Jews *or* Gentiles that He prophesied during His earthly ministry:

> **John 7:37-39** - *In the last day, that great day of the feast, Jesus stood and cried, saying, If any man thirst, let him come unto me, and drink. He that believeth on me, as the scripture hath said, out of his belly shall flow rivers of living water. (But this spake he of the Spirit, which they that believe on him should receive: for the Holy Ghost was not yet given; because that Jesus was not yet glorified.)*

Two Different Types of Response

> **Acts 2:12-13** - *And they were all amazed, and were in doubt, saying one to another, What meaneth this? Others mocking said, These men are full of new wine.*

When the apostles spoke in foreign languages, many of the people were so perplexed and amazed that they wanted to know what all of this meant. We must keep in mind that this was a supernatural move of the Holy Spirit, and the people had never heard anything like this. It was a phenomenon! Some doubted and mocked the apostles by saying they were drunk with *new wine*. New wine refers to wine that had begun to ferment, but had not completed the fermentation process. There will always be some seekers and some scoffers.

Peter's First Sermon

> **Acts 2:14-21** - *But Peter, standing up with the eleven, lifted up his voice, and said unto them, Ye men of Judaea, and all ye that dwell at Jerusalem, be this known unto you, and hearken to my words: For these are not drunken, as ye suppose, seeing it is but the third hour of the day. But this is that which was spoken by the prophet Joel; And it shall come to pass in the last days, saith God, I will pour out of my Spirit upon all flesh: and your sons and your daughters shall prophesy, and your young men shall see visions, and your old men shall dream dreams:*

> *And on my servants and on my handmaidens I will pour out in those days of my Spirit; and they shall prophesy: And I will shew wonders in heaven above, and signs in the earth beneath; blood, and fire, and vapour of smoke: The sun shall be turned into darkness, and the moon into blood, before the great and notable day of the Lord come: And it shall come to pass, that whosoever shall call on the name of the Lord shall be saved.*

The fact that the other 11 are mentioned shows that Matthias had been accepted to replace Judas. Jesus had given Simon Peter the *keys to the kingdom,* and this would be the first time that Peter would use the keys and open the door to the men of Judea and the inhabitants of Jerusalem:

> *And I will give unto thee the keys of the kingdom of heaven: and whatsoever thou shalt bind on earth shall be bound in heaven: and whatsoever thou shalt loose on earth shall be loosed in heaven.* **(Matthew 16:19)**

The first thing that Peter did was to address their mocking by referring to the Jewish customs of the feast of Pentecost. The *third hour,* or nine o'clock in the morning, is when they offered prayers and special sacrifices, and it was not the time to be drinking. They drank wine in the evening.

The second point that Peter makes is the *partial* fulfillment of **Joel 2:28-32**. Not everything that Joel wrote about happened during the initial coming of the Holy Spirit, but in Hebrew thought, just one truth or point from a text results in a fulfillment of that passage, even if it is a *partial* fulfillment. Notice that Peter said, *this is that which was spoken by the prophet Joel.* The words that *whosoever shall call on the name of the Lord* are referring to the diverse multitude who will believe Peter's message, which also can be applied to *whosoever* today.

The entire prophecy in Joel is actually going to be ultimately fulfilled at the end of the great tribulation period when national Israel will be restored when the Holy Spirit will be *poured out* again. At the end of the great tribulation, there will be great signs in the heavens before the Lord will return. The primary reason why the Holy Spirit inspired Peter to quote from Joel is because the Holy Spirit had been *poured out* on not only the apostles, but also some of God's *servants and handmaidens.*

Proof that Jesus is the Messiah of Israel

> **Acts 2:22-24 - *Ye men of Israel, hear these words; Jesus of Nazareth, a man approved of God among you by miracles and wonders and signs, which God did by him in the midst of you, as ye yourselves also know: Him, being delivered by the determinate counsel and foreknowledge of God, ye have taken, and by wicked hands have crucified and slain: Whom God hath raised up, having loosed the pains of death: because it was not possible that he should be holden of it.***

Peter calls Jesus, *Jesus of Nazareth,* which was the most humble title that Jesus carried. Peter was showing the men of Israel that they had misunderstood the mission of Israel's Messiah. He was *a man approved of God*! In the very midst of you He performed *miracles, wonders, and signs.* These miracles were *messianic* in nature, and the religious leaders should have known that Jesus of Nazareth was the One the prophets foretold would come.

On the *divine* side, God used the wicked, unbelieving leaders of the nation of Israel to fulfill His divine plan for the world. Jesus came into the world at the right time, when the nation would reject Him.

> *But when the fulness of the time was come, God sent forth his Son, made of a woman, made under the law.* **(Galatians 4:4)**

It was God in heaven who sent His Son into the world, and it was God in heaven who gave Him to be fastened to a tree for the sins of the world. Christ was crucified before the foundation of the world:

> *Who verily was foreordained before the foundation of the world, but was manifest in these last times for you.* **(I Peter 1:20)**

This did not take away or excuse the wickedness of the leaders of Israel. If Israel had received Jesus as their Messiah, He would have still died on the cross; His death was inevitable.

"the pains of death" – The original wording, *odin,* here means *birth pangs,* and Jesus was born out of death. He came into the world to taste the *pangs* of death for all of those who will embrace Him:

> *Forasmuch then as the children are partakers of flesh and blood, he also himself likewise took part of the same; that through death he might destroy him that had the power of death, that is, the devil; And deliver them who through fear of death were all their lifetime subject to bondage.* **(Hebrews 2:14-15)**

It was not possible that death should hold Jesus. Jesus was the Creator of life, and death could not hold life. Jesus was identified with His people and was born into this world. He knows what it is like to be birthed into this sinful world without the sinful nature. He was identified with His people by dying on a tree not for His sin, but for our sin. He became the perfect sacrifice! Jesus was identified with His people being buried to show that we do not have to fear going to the grave. He arose from the grave to give us the assurance of everlasting life. This is the essence of the gospel!

DAVID FORETOLD OF THE MESSIAH'S RESURRECTION

> **Acts 2:25-31** - *For David speaketh concerning him, I foresaw the Lord always before my face, for he is on my right hand, that I should not be moved: Therefore did my heart rejoice, and my tongue was glad; moreover also my flesh shall rest in hope: Because thou wilt not leave my soul in hell, neither wilt thou suffer thine Holy One to see corruption. Thou hast made known to me the ways of life; thou shalt make me full of joy with thy countenance. Men and brethren, let me freely speak unto you of*

> *the patriarch David, that he is both dead and buried, and his sepulchre is with us unto this day. Therefore being a prophet, and knowing that God had sworn with an oath to him, that of the fruit of his loins, according to the flesh, he would raise up Christ to sit on his throne; He seeing this before spake of the resurrection of Christ, that his soul was not left in hell, neither his flesh did see corruption.*

It is very important for us to connect the scriptures together that Peter uses. It proves how divinely inspired the Holy Bible really is. David was in deep meditation and prayer and was writing about His own assurance about death, but it was also a prophecy concerning the first coming of Israel's Messiah. We must be reminded that Jesus was the Son of David and the fulfillment of God's covenant that He had made with David. **(Connect 2 Samuel 7 with Acts 2:30)** No doubt, Peter had been taught by Jesus how to take the Old Testament and explain that He was the Messiah. **(Luke 24:44-46)**

> *I have set the Lord always before me: because he is at my right hand, I shall not be moved. Therefore my heart is glad, and my glory rejoiceth: my flesh also shall rest in hope. For thou wilt not leave my soul in hell; neither wilt thou suffer thine Holy One to see corruption. Thou wilt shew me the path of life: in thy presence is fulness of joy; at thy right hand there are pleasures for evermore.* **(Psalm 16:8-11)**

While David was writing about the hope that he had with the God of Israel being his Shepherd, it was the *resurrection of Christ* that he is ultimately writing about. Peter told them that David died, was buried, and his ★ *sepulcher* is with us here today. It's interesting that according to Jewish tradition, David died on the feast of Pentecost.

★ *(There is a place just outside of the Old City, on Mount Zion, in Jerusalem, called David's Tomb. While religious Jews go there to worship and it is in the corner of a Roman-era synagogue, it is not the actual tomb of David. It actually dates back to the 9th century.)*

"neither his flesh did see corruption" - **Psalm 16** is one of the Psalms that is meditated upon when the religious Jews hold a custom called *shemira*, or guarding the body of the dead. They watch over the body to protect it from wild beasts or from being stolen. It is their custom that a body begins to decompose and see *corruption* on the fourth day. Peter is letting the men of Israel know that the fleshly body of Jesus did not see *corruption*.

When we study the scriptures from the Jewish, Hebrew culture, many times a passage of scripture can hold four different types of interpretations:

★ *p shat - historical*
★ *midrash - application*
★ *remez – hint of the Messiah*
★ *sod – hidden meaning*

Someone once asked, *"how could God use a man like David, who committed such sinful acts of adultery and murder?"* It was because God's covenant was unconditional and was not based on David's performance. We must remember that in spite of David's moral failures, he was a man after God's own heart. **(I Samuel 13:14, Acts 13:22)**

Jesus Is Both Lord and Christ

Acts 2:32-36 - *This Jesus hath God raised up, whereof we all are witnesses. Therefore being by the right hand of God exalted, and having received of the Father the promise of the Holy Ghost, he hath shed forth this, which ye now see and hear. For David is not ascended into the heavens: but he saith himself, The Lord said unto my Lord, Sit thou on my right hand, Until I make thy foes thy footstool. Therefore let all the house of Israel know assuredly, that God hath made the same Jesus, whom ye have crucified, both Lord and Christ.*

The disciples were chosen to be *eyewitnesses* of the resurrection of Jesus. He is the One David wrote about; He is Jesus of Nazareth, who was rejected and crucified.

And said unto them, Thus it is written, and thus it behooved Christ to suffer, and to rise from the dead the third day: And that repentance and remission of sins should be preached in his name among all nations, beginning at Jerusalem. And ye are witnesses of these things. **(Luke 24:46-48)**

The same Jesus has been exalted to sit down at *the right hand of God,* a place of honor, glory, authority, dominion, and rulership. Peter is telling them that what they are now *seeing and hearing* is a result of the finished work of Jesus and His promise of the Holy Spirit that He gave to them before He ascended. Peter again refers to what David said in the Psalms:

> *The Lord said unto my Lord, Sit thou at my right hand, until I make thine enemies thy footstool.* **(Psalm 110:1)**

To paraphrase the verse so we can better understand it, the God of heaven invited David's Lord *(Messiah)* to sit at His right hand. Jesus is addressed as *Lord* because He was the God of heaven who came down to this earth in the form of a man. What may sound like double talk to us on earth is the mysterious workings of the *Triune Godhead* in the counsels of heaven.

Jesus will remain at the right hand of God until His enemies have been made His footstool. The apostle Paul used this terminology when he wrote to the believers in Corinth. Jesus will return as the Son of Man, and His feet will be like *fine brass,* representing judgment. **(Revelation 1:15)**

> *Then cometh the end, when he shall have delivered up the kingdom to God, even the Father; when he shall have put down all rule and all authority and power. For he must reign, till he hath put all enemies under his feet. The last enemy that shall be destroyed is death. For he hath put all things under his feet. But when he saith all things are put under him, it is manifest that he is excepted, which did put all things under him. And when all things shall be subdued unto him, then shall the Son also himself be subject unto him that put all things under him, that God may be all in all.* (I Corinthians 15:24-28)

"Therefore let all the house of Israel know assuredly, that God hath made the same Jesus, whom ye have crucified, both Lord and Christ." – Here Peter wants *all of the house of Israel to know* that Jesus is the Lord Messiah! He is David's Lord! Everyone who professes to be a Christian needs to be reminded of the words LORD JESUS CHRIST and what they mean! Those words mean that Jesus is *the Messiah*, but He is much more. He is *the Lord God* of the Old Testament! Wow! Peter is emphasizing the Jewish guilt in crucifying the Lord, and later He will emphasize the Gentile guilt.

THE RESULTS OF PETER'S FIRST SERMON

Acts 2:37-41 - *Now when they heard this, they were pricked in their heart, and said unto Peter and to the rest of the apostles, Men and brethren, what shall we do? Then Peter said unto them, Repent, and be baptized every one of you in the name of Jesus Christ for the remission of sins, and ye shall receive the gift of the Holy Ghost. For the promise is unto you, and to your children, and to all that are afar off, even as many as the Lord our God shall call. And with many other words did he testify and exhort, saying, Save yourselves from this untoward generation. Then they that gladly received his word were baptized: and the same day there were added unto them about three thousand souls.*

"they were pricked in their heart" – The verb used here, *katenygesan*, means *"to pierce"* in the heart. The preaching of Peter was so filled with the powerful Holy Spirit that it brought conviction to their hearts. This is what happens when a preacher has the power of the Holy Spirit. Peter is overshadowed many times by the educated apostle Paul, but Peter was certainly one of the most powerful preachers the world has ever known.

"and said unto Peter and to the rest of the apostles, Men and brethren, what shall we do?"- They were responding not only to Peter, but to *the rest of the apostles*, and the *brethren*. Peter had the keys to the kingdom and was recognized as being the leader, but the people were cut to the heart to know that they were fellow Jews, but in a different group than the 120 who had received the Holy Spirit. They wanted to know, *what shall we do?* In the Jewish mind there had to be conduct to back up your words.

"Then Peter said unto them, Repent, and be baptized every one of you in the name of Jesus Christ for the remission of sins, and ye shall receive the gift of the Holy Ghost." - Because some misguided churches try to build their theology on a misinterpretation of this verse, it is needful to spend some time and explain it within its proper context.

The Greek word for repent here is *metanoeo,* and it means *to change one's mind*. Peter was most likely speaking in the Galilean Aramaic, or since they were in the religious Jerusalem, he could have been speaking the Hebrew word, *t'shuvah*, which means *to turn from your sins and return to God*. Peter is telling the men of Israel that they need to change their minds about who Jesus is. *That generation* had committed the unpardonable sin by accusing the Son of God of being demon possessed:

> *But when the Pharisees heard it, they said, This fellow doth not cast out devils, but by Beelzebub the prince of the devils. And Jesus knew their thoughts, and said unto them, Every kingdom divided against itself is brought to desolation; and every city or house divided against itself shall not stand: And if Satan cast out Satan, he is divided against himself; how shall then his kingdom stand? And if I by Beelzebub cast out devils, by whom do your children cast them out? therefore they shall be your judges. But if I cast out devils by the Spirit of God, then the kingdom of God is come unto you. Or else how can one enter into a strong man's house, and spoil his goods, except he first bind the strong man? and then he will spoil his house. He that is not with me is against me; and he that gathereth not with me scattereth abroad. Wherefore I say unto you, All manner of sin and blasphemy shall be forgiven unto men: but the blasphemy against the Holy Ghost shall not be forgiven unto men. And whosoever speaketh a word against the Son of man, it shall be forgiven him: but whosoever speaketh against the Holy Ghost, it shall not be forgiven him, neither in this world, neither in the world to come.* **(Matthew 12:24-32)**

The nation was under God's hand of judgment, and Jerusalem would be destroyed in 70AD. Individuals could be saved spiritually if they would change their minds about who Jesus was.

Now they are being told by Peter to do something to prove their minds have been changed about Jesus. We must keep in mind that this is a Jew preaching to Jewish people in Jerusalem. The English transliterated word *baptize* comes from the Greek word *baptizo*, which means *to dip or immerse*. Once again, the Jewish Peter probably used the word *tevilah*, which means to fully immerse one's body in a *mikveh*, or ritual bath.

By being immersed in a * mikveh, *in the name of Yeshua Ha Maschiach, (It's not likely that Peter used the Greek name Iesous, or English Jesus, for Yeshua)* they would be separating themselves from *that generation* who had rejected *Yeshua*. It was a Jewish way of identification. *In the name of* was a Hebrew idiom for saying they believed in *Yeshua* as their Messiah, His divine miracles, His authority, and His death, burial, and resurrection. They were believing everything that Peter had told them concerning *Yeshua*.

* *(Over 60 mikveots (Jewish ritual baths) have been discovered just below the Southern Steps leading up the Temple compound in Jerusalem from the first century.)*

"*for the remission of sins, and ye shall receive the gift of the Holy Ghost*" - The original wording is *unto,* or the Greek *eis,* which means, *on the basis of,* or *because of.* Because their sins had been forgiven, they were to go ahead and be immersed and then they would receive the Holy Spirit. In other places Peter later promised the forgiveness of sins on the basis of faith alone. **(Acts 5:31, 10:43, 13:38)** Water baptism never took anyone's sins away, but several times in the Bible the wording is closely connected to salvation when addressing a Jewish audience. **(Mark 16:16, Acts 2:38, 22:16)**

"For the promise is unto you, and to your children, and to all that are afar off, even as many as the Lord our God shall call." - The promise of the Holy Spirit for Israel is evident. The *call* goes out to *whosoever will*, but the Holy Spirit gives a divine call to those who have a desire to know the Lord.

"Save yourselves from this untoward generation." - The men of Israel to whom Peter was preaching couldn't stop the physical judgment that was coming upon Jerusalem, but they could separate themselves from the crooked generation that was guilty of the unpardonable sin. They certainly could not *save themselves* spiritually, but physically.

"Then they that gladly received his word were baptized: and the same day there were added unto them about three thousand souls." — About 3,000 precious souls became a part of the Jewish remnant that was saved. It could have been that the 12 apostles *(including Matthias)* immersed about 250 people each, or there could have been other members of the 120 disciples who participated in the ★ immersions. We are reminded of the words that Jesus spoke:

"Verily, verily, I say unto you, He that believeth on me, the works that I do shall he do also; and greater works than these shall he do; because I go unto my Father." **(John 14:12)** These works are not greater in quality, but greater in quantity.

Try to imagine how Peter and the other apostles must have felt when they saw these thousands of Jews believing in Jesus as their Messiah! Many of the things that Jesus had told them were coming true before their very eyes. They were now realizing the monumental task of taking the gospel into the known world!

(When churches take away the Jewish context, water baptism can give people a real false sense of security. Gentiles also need to be water baptized after they have received Christ, but not as a means of salvation, but a means of identifying themselves with Christ.)

THE FIRST CHURCH

Acts 2:42-47 - *And they continued stedfastly in the apostles' doctrine and fellowship, and in breaking of bread, and in prayers. And fear came upon every soul: and many wonders and signs were done by the apostles. And all that believed were together, and had all things common; And sold their possessions and goods, and parted them to all men, as every man had need. And they, continuing daily with one accord in the temple, and breaking bread from house to house, did eat their meat with gladness and singleness of heart, Praising God, and having favour with all the people. And the Lord added to the church daily such as should be saved.*

To prove that the thousands who had been immersed were truly born again, they *continued* in their devotion to Christ and to each other. Most of the Jews who accepted the preaching of Simon Peter and embraced Jesus as their Messiah returned to the country where they lived and *continued* to spread the message of the gospel. **(Romans 2:9-11)** The world would never be the same!

Those who lived in Israel *continued* in Jerusalem devoting themselves to the *apostle's doctrine*. They continued in spiritual *fellowship, breaking bread* together, and in *prayers*. This *first church* in Jerusalem probably ate meals together in their private homes, but the primary meaning here is that they partook of the Lord's Supper together. In the Jewish culture of that day, the Lord's Supper was not just a religious ritual, it was a real spiritual experience. Their prayers were filled with the Holy Spirit and as they broke the bread, they were truly remembering how Christ had broken bread with the apostles and then sacrificed Himself on the tree for their sins. **(Matthew 26:26-28, John 6:1-14, Luke 24:30-31)**

"And fear came upon every soul: and many wonders and signs were done by the apostles." - Those first followers of Jesus had the *afterglow* of Pentecost on their faces. Here is a perfect example that while Luke was writing in *Koine* Greek, his thoughts were really Hebrew. The Greek word for *fear* in this verse is, *phobos*, and means, *panic or flight or terror*. But the Hebrew word for *fear* is, *yirah*, and means *reverent awe*. In Hebrew thought, it meant that those early believers knew that they were experiencing something outside the realm of reasoning and understanding. This was a real divine act of God, not of man!

The only ones who were able to perform miracles were the *apostles* and those they delegated, such as *Stephen*. **(Acts 6:8)** The individual believers in the church were not able to perform *signs and wonders*.

"And sold their possessions and goods, and parted them to all men, as every man had need." - One of the most important

things this *first church* had was *unity*. The Holy Spirit had given them such a heavenly love for each other that they *sold their possessions* and distributed them to the ones who were in need. This was not a commandment from God. They were so filled with such unity, it was of their own free will. If the modern-day church had this kind of unity, there would be no need for welfare from the government.

"Praising God, and having favour with all the people. And the Lord added to the church daily such as should be saved." - Their *fellowship*, their *praise*, and their sense of *unity* were infectious. This is how a church is supposed to be. Their daily lives were a testimony of their faith in Christ. What the world calls "church" today has drifted far from what the first Jewish community of believers was really all about.

Several years ago this author was leading a group to Israel, and we were at the Southern Steps in Jerusalem. When we reflected upon **Acts 2:42-47**, this Hebrew thought came to mind to describe the *first church* in Jerusalem:

* *Beit Midrash = House of Study*
* *Beit Knesset = House of Fellowship*
* *Beit Tephillah = House of Prayer*
* *Beit Echod = House of One*
* *Beit Pele = House of Wonder*
* *Beit Simchah = House of Joy*
* *Beit Yirah = House of Fear*
* *Beit Halal = House of Praise*
* *Beit Yeshua = House of Salvation*

CHAPTER THREE

THE FIRST RECORDED APOSTOLIC MIRACLE

Acts 3:1-11 - *Now Peter and John went up together into the temple at the hour of prayer, being the ninth hour. And a certain man lame from his mother's womb was carried, whom they laid daily at the gate of the temple which is called Beautiful, to ask alms of them that entered into the temple; Who seeing Peter and John about to go into the temple asked an alms. And Peter, fastening his eyes upon him with John, said, Look on us. And he gave heed unto them, expecting to receive something of them. Then Peter said, Silver and gold have I none; but such as I have give I thee: In the name of Jesus Christ of Nazareth rise up and walk. And he took him by the right hand, and lifted him up: and immediately his feet and ankle bones received strength. And he leaping up stood, and walked, and entered with them into the temple, walking, and leaping, and praising God. And all the people saw him walking and praising God: And* *they knew that it was he which sat for alms at the Beautiful gate of the temple: and they were filled with wonder and amazement at that which had happened unto him. And as the lame man which was healed held Peter and John, all the people ran together unto them in the porch that is called Solomon's, greatly wondering.*

"Now Peter and John went up together into the temple at the hour of prayer, being the ninth hour." - Peter and John were used to going up to the Temple to pray at *the ninth hour*, or *three o'clock* in the afternoon. The first followers of Jesus saw no contradiction in the Temple traditions of worship and believing in Jesus as their Messiah. It was a Jewish community who had come to be *complete* in its faith. **(Romans 2:28-29)** Jesus talked about the kingdom of God being taken away from the unbelieving scribes and Pharisees and being given to a *new community*. The *new community* would consist of believing Jews and Gentiles:

"Therefore say I unto you, The kingdom of God shall be taken from you, and given to a nation (people) bringing forth the fruits thereof." **(Matthew 21:43)**

"And a certain man lame from his mother's womb was carried, whom they laid daily at the gate of the temple which is called Beautiful" - According to **Acts 4:22**, this man was over 40 years of age and had never known what it was like to walk one step. He had to be carried everywhere he went. One note of interest here is that Jesus did not heal this man who had been in the Temple precincts during Jesus' earthly ministry.

Jesus did not heal everyone as some supposed. The *Beautiful* gate is believed to have been the *Nicanor Gate* that went from the Outer Court of the Gentiles to the Inner Court of the Women close to the Temple itself.

"Then Peter said, Silver and gold have I none; but such as I have give I thee: In the name of Jesus Christ of Nazareth rise up and walk." – The apostles were not rich as the prosperity preachers tried to get people to believe. They had something that money could not buy; they had the power of the Holy Spirit, *in the name of, in the authority of, Jesus Christ of Nazareth*.

"And he took him by the right hand, and lifted him up: and immediately his feet and ankle bones received strength." – Peter wanted the lame man to look him and John right in the eyes. In the Jewish mind the eyes were the gateway into the soul of a man. **(Matthew 6:22-23)** When he did, Peter took him by the *right hand*, which was the Jewish symbol of strength, and *lifted the man up*. Not leaving out what specifically happened to the man, notice the physician Luke describes the results of the miracle in medical terms; *immediately his feet and ankle bones received strength*. The healed man started *walking with Peter and John into the Temple*. He wasn't just walking, he was *leaping*! What a sight that must have been!

"And all the people saw him walking and praising God: And they knew that it was he which sat for alms at the Beautiful gate of the temple: and they were filled with wonder and amazement at that which had happened unto him." – The people knew that this was the very same man who had been at the gate for many years begging for alms. Now they see him not just *walking*, but also *praising* God. The Bible tells us that this healed man was *walking, leaping, and praising God*.

"And as the lame man which was healed held Peter and John, all the people ran together unto them in the porch that is called Solomon's, greatly wondering." - While Peter and John certainly did not want anyone to worship them, one can understand why this thankful man was holding on to them. The *porch that is called Solomon's* was located on the southern end of the Outer Court of the Gentiles. It had been built on the ancient foundations of the temple that Solomon built. One of the purposes of this miracle was to draw a crowd so Peter could deliver his second sermon.

Israel's Rejection of Jesus as their Messiah

Acts 3:12-18 - *And when Peter saw it, he answered unto the people, Ye men of Israel, why marvel ye at this? or why look ye so earnestly on us, as though by our own power or holiness we had made this man to walk? The God of Abraham, and of Isaac, and of Jacob, the God of our fathers, hath glorified his Son Jesus; whom ye delivered up, and denied him in the presence of Pilate, when he was determined to let him go. But ye denied the Holy One and the Just, and desired a murderer to be granted unto you; And killed the Prince of life, whom God hath raised from the dead; whereof we are witnesses. And his name through faith in his name hath made this man strong, whom ye see and know: yea, the faith which is by him hath given him this perfect soundness in* *the presence of you all. And now, brethren, I wot that through ignorance ye did it, as did also your rulers. But those things, which God before had shewed by the mouth of all his prophets, that Christ should suffer, he hath so fulfilled.*

"Ye men of Israel, why marvel ye at this? or why look ye so earnestly on us, as though by our own power or holiness we had made this man to walk?" - This was a different group of Jews from when Peter preached his first sermon. They were located at a different part of the Temple compound and at a different time. Peter wanted them to know first that the miracle of the lame man had nothing to do with him or with John. Peter wanted to draw attention to Jesus immediately.

"The God of Abraham, and of Isaac, and of Jacob, the God of our fathers, hath glorified his Son Jesus;" - Peter is reminding them of the Abrahamic Covenant, and Jesus is the Seed of Abraham that would bless the entire world. **(Galatians 3:16)** *The God of Abraham, Isaac, and Jacob* has a Son, and his name is *Yeshua/Jesus*:

> *For unto us a child is born, unto us a son is given: and the government shall be upon his shoulder: and his name shall be called Wonderful, Counsellor, The mighty God, The everlasting Father, The Prince of Peace.* **(Isaiah 9:6)**
>
> *Who hath ascended up into heaven, or descended? who hath gathered the wind in his fists? who hath bound the waters in a garment? who hath established*

all the ends of the earth? what is his name, and what is his son's name, if thou canst tell? **(Proverbs 30:4)**

"whom ye delivered up, and denied him in the presence of Pilate, when he was determined to let him go." - The people that Peter was speaking to were the guilty ones who had delivered Jesus up to Pilate. Even the pagan Roman Procurator, *Pontius Pilate, was determined to let Him go,* and He was rejected by you, His own people!

"But ye denied the Holy One and the Just, and desired a murderer to be granted unto you;" - Peter is drawing their attention to the divinity of Christ, *ye denied the Holy One and the Just.* They not only denied the divine Jesus, but they also desired the murderer, Barabbas, to be released. The Holy Spirit was using Peter to carefully choose his words that would cut to their hearts.

"And killed the Prince of life, whom God hath raised from the dead; whereof we are witnesses." - Here Peter calls Jesus the *Prince of life,* or the One who created life in the first place. **(John 1:1-4)** Because He is the Originator of life, death could not hold Him. Peter said we are not just preaching to you about some man-made legend, we are *eyewitnesses* of His resurrection.

"And his name through faith in his name hath made this man strong, whom ye see and know: yea, the faith which is by him hath given him this perfect soundness in the presence of you all." - Now Peter is telling them who is responsible for the healing of the lame man. This man that you have seen walking had *faith* in this Jesus. He had probably seen or heard about Jesus teaching in the Temple during His earthly ministry. When the lame man heard Peter say that *Jesus of Nazareth* was the *Messiah*, he believed and was a witness of the power and authority in His name.

"And now, brethren, I wot that through ignorance ye did it, as did also your rulers. But those things, which God before had shewed by the mouth of all his prophets, that Christ should suffer, he hath so fulfilled." - Peter is not saying that everyone who rejected Jesus did it in *ignorance*. Some such as *Judas, Caiaphas, and Annas* knew exactly what they were doing. Most of the people who rejected Jesus were *ignorant* of who He was. **(I Corinthians 2:8)** Being *ignorant* did not erase their guilt because if they had known the scriptures, they would have known who Jesus was. God told the *prophets* of old that when the Messiah came into the world, He would *suffer*. Peter is saying that God used your *ignorance* to fulfill the prophecies, but you are still guilty and need to turn from your sins.

Israel is Responsible for Their Sins

Acts 3:19-26 - *Repent ye therefore, and be converted, that your sins may be blotted out, when the times of refreshing shall come from the presence of the Lord. And he shall send Jesus Christ, which before was preached unto you: Whom the heaven must receive until the times of restitution of all things, which God hath spoken by the mouth of all his holy prophets since the world began. For Moses truly said unto the fathers, A prophet shall the Lord your God raise up unto you of your brethren, like unto me; him shall ye hear in all things whatsoever he shall say unto you.*

And it shall come to pass, that every soul, which will not hear that prophet, shall be destroyed from among the people. Yea, and all the prophets from Samuel and those that follow after, as many as have spoken, have likewise foretold of these days. Ye are the children of the prophets, and of the covenant which God made with our fathers, saying unto Abraham, And in thy seed shall all the kindreds of the earth be blessed. Unto you first God, having raised up his Son Jesus, sent him to bless you, in turning away every one of you from his iniquities.

"*Repent ye therefore, and be converted, that your sins may be blotted out*" – As we looked at earlier, repentance in the Jewish mind means *to turn from your sins and return to God*. True repentance for the *individual* will result in his/her *sins being blotted out*. True faith in Christ alone will remove all sin! The *national* sin of Israel will still be judged by the Roman invasion in 70AD, and Peter was not reoffering Jesus to the generation who had committed the unpardonable sin, but he was simply offering the individuals their Messiah. Individual Jewish salvation is different from the restoration of national Israel.

"*when the times of refreshing shall come from the presence of the Lord. And he shall send Jesus Christ, which before was preached unto you: Whom the heaven must receive until the times of restitution of all things, which God hath spoken by the mouth of all his holy prophets since the world began.*" – When the nation of Israel repents as a whole, then the Messiah will return and restore all things. Peter may have been saying *if* there could be a national revival and all of the Jews repent, then the *times of refreshing would come.* The same Jesus that Peter was preaching to them will be the One who will come one day and establish the Messianic Kingdom that the prophets wrote about. Jesus ascended back to heaven and *will remain in heaven* until the sin ledger is full and the time is fulfilled. Jesus talked specifically about this time:

> *And Jesus said unto them, Verily I say unto you, That ye which have followed me, in the regeneration when the Son of man shall sit in the throne of his glory, ye also shall sit upon twelve thrones, judging the twelve tribes of Israel.* **(Matthew 19:28)**

Many times the Gentile Christians forget that Israel must repent as a nation before Jesus will return:

> *For I say unto you, Ye shall not see me henceforth, till ye shall say, Blessed is he that cometh in the name of the Lord.* **(Matthew 23:39)**

This will happen at the very end of the great tribulation period, after Israel has gone through the time of *Jacob's Trouble.* **(Jeremiah 30:7)** Only one-third of Israel will be ushered into the new *Davidic Kingdom*:

> *And it shall come to pass, that in all the land, saith the Lord, two parts therein shall be cut off and die; but the third shall be left therein. And I will bring the third part through the fire, and will refine them as silver is refined, and will try them as gold is tried: they shall call on my name, and I will hear them:*

I will say, It is my people: and they shall say, The Lord is my God. **(Zechariah 13:8-9)**

"For Moses truly said unto the fathers, A prophet shall the Lord your God raise up unto you of your brethren, like unto me; him shall ye hear in all things whatsoever he shall say unto you. And it shall come to pass, that every soul, which will not hear that prophet, shall be destroyed from among the people." - The Holy Spirit is prompting Peter to quote passages from Moses; **Deuteronomy 18:15, 18:19**. Deuteronomy 18:15 is alluded to many times in the New Testament, but quoted again in **Acts 7:37**. Here Jesus is called *a prophet*, and if the people decide to reject Jesus, *every soul shall be destroyed*.

"Yea, and all the prophets from Samuel and those that follow after, as many as have spoken, have likewise foretold of these days." - Most of the time Peter uses the term *all of the prophets*, but here he adds *from Samuel and those that follow after*. Why? Samuel is considered to be one of the most holy of the prophets of Israel, and he was the one who anointed David to be king over Israel. Jesus is the Son of David, and thus Samuel holds a very special place in the Jewish culture.

"Ye are the children of the prophets, and of the covenant which God made with our fathers, saying unto Abraham, And in thy seed shall all the kindreds of the earth be blessed." - Peter wasn't saying that the people he was preaching to were direct descendants of the prophets, but they were descendants in the sense of inheritance of the covenant that God made with Abraham. If they would embrace Jesus as their Messiah, they would not just be a part of *natural Israel*, but a part of *spiritual*

Israel, and true children of Abraham. The apostles would see the Abrahamic Covenant start to unfold within their lifetime.

"Unto you first God, having raised up his Son Jesus, sent him to bless you, in turning away every one of you from his iniquities." - This is a powerful truth that has been lost over the centuries in the Gentile world. Jesus was sent first to Israel, then to the Gentiles. This pattern we will see as we go through the rest of the book of Acts. The apostle Paul made this statement in the book of Romans:

> *For I am not ashamed of the gospel of Christ: for it is the power of God unto salvation to every one that believeth; to the Jew first, and also to the Greek.* **(Romans 1:16)**

Peter uses six different titles for Jesus within the second sermon:
* *Son Jesus*
* *The Holy One*
* *The Just*
* *The Prince of Life*
* *Jesus Christ*
* *Prophet like unto Moses*

CHAPTER FOUR

FIVE THOUSAND MORE & THE APOSTLES ARRESTED

Acts 4:1-4 - *And as they spake unto the people, the priests, and the captain of the temple, and the Sadducees, came upon them, Being grieved that they taught the people, and preached through Jesus the resurrection from the dead. And they laid hands on them, and put them in hold unto the next day: for it was now eventide. Howbeit many of them which heard the word believed; and the number of the men was about five thousand.*

This marks the beginning of the rejection of Peter's message. As the apostles were speaking, they were interrupted by the *priests,* the *Temple captain,* and the *Sadducees* who ruled over the Temple. The *captain of the Temple* was called the Overseer of the Temple Mount, or *ish har ha-bayit,* and he was second in authority to the high priest himself.

There were several reasons why the religious rulers were indignant with the apostles:

* *The apostles were teaching the people*
* *The apostles were uneducated Galileans*
* *The apostles were in the Temple compound*
* *The apostles were preaching about Jesus' resurrection*
* *The Sadducees did not believe in any resurrection*

"And they laid hands on them, and put them in hold unto the next day: for it was now eventide." - It was already late in the day and by Jewish law, no trial could be conducted in the evening.

"Howbeit many of them which heard the word believed; and the number of the men was about five thousand." - Glory to God! In the midst of a religious establishment who was jealous and hated what was going on, the God of heaven was still doing His great work. *Five thousand* more men received Jesus as their Messiah, not counting the women and children. One has to also consider the fact that in some areas of the Temple compound, women were not allowed. No doubt many of the members of their families would have followed Christ as well.

The Sanhedrin Question the Apostles

Acts 4:5-7 - *And it came to pass on the morrow, that their rulers, and elders, and scribes, And Annas the high priest, and Caiaphas, and John, and Alexander, and as many as were of the kindred of the high priest, were gathered together at Jerusalem. And when they had set them in the midst, they asked, By what power, or by what name, have ye done this?*

The ruling body of the religious Jews was made up of 71 men called the *Sanhedrin*. It was *rulers, priests,* and *teachers. Annas* was the high priest from 6-15AD, and one of his sons was named Jonathan, or *John,* who served from 36-37AD. *Caiaphas* served as high priest from 18-36AD. Nothing is recorded about *Alexander.* They were in a lucrative money-changing and sacrifice-selling business. They undoubtedly had not forgotten about Jesus overthrowing their tables twice during His ministry.

It's astounding that a group of common Galileans preaching about the King of Israel could cause such uproar in Jerusalem that was called *the city of the Great King.* **(Psalm 48:2)** Satan always works through religious systems to corrupt the people and to attack what the precious Lord is doing.

"And when they had set them in the midst, they asked, By what power, or by what name, have ye done this?" - The religious leaders admitted that the lame man had been healed, but they were saying that the apostles did it through some kind of magic or evil power. They were quick to accuse Jesus of doing His works in the name of Beelzebub. **(Matthew 12:24)**

FIRST TIME PETER ADDRESS THE LEADERS OF ISRAEL

Acts 4:8-12 - *Then Peter, filled with the Holy Ghost, said unto them, Ye rulers of the people, and elders of Israel, If we this day be examined of the good deed done to the impotent man, by what means he is made whole; Be it known unto you all, and to all the people of Israel, that by the name of Jesus Christ of Nazareth, whom ye crucified, whom God raised* *from the dead, even by him doth this man stand here before you whole. This is the stone which was set at nought of you builders, which is become the head of the corner. Neither is there salvation in any other: for there is none other name under heaven given among men, whereby we must be saved.*

Peter's words were not his own thoughts for he was filled with the Holy Spirit! This is a fulfillment of **Luke 21:12-15**. Peter's boldness told them that it was by the *name of Jesus Christ of Nazareth* that the lame man had been made whole. Peter is charging them with murdering the Messiah by crucifixion, but God answered them by raising Him from the dead. The same One you killed was healed by His resurrection power. The phrase, *even by him doth this man stand here before you whole,* implies that the healed man had been in jail with the apostles.

"This is the stone which was set at nought of you builders, which is become the head of the corner." - The *builders* who rejected Christ were the religious leaders that Peter was speaking to. Peter is paraphrasing a verse from Psalms that Jesus also used when talking to the religious leaders, and then Peter referred to it again almost 30 years later. **(Read Psalm 118:22, Matthew 21:42, I Peter 2:6-8)**

"Neither is there salvation in any other: for there is none other name under heaven given among men, whereby we must be saved." - The very name by which the lame man was healed is the very same *name* and only *name* by which one *must* be saved. We are reminded of what Jesus said:

Jesus saith unto him, I am the way, the truth, and the life: no man cometh unto the Father, but by me. **(John 14:6)**

Peter's address to the religious leaders can be summarized as follows:

* *Jesus is the Messiah*
* *You crucified Him*
* *You rejected Him*
* *God raised him from the dead*
* *God has exalted Him*
* *Jesus is the only name whereby one can be saved*
* *Salvation is a must, not an option to enter heaven*

THE RELIGIOUS LEADERS MARVELED

Acts 4:13-14 - *Now when they saw the boldness of Peter and John, and perceived that they were unlearned and ignorant men, they marvelled; and they took knowledge of them, that they had been with Jesus. And beholding the man which was healed standing with them, they could say nothing against it.*

The boldness of Peter and John came from being filled with the Holy Spirit. They had not been taught in the rabbinic schools and they were unrefined, but they had something that every child of God needs. The religious leaders *marveled* at their boldness, and they began to recognize them as men who had been with Jesus. There should be enough of the Holy

Spirit within our lives that even the lost people in the world will know that we have been walking with Jesus!

"And beholding the man which was healed standing with them, they could say nothing against it." - The man who had never walked was *standing* with Peter and John, and the unbelieving Jewish leaders could say nothing. There are great hosts of people when they see the power of God at work can say nothing against it, but they refuse to repent themselves. The darkest type of blindness is religious blindness.

THE DECISION AND RESPONSE

Acts 4:15-22 - *But when they had commanded them to go aside out of the council, they conferred among themselves, Saying, What shall we do to these men? for that indeed a notable miracle hath been done by them is manifest to all them that dwell in Jerusalem; and we cannot deny it. But that it spread no further among the people, let us straitly threaten them, that they speak henceforth to no man in this name. And they called them, and commanded them not to speak at all nor teach in the name of Jesus. But Peter and John answered and said unto them, Whether it be right in the sight of God to hearken unto you more than unto God, judge ye. For we cannot but speak the things which we have seen and heard. So when they had further threatened them, they let them go, finding nothing how they might punish them, because of the people: for all men glorified God for that which*

was done. For the man was above forty years old, on whom this miracle of healing was shewed.

The religious leaders decided it was time to have a private council. They were in a predicament because this miracle of the lame man has caused thousands to be converted to Christ as their Lord Messiah and the *notable miracle hath been done by them is manifest to all them that dwell in Jerusalem*. The apostles had not broken any law, so they decided to *threaten them, that they speak henceforth to no man in this name. And they called them, and commanded them not to speak at all nor teach in the name of Jesus*. Notice that the leaders said *in this name*. They wouldn't even speak His name. Even today many of the unbelieving Jews call *Yeshua, "Yeshu"*, which means, *may his name be blotted out*. If they do say *"Yeshua"* or *"Jesus,"* it is in a derogatory, mocking way.

"But Peter and John answered and said unto them, Whether it be right in the sight of God to hearken unto you more than unto God, judge ye. For we cannot but speak the things which we have seen and heard." - There was no way they would silence the apostles who had been commanded by Jesus to be witnesses. This is a major theme in the book of Acts. What God had called them to do was a much greater command than the orders of unbelieving leaders of Israel. We are reminded of what the prophet Jeremiah said:

Then I said, I will not make mention of him, nor speak any more in his name. But his word was in mine heart as a burning fire shut up in my bones, and

> *I was weary with forbearing, and I could not stay.* **(Jeremiah 20:9)**

"So when they had further threatened them, they let them go, finding nothing how they might punish them, because of the people: for all men glorified God for that which was done." - Several reasons why the religious leaders had to let the apostles go:

> *★ No law had been broken*
> *★ The healing of the lame man was real*
> *★ All men were glorifying God*
> *★ Over 5,000 more had received Jesus as their Messiah*

This was the beginning of a stirring up of the religious establishment that eventually led to a major scattering of the Jewish believers.

A Time for Praise and Prayer

Acts 4:23-30 - *And being let go, they went to their own company, and reported all that the chief priests and elders had said unto them. And when they heard that, they lifted up their voice to God with one accord, and said, Lord, thou art God, which hast made heaven, and earth, and the sea, and all that in them is: Who by the mouth of thy servant David hast said, Why did the heathen rage, and the people imagine vain things? The kings of the earth stood up, and the rulers were gathered together against the Lord, and against his Christ. For of a truth against thy holy child Jesus, whom thou hast anointed, both*

Herod, and Pontius Pilate, with the Gentiles, and the people of Israel, were gathered together, For to do whatsoever thy hand and thy counsel determined before to be done. And now, Lord, behold their threatenings: and grant unto thy servants, that with all boldness they may speak thy word, By stretching forth thine hand to heal; and that signs and wonders may be done by the name of thy holy child Jesus.

After the apostles were released, Peter and John reported to the other apostles and told them what the religious leaders had said. They began to praise the God of heaven; *And when they heard that, they lifted up their voice to God with one accord, and said,* ★ *Lord, thou art God, which hast made heaven, and earth, and the sea, and all that in them is.* We can learn a powerful lesson about prayer from these early believers. When we pray, we need to begin by *praising* the Lord for creation! All through the Old Testament the saints of God praised God for everything that He had made.

★ *(This author likes to take a walk and pray looking up to the clouds and the blue sky. A reminder that the One who died for us on the tree is none other than the Creator Himself, who helps us increase our faith. It reminds us how big God really is in that we are in the hands of the One who created the heavens and the earth and the One who gives us the blessed assurance that no matter what happens, we are never out of His eyes.)*

"*Who by the mouth of thy servant David hast said, Why did the heathen rage, and the people imagine vain things? The kings of the earth stood up, and the rulers were gathered together against the Lord, and against his Christ.* (mashiach) *For of a truth against thy holy child Jesus, whom thou hast anointed, both Herod, and Pontius Pilate, with the Gentiles, and the people of Israel, were gathered together,"* – The apostles start quoting **Psalm 2:1-2.** Again, we can see the dual authorship of God's Holy Word. The words that *David* wrote down were inspired by God and many times hold profound prophecies into the future, sometimes with two or three different meanings. We need to be reminded that Jesus is the Son of David and make the mysterious correlation between David's writings and Jesus' life and ministry. The Hebrew word in **Psalm 2:2** is *mashiach*, translated *anointed*, which means *Messiah* in Hebrew, *Christos* in Greek, and *Christ* in English. This strong passage in **Psalm 2** is connected to the first *and* second comings of Jesus:

* *The people of Israel who rejected Jesus*
* *Herod, Pilate, and the Roman soldiers who help to crucify Jesus*
* *The kings of the earth will fight against Jesus at the Battle of Armageddon.* **(Revelation 16:14-16)**

"For to do whatsoever thy hand and thy counsel determined before to be done." – There was a *human* responsibility and a *Divine* responsibility in the death of Christ. Both the *Jews* and *Gentiles* were guilty, but what happened was what God had predetermined to come to pass. God knew the Jewish religious establishment was corrupt, and He would use the pagan Romans to accomplish His will. Crucifixion was prophesied centuries before it was invented by the Persians. (300-400BC) Why didn't Jesus come into the world 100 years earlier? Why didn't He come 100 years later? The time on the historical clock was perfect for everything to be fulfilled. Even in the darkest

hours of our world when evil men think they are in control, God is still at work accomplishing His master plan.

"And now, Lord, behold their threatenings: and grant unto thy servants, that with all boldness they may speak thy word, By stretching forth thine hand to heal; and that signs and wonders may be done by the name of thy holy child Jesus." - The apostles made three prayer requests:

* *Lord remember the threatenings against us*
* *Give us boldness*
* *Stretch forth thine hand to heal with signs and wonders*

GOD'S ANSWER TO THEIR PRAYER

Acts 4:31 - *And when they had prayed, the place was shaken where they were assembled together; and they were all filled with the Holy Ghost, and they spake the word of God with boldness.*

The place was *shaken*! They were all filled with the Holy Ghost! They had been baptized in the Holy Spirit, and now they experience a fresh filling of the Holy Spirit. There is only one time a believer is baptized in the Holy Spirit, when we are born again. There are many fillings of the Holy Spirit along our spiritual journey. We are commanded in God's Word to be filled with the Holy Spirit. **(Ephesians 5:18)** The apostles were given the boldness to speak God's Word as they had requested. In spite of the threats, the apostles would continue to be a witness for Jesus with supernatural power! Hallelujah!

Holy Spirit Working in the Community of Believers

Acts 4:32-35 - *And the multitude of them that believed were of one heart and of one soul: neither said any of them that ought of the things which he possessed was his own; but they had all things common. And with great power gave the apostles witness of the resurrection of the Lord Jesus: and great grace was upon them all. Neither was there any among them that lacked: for as many as were possessors of lands or houses sold them, and brought the prices of the things that were sold, And laid them down at the apostles' feet: and distribution was made unto every man according as he had need.*

After the conversion of over 5,000 more Jews, there was now *a multitude of them that believed*. Only the Holy Spirit could provide such a unity of spirit among this great number of people. At the beginning of this early church, there were no bad or negative spirits within the community. They all had *one heart and one soul*.

"neither said any of them that ought of the things which he possessed was his own; but they had all things common....... Neither was there any among them that lacked: for as many as were possessors of lands or houses sold them, and brought the prices of the things that were sold, And laid them down at the apostles' feet: and distribution was made unto every man according as he had need." - The Holy Spirit had given them the spirit of sharing their material possessions with those who had need. We can see clearly the apostolic authority as they sold their lands or houses and laid the money down at the apostles' feet. The apostles themselves had no desire to be wealthy; they distributed the money to the ones who had been less fortunate. This was not a

doctrine for communism; it was simply the love of Jesus coming out of the hearts of the Jewish believers toward each other. Most likely they were also looking for Christ to return soon, and they didn't want to lay up any treasures on this earth. While this is not a *prescription* for the church today, it is a beautiful *description* of that early church. When believers are filled with the Holy Spirit, they want to share their possessions with others. Every local church should have this spirit. It has been said that one of the greatest hindrances of a spiritual revival in our world is the greed and selfishness that is so prevalent in the lives of so many professing Christians. Later on the church in Jerusalem would need financial help from the Gentile churches. **(Acts 11:27-30, 24:17, Romans 15:25-27, Gal.2:10)**

"And with great power gave the apostles witness of the resurrection of the Lord Jesus: and great grace was upon them all." – The apostles *continued* to preach about the *Lord Jesus*, in spite of the threats by the religious leaders. Their message was centered on the *resurrection* of Jesus. Early Jewish history of those first Jewish Christians reveals that every time they gathered together, they focused on the resurrection of Christ. Without the resurrection of Christ, there would be no Christianity and no hope of heaven. We are reminded of what the apostle Paul would later write:

> *"And if Christ be not risen, then is our preaching vain, and your faith is also vain. Yea, and we are found false witnesses of God; because we have testified of God that he raised up Christ: whom he raised not up, if so be that the dead rise not. For if the dead rise not, then is not Christ raised: And if Christ be not raised, your faith is vain; ye are yet in your sins. Then they also*

which are fallen asleep in Christ are perished. If in this life only we have hope in Christ, we are of all men most miserable." **(I Corinthians 15:14-19)**

This early believing community had *the grace of God upon them all*. All of the preaching, signs and wonders, and sharing were not just because the people were talented individuals, or just plain good folks. It was not because they were trying to keep the Law of Moses or trying to have a good reputation. It was because they had believed in Jesus as their Messiah and were filled with the Holy Spirit. It was the *unmerited favor* of God upon them. God was pleased, and He accepted their worship!

THE INTRODUCTION OF BARNABAS

Acts 4:36-37 - *And Joses, who by the apostles was surnamed Barnabas, (which is, being interpreted, The son of consolation,) a Levite, and of the country of Cyprus, Having land, sold it, and brought the money, and laid it at the apostles' feet.*

The general account of the early believers now changes to one specific person, *Barnabas*. This man is mentioned specifically because of the role he played later on in the book of Acts. He is one of the most underrated people in the Bible. His Aramaic name can mean *son of consolation*, or *son of exhortation*. His original name was the Hebrew *Joseph*, and he was *surnamed Barnabas by the apostles* because of his gift of comforting others. What a precious gift to have!

It is very interesting that he was a Jew from the tribe of Levi who had lived on the island of Cyprus, about 300 miles out in the Mediterranean Sea west of Israel. Jews first settled on the island of Cyprus as far back as the second century BC. Barnabas was now living in Jerusalem.

Barnabas is the important man who persuaded the church of Jerusalem to receive Paul. **(Acts 9:27)** He was sent by the church of Jerusalem to investigate Gentile salvation in Antioch. **(Acts 11:19-24)** Barnabas was a man filled with the Holy Spirit. **(Acts 11:24)** He is also the one who brought Paul from Tarsus to Antioch. **(Acts 11:25-26)** According to **Acts 14:12**, he must have had a commanding appearance. Barnabas was called an apostle in a second category of apostles, such as Paul. **(Acts 14:14)** The name ★ Barnabas appears some 23 times in the book of Acts and five times in other books of the New Testament. **(I Cor.9:6, Gal.2:1, 9, 13, and Col.4:10)** Barnabas was the cousin of John Mark. **(Col.4:10)** It is strongly believed that Barnabas was one of the 500 who saw the resurrected Christ in **I Cor.15:6**.

★ *(While most scholars and colleges do not teach this, the prolific Christian author, Tertullian, from Carthage, a province in Africa, stated that Barnabas was the author of the book of Hebrews.)*

"Having land, sold it, and brought the money, and laid it at the apostles' feet." - Within the land of Israel, a Levite was forbidden to own land. **(Num.18:20, Deut.10:9)** Evidently he owned land on the island of Cyprus and sold it. He brought the money to the apostles. He was a wonderful example of someone who had the love of Jesus in his heart for the brethren.

CHAPTER FIVE

THE BAD EXAMPLE OF ANANIAS & SAPPHIRA

Acts 5:1-11 - *But a certain man named Ananias, with Sapphira his wife, sold a possession, And kept back part of the price, his wife also being privy to it, and brought a certain part, and laid it at the apostles' feet. But Peter said, Ananias, why hath Satan filled thine heart to lie to the Holy Ghost, and to keep back part of the price of the land? Whiles it remained, was it not thine own? and after it was sold, was it not in thine own power? why hast thou conceived this thing in thine heart? thou hast not lied unto men, but unto God. And Ananias hearing these words fell down, and gave up the ghost: and great fear came on all them that heard these things. And the young men arose, wound him up, and carried him out, and buried him. And it was about the space of three hours after, when his wife, not knowing what was done, came in. And Peter answered unto her, Tell me whether ye sold the land for so much? And she said,*

Yea, for so much. Then Peter said unto her, How is it that ye have agreed together to tempt the Spirit of the Lord? behold, the feet of them which have buried thy husband are at the door, and shall carry thee out. Then fell she down straightway at his feet, and yielded up the ghost: and the young men came in, and found her dead, and, carrying her forth, buried her by her husband. And great fear came upon all the church, and upon as many as heard these things.

The first word *But* lets us know the sharp contrast between the good example of *Barnabas* and the bad examples of *Ananias and Sapphira*. Ironically, the original Hebrew name of *Ananias,* is *Chananyah*, which means, *Jehovah is gracious*. The name *Sapphira* in Hebrew is * *Shaphirah,* and it means *beautiful.* Even though God was gracious to both of them, they lied to the Holy Spirit and caused the first internal problems for the early church in Jerusalem. Their deaths seem such a harsh treatment to us today. It was a severe case of promising God something, and then they let greed come into their hearts. Their deceit interrupted the progress of the program of God. While Barnabas had a true love for the brethren, *Ananias and Sapphira* did not. Twice it says that they *kept back part* of the price of the land they had promised to the Lord. *Satan had filled their hearts.* While prosperity can be a good thing if it used for God's kingdom, many times when people see the chance to keep money or possessions, Satan tempts them the way he tempted Jesus. **(Matthew 4:8)**

The selling of the land and promising to give all of the money to the apostles was purely voluntary. Their sin was that they claimed to have given it all but lied about it. Peter had the gift of discernment, and Christ had given him the power *to bind or to loose. To bind* meant to pronounce judgment, and *to loose* meant that he could free people from punishment.

> **And I will give unto thee the keys of the kingdom of heaven: and whatsoever thou shalt bind on earth shall be bound in heaven: and whatsoever thou shalt loose on earth shall be loosed in heaven. (Matthew 16:19)**

The other apostles were also given this power:

> **Whose soever sins ye remit, they are remitted unto them; and whose soever sins ye retain, they are retained. (John 20:23)**

"about the space of three hours after, when his wife, not knowing what was done, came in." - It is believed that Ananias' body was taken outside the city limits for burial, and this may help to explain the three-hour period.

★ *(On the Mount of Olives, hundreds of ossuaries (small boxes containing the bones of the deceased from the first century) were found in a Jewish Christian cemetery. Among the many names that were found inscribed on the ossuaries was the name Sapphira. While we cannot be certain that this was the biblical Sapphira, it was not such a common name for a woman during the first century.)*

"And great fear came upon all the church, and upon as many as heard these things." - Because of the death of *Ananias and Sapphira*, the early believers were struck with a *reverent fear* and seriousness of how to have respect for holy things. One of the problems we face today is that there is no separation between carnal things and spiritual things. The world has come into the church, and the Holy Spirit has been quenched! The church system of today has lost that awesome *fear* of God's holiness. The work of the Holy Spirit is sacred!

This is the first mention in the book of Acts of the term for the *church*, the Greek word, *ekklesia*, and is found some 23 times in the book of Acts. The word that Jesus would have used for the *church* would have probably been the Hebrew word, *qahal*. In either case, both words are referring to *the called out people*, not a building or any denomination.

We can gather four important lessons from the death of *Ananias and Sapphira:*

* *Peter's apostolic authority*
* *Discipline was strict during the start of the early church*
* *God desires a pure church*
* *It produced godly fear*

God will judge sin, as Peter would later write:

For the time is come that judgment must begin at the house of God: and if it first begin at us, what shall the end be of them that obey not the gospel of God? (I Peter 4:17)

A congregation of true born again believers should practice discipline according to what Jesus said:

Moreover if thy brother shall trespass against thee, go and tell him his fault between thee and him alone: if he shall hear thee, thou hast gained thy brother. But

if he will not hear thee, then take with thee one or two more, that in the mouth of two or three witnesses every word may be established. And if he shall neglect to hear them, tell it unto the church (assembly)*: but if he neglect to hear the church, let him be unto thee as an heathen man and a publican. Verily I say unto you, Whatsoever ye shall bind on earth shall be bound in heaven: and whatsoever ye shall loose on earth shall be loosed in heaven. Again I say unto you, That if two of you shall agree on earth as touching any thing that they shall ask, it shall be done for them of my Father which is in heaven. For where two or three are gathered together in my name, there am I in the midst of them.* **(Matthew 18:15-20)**

GOD'S POWER CONTINUED

Acts 5:12-16 - *And by the hands of the apostles were many signs and wonders wrought among the people; (and they were all with one accord in Solomon's porch. And of the rest durst no man join himself to them: but the people magnified them. And believers were the more added to the Lord, multitudes both of men and women.) Insomuch that they brought forth the sick into the streets, and laid them on beds and couches, that at the least the shadow of Peter passing by might overshadow some of them. There came also a multitude out of the cities round about unto Jerusalem, bringing sick folks, and them which*

were vexed with unclean spirits: and they were healed every one.

The death of *Ananias and Sapphira* purged the church, and God's power and unity would continue through the apostles to the believing community. Because there were now thousands of believers, they could not meet in a room, but in *Solomon's Porch*. This area was a long covered hallway stretching along the whole length of the south end of the Temple compound. It's interesting that the early church was meeting for a time in the precincts of the Jewish Temple. The contrast is given of the unbelieving religious establishment who controlled the Temple and the new *messianic* Jews who were meeting on the same Mount Moriah where Abraham brought Isaac. God's covenant that He made with Abraham centuries before was now coming to fruition.

"And of the rest durst no man join himself to them: but the people magnified them."- The unbelieving Jews would not join with the new community for fear of being persecuted by the religious leaders. However, the believers in Jesus as their Messiah had a good report among the unbelievers. Even the unbelieving Jews could see the signs and wonders of the apostles were real, and they also saw the unity among the brethren.

"And believers were the more added to the Lord, multitudes both of men and women.)" – In spite of the unbelief of the general population, Jews were still being converted to Christ. *Multitudes of people continued to be added, both men and women.*

"Insomuch that they brought forth the sick into the streets, and laid them on beds and couches, that at the least the shadow

of Peter passing by might overshadow some of them." - What a unique gift was given to the apostle Peter! All of the apostles had supernatural power, but Peter was the chief of the apostles. We need to remember the four gospels when Jesus called the ★ fisherman Simon Peter, and how He saw something in Peter that would be great one day. Peter was a flawed and simple man, but he became one of the world's most powerful preachers. Peter had such power that the people believed that even *his shadow* would heal them. Wow! We all need to remember that God sees what we can become through His mercy and grace.

★ *(One of the major symbols of the early Jewish Christian movement was the Greek, ichthus, or fish. Inside the fish were the Greek letters; IXOYC, which stand for "Jesus Christ, Son of God, Savior." It affirmed the belief that Jesus was both fully God and fully Man.)*

"There came also a multitude out of the cities round about unto Jerusalem, bringing sick folks, and them which were vexed with unclean spirits: and they were healed every one." - Notice the two categories of people who came from the surrounding cities, *sick folks* and the ones who were *vexed with unclean spirits*. Most sicknesses are caused simply by human frailty, but some sicknesses are caused by demons. The Holy Spirit was showing through the apostles that the kingdom of God was greater than the kingdom of darkness.

It is sad that so-called faith healers today claim to have the same power that the apostles had. Just saying the words and positive thinking may help someone temporarily with psychosomatic problems, but no one today has the power that the apostles had, who walked with the very Son of God. God still heals today through our own personal faith, sometimes with the aid of a physician, but it is always within His own choosing and timing. All physical healing is temporary, and there must come a time for all of the saved to leave this physical world and enter into God's glorious presence.

The Second Arrest of the Apostles

Acts 5:17-26 - *Then the high priest rose up, and all they that were with him, (which is the sect of the Sadducees,) and were filled with indignation, And laid their hands on the apostles, and put them in the common prison. But the angel of the Lord by night opened the prison doors, and brought them forth, and said, Go, stand and speak in the temple to the people all the words of this life. And when they heard that, they entered into the temple early in the morning, and taught. But the high priest came, and they that were with him, and called the council together, and all the senate of the children of Israel, and sent to the prison to have them brought. But when the officers came, and found them not in the prison, they returned and told, Saying, The prison truly found we shut with all safety, and the keepers standing without before the doors: but when we had opened, we found no man within. Now when the high priest and the captain of the temple and the chief priests heard these things, they doubted of them whereunto this would grow. Then came one and told them, saying, Behold, the men whom ye put in prison are standing in the* *temple, and teaching the people. Then went the captain with the officers, and brought them without violence: for they feared the people, lest they should have been stoned.*

The second persecution of the apostles starts because of the *high priest* and was instigated by *the Sadducees*. Through the inspiration of the Holy Spirit, Luke is writing to let us know that the ones who were in charge of the Temple to the God of Israel were persecuting the *true* followers of God.

"were filled with indignation" – The Greek word that Luke uses here for *indignation* is *zelos*, and it means envy or jealousy. The success of the apostles had created jealousy in the hearts of the religious establishment. Their jealousy was so noticeable that even the pagan Pontius Pilate knew their motive for crucifying Jesus:

For he knew that for envy they had delivered him. **(Matthew 27:18)**

"But the angel of the Lord by night opened the prison doors" – It was a divine rescue! One has to wonder if this *angel* was one of the angels at the tomb of our Risen Lord?

And it came to pass, as they were much perplexed thereabout, behold, two men stood by them in shining garments: **(Luke 24:4)**

Luke mentions several other angelic interventions in the book of Acts. **(Acts 8:26, 12:7-10, 23)**

"and said, Go, stand and speak in the temple to the people all the words of this life" – These are the words of the angel to the apostles! The angel is telling them not to speak in a secret place, but in a public place. It is astounding that the angel told them to tell the people *all the words of this life*. This is a Hebraism for *resurrection life*, which is exactly what the Sadducees did not believe.

"early in the morning, and taught." – This was when the people were pouring into the Temple compound. Being told by the angel, their teaching must have been filled with even a greater boldness.

"But the high priest came, and they that were with him, and called the council together, and all the senate of the children of Israel, and sent to the prison to have them brought. But when the officers came, and found them not in the prison, they returned and told, Saying, The prison truly found we shut with all safety, and the keepers standing without before the doors: but when we had opened, we found no man within. – The entire body of the Sanhedrin convened for the purpose of putting the apostles on trial. This again shows that the persecution was by both the Sadducees and the Pharisees, who made up the *council*. Not only did the *officers* find the prison doors shut tightly with no possible way of escape, they also found the guards still standing in front of the doors. It was clear that the apostles had been visited and rescued by a heavenly visitor.

"Now when the high priest and the captain of the temple and the chief priests heard these things, they doubted of them whereunto this would grow." – Now we find the second most important person in the Temple compound, *the captain of the Temple*. Not only were they perplexed and puzzled by what had happened, they were worried about what might happen if the news of this miracle got out to the public. It is amazing that the so-called leaders of Israel were trying to stop the gospel of Christ from continuing to be proclaimed. The real enemies of Christ were the religious leaders who were being controlled by Satan.

"Then came one and told them, saying, Behold, the men whom ye put in prison are standing in the temple, and teaching the people. Then went the captain with the officers, and brought them without violence: for they feared the people, lest they should have been stoned." - Try to imagine the looks on their faces when some unnamed person told the rulers that the men they had locked up were standing in the Temple and teaching the people again! In the first arrest the apostles were taken by force, but this time they took them slowly and solemnly. Why? They were afraid of the people. The apostles still had a good reputation among the common people who had been followers of the Pharisees. The people were finding out the true hearts of their leaders.

THE APOSTLES BEFORE THE COUNCIL

Acts 5:27-33 - *And when they had brought them, they set them before the council: and the high priest asked them, Saying, Did not we straitly command you that ye should not teach in this name? and, behold, ye have filled Jerusalem with your doctrine, and intend to bring this man's blood upon us. Then Peter and the other apostles answered and said, We ought to obey God rather than men. The God of our fathers raised up Jesus, whom ye slew and hanged on a tree. Him* *hath God exalted with his right hand to be a Prince and a Saviour, for to give repentance to Israel, and forgiveness of sins. And we are his witnesses of these things; and so is also the Holy Ghost, whom God hath given to them that obey him. When they heard that, they were cut to the heart, and took counsel to slay them.*

"**And when they had brought them, they set them before the council:**" – The apostles are looked upon and treated as prisoners. This connects us to what Jesus told them:

But before all these, they shall lay their hands on you, and persecute you, delivering you up to the synagogues, and into prisons, being brought before kings and rulers for my name's sake. **(Luke 21:12)**

"**Did not we straitly command you that ye should not teach in this name?**" – The high priest probably spoke in Hebrew because the Greek text contains a Hebraism saying, *"with charging we charged you."* The first charge was given in **Acts 4:17-18**. Notice that the high priest does not call the name of Yeshua; he says *this name*.

"**and, behold, ye have filled Jerusalem with your doctrine, and intend to bring this man's blood upon us**" – The doctrine of the apostles was the death, burial, and resurrection of Jesus. **(Acts 2:42, 4:33)** The apostles were not bringing the blood of Christ upon them; they were bringing it upon themselves by rejecting Jesus their Messiah:

> *Then answered all the people, and said, His blood be on us, and on our children.* **(Matthew 27:25)**

"Then Peter and the other apostles answered and said, We ought to obey God rather than men." – The apostles had been given a commandment by Jesus Himself and by the angel to preach the gospel to the people. (*Jesus*– **Luke 24:47**, *Angel*– **Acts 5:20**) The apostles were left with no other choice!

"The God of our fathers raised up Jesus, whom ye slew and hanged on a tree." – This is a powerful section of scripture because Peter is saying that the same God who made covenants with Israel is the one who sent Jesus into the world and brought Him to the *forefront*, by raising Him from the dead. Peter does not say that Jesus was killed on a cross, but *on a *tree*. Peter would use this word again in **Acts 10:39**, and **I Peter 2:24**. During the 40 days that Jesus stayed on the earth after the resurrection, He taught the apostles that He was crucified on a *tree* to fulfill the Mosaic Law. This was later mentioned by the apostle Paul:

> *And if a man have committed a sin worthy of death, and he be to be put to death, and thou hang him on a tree: His body shall not remain all night upon the tree, but thou shalt in any wise bury him that day; (for he that is hanged is accursed of God;) that thy land be not defiled, which the* Lord *thy God giveth thee for an inheritance.* **(Deut.21:22-23)**

> *Christ hath redeemed us from the curse of the law, being made a curse for us: for it is written, Cursed is every one that hangeth on a tree.* **(Galatians 3:13)**

* *(A Jewish tomb was found in 1968, just north of Jerusalem with the Hebrew name, Jehohanan ben Ha'galqol, who had been crucified in the first century. A nail was found in his anklebone with a trace of olive wood on the nail. This led archaeologists to believe that most people who were crucified by the Romans, were nailed to a tree, not a square-timbered cross. Since olive trees were so plentiful in the area, it is believed that the victim's hands would have been nailed to a crossbeam, called a patibulum. The crossbeam would have then been nailed to an olive tree, where also long nails would have been used to fasten the victim's ankles to the tree.)*

"Him hath God exalted with his right hand to be a Prince and a Saviour" - Jesus of Nazareth had been nailed to a tree and was now exalted by God the Father. Let's reflect on the exaltation of Jesus:

* *His resurrection*
* *His ascension*
* *At the right hand of the Father*
* *He is now Prince*
* *He is now Savior*

"for to give repentance to Israel, and forgiveness of sins. And we are his witnesses of these things; and so is also the Holy Ghost, whom God hath given to them that obey him." - With Jesus being the perfect sacrifice for the sins of Israel and the world, Israel could have *forgiveness of sins* if it would *repent*. While the present work of Christ is to forgive individuals of their sins, one day national Israel will repent and usher in the second coming of the Lord Jesus Christ:

And I will pour upon the house of David, and upon the inhabitants of Jerusalem, the spirit of grace and of supplications: and they shall look upon me whom they have pierced, and they shall mourn for him, as one mourneth for his only son, and shall be in bitterness for him, as one that is in bitterness for his firstborn. **(Zechariah 12:10)**

For I say unto you, Ye shall not see me henceforth, till ye shall say, Blessed is he that cometh in the name of the Lord. **(Matthew 23:39)**

There were two witnesses of the finished work of Christ:

* **The apostles**
* **The Holy Spirit**

"When they heard that, they were cut to the heart, and took counsel to slay them." - The original Greek words here mean that they were cut like being sawn into. In **Acts 2:37**, the crowd was cut to the heart under *conviction*, but here the religious rulers were cut to the heart in *rage*. They wanted to kill the apostles! However, there was a problem with their Jewish law. Just because someone disobeyed the Sanhedrin, it did not carry the penalty of death.

THE STRANGE ADVICE OF GAMALIEL

Acts 5:34-39 - *Then stood there up one in the council, a Pharisee, named Gamaliel, a doctor of the law, had in reputation among all the people, and commanded to put the apostles forth a little* *space; And said unto them, Ye men of Israel, take heed to yourselves what ye intend to do as touching these men. For before these days rose up Theudas, boasting himself to be somebody; to whom a number of men, about four hundred, joined themselves: who was slain; and all, as many as obeyed him, were scattered, and brought to nought. After this man rose up Judas of Galilee in the days of the taxing, and drew away much people after him: he also perished; and all, even as many as obeyed him, were dispersed. And now I say unto you, Refrain from these men, and let them alone: for if this counsel or this work be of men, it will come to nought: But if it be of God, ye cannot overthrow it; lest haply ye be found even to fight against God.*

The book of Acts portrays Jewish opposition to the first Christian movement, contrary to *traditional* Judaism. In reality, those first followers of Christ were not trying to go against the Law of Moses, but considered themselves *complete in Jesus* as their Messiah. We must keep in mind that Jesus taught the apostles after His resurrection how to explain the Old Testament concerning His first and second comings. The reason why the religious leaders were against them is because their prideful, religious positions were being threatened. Instead of embracing what the apostles were teaching concerning the Old Testament about Jesus, they saw a movement that was growing so fast that they could lose their authority over the people. Eventually their positions of authority were lost in 70AD, when the Romans leveled the Temple in Jerusalem to the ground. *Gamaliel* died 18 years before the destruction of the Temple.

"Then stood there up one in the council, a Pharisee, named Gamaliel, a doctor of the law, had in reputation among all the people," - While the Jewish religious council was making plans to do away with the apostles of Jesus, its plans were interrupted by a man named *Gamaliel*. It helps us to acquaint ourselves with who *Gamaliel* really was.

Gamaliel was a member of the Sanhedrin. He was a Pharisee, and known as *Gamaliel the Elder*. Most of the Jewish teachers were called simply, *rabbi*, but *Gamaliel* was called *Rabban*, which was above the normal *rabbi* teacher. He was the grandson of *Hillel*, one of the most famous sages and scholars. (110BC-10AD) He was paralleled with Moses because he lived 120 years. Being the head of the School of Hillel, he was the first one to have the title, *Rabban*. According to **Acts 22:3**, he was the teacher of Paul. *Gamaliel* was a man who held a moral force, who held high reverence for the Law of Moses. The other rabbis followed him. His knowledge of the Law of Moses and wisdom were deeply respected. There is no evidence that he became a follower of Christ, but God certainly used him to spare the apostles so they could continue spreading the gospel.

"and commanded to put the apostles forth a little space;" - The apostles were put outside of the council chamber of the Sanhedrin so they could have a private discussion.

"And said unto them, Ye men of Israel, take heed to yourselves what ye intend to do as touching these men." - Gamaliel told them to use caution and to consider carefully what they were about to do to the apostles. One of Gamaliel's motives may have been that killing the apostles could cause a riot on the Temple Mount, and Rome could intervene. Another motive could have been that Gamaliel was a Pharisee who did believe in *a* resurrection, and the Sadducees did not. His theological differences with the Sadducees may have been a driving force behind his defense of the apostles.

"For before these days rose up Theudas, boasting himself to be somebody; to whom a number of men, about four hundred, joined themselves: who was slain; and all, as many as obeyed him, were scattered, and brought to nought." – The first illustration that Gamaliel gives the council is about a man named *Theudas*. There is nothing written in Jewish history about this man * *Theudas*. There were thousands of revolts during and after the time of Herod the Great, and he is believed to have been one who led a revolt against the wicked king Herod, who reigned in Judaea from 37-1BC. *Theudas* may have been a false Messiah figure.

* *(Flavius Josephus records a revolt that took place in 44AD and was led by a man also named Theudas. The man who Gamaliel is speaking about lived during a much earlier time. Theudas was a very common Jewish name.)*

"After this man rose up Judas of Galilee in the days of the taxing, and drew away much people after him: he also perished; and all, even as many as obeyed him, were dispersed." – Sometime after *Theudas*, another man rose up whose name was *Judas of Galilee*, from the town of Gamala in the mountains on the northeastern side of the Sea of Galilee. Judas of Galilee started a revolt against the Romans when the census was ready for taxation by the Romans in 6AD. The census to be registered was *first* ordered by *Caesar Augustus*, that sent Joseph and Mary to Bethlehem in 2BC. It took many years for a census to be completed in those days:

> ***And it came to pass in those days, that there went out a decree from Caesar Augustus that all the world should be taxed. (And this taxing was first made when Cyrenius was governor of Syria.) (Luke 2:1-2)***

The revolt by Judas of Galilee is what started the * *Zealot* movement in 6AD. The revolt was crushed, and Judas was beheaded and all who followed him were killed. The *Zealot* survived for several more years, and the movement made their last stand at Masada in 73AD. Gamaliel is saying that these two so-called Messianic movements failed.

* *(The Arbel Cliffs in Galilee are some 594 ft. above the Galilean sea level. They are dotted with caves where the Zealots hid out from Herod the king and against the taxation of Rome. Herod ordered many armed Roman soldiers to be placed into large baskets and to be let down by ropes over the cliffs to the caves. They burned out many of the Zealots, while others chose to jump to their death.)*

"And now I say unto you, Refrain from these men, and let them alone: for if this counsel or this work be of men, it will come to nought: But if it be of God, * ***ye cannot overthrow it; lest haply ye be found even to fight against God."*** – Gamaliel is telling the council to *let the apostles alone*. If the apostles were true and Jesus was the Messiah, there was nothing they could do that would stop them. Gamaliel really got their attention when he closed his argument by saying that if the apostles were true followers of the God of Israel, then the council would be *fighting against God*.

★ *(Some have taken the opinion of Gamaliel and tried to turn it into divine truth. There are many false religions and cults who have prospered and have led countless people astray. In a fallen world sometimes Satan's followers have a large following. WE must be careful not to take someone's opinion and twist it into being truth.)*

GAMALIEL CONVINCED THE COUNCIL

Acts 5:40-42 - And to him they agreed: and when they had called the apostles, and beaten them, they commanded that they should not speak in the name of Jesus, and let them go. And they departed from the presence of the council, rejoicing that they were counted worthy to suffer shame for his name. And daily in the temple, and in every house, they ceased not to teach and preach Jesus Christ.

The council agreed with Gamaliel. When they called the apostles back to the meeting, they had them beaten. We can suppose that they followed the Torah's teaching of how much to beat the apostles:

And it shall be, if the wicked man be worthy to be beaten, that the judge shall cause him to lie down, and to be beaten before his face, according to his fault, by a certain number. <u>Forty stripes he may give him</u>, and not exceed: lest, if he should exceed, and beat him above these with many stripes, then thy brother should seem vile unto thee. **(Deut. 25:2-3)**

"they commanded that they should not speak in the name of Jesus, and let them go." - After being stirred by the advice of the revered Gamaliel, the Jewish council commanded the apostles once again not to speak, but this time they thought they had better use the name of *Yeshua*. The apostles were released.

"And they departed from the presence of the council, rejoicing that they were counted worthy to suffer shame for * his name. And daily in the temple, and in every house, they ceased not to teach and preach Jesus Christ." - The apostles not only continued to preach about *Jesus Christ,* but they had even a greater zeal and joy! They thought that they were being highly favored by God to be able to *suffer* for Christ. The apostles were arrested and beaten, *and they continued!*

★ (The word, "name" in the original is written, "Name" and was equated to the four letters of God's name: YHVH. When the vowels were later added to the Hebrew 22 consonants by the Masoretic Jews in the 5th-10th century AD, the Name became YEHOVAH. Here in the book of Acts, <u>the Name</u> is being applied to <u>Yeshua; astounding!</u>)

CHAPTER SIX

THE APPOINTMENT OF THE FIRST DEACONS

Acts 6:1-7 - *And in those days, when the number of the disciples was multiplied, there arose a murmuring of the Grecians against the Hebrews, because their widows were neglected in the daily ministration. Then the twelve called the multitude of the disciples unto them, and said, It is not reason that we should leave the word of God, and serve tables. Wherefore, brethren, look ye out among you seven men of honest report, full of the Holy Ghost and wisdom, whom we may appoint over this business. But we will give ourselves continually to prayer, and to the ministry of the word. And the saying pleased the whole multitude: and they chose Stephen, a man full of faith and of the Holy Ghost, and Philip, and Prochorus, and Nicanor, and Timon, and Parmenas, and Nicolas a proselyte of Antioch: Whom they set before the apostles: and when they had prayed, they laid their hands on them. And the word of God increased; and* *the number of the disciples multiplied in Jerusalem greatly; and a great company of the priests were obedient to the faith.*

"And in those days, when the number of the disciples was multiplied, there arose a murmuring of the Grecians against the Hebrews, because their widows were neglected in the daily ministration." - The timing of the need for deacons occurred when the ★ *disciples* were increasing in great number. The first internal problem in the early church was with Ananias and Sapphira, and the second internal problem was murmuring about the widows not being taken care of properly. It was because they were *Grecian Jews,* or Greek-speaking Hellenized Jews, who were born outside of Israel, and had moved to Jerusalem. They had moved into Israel and were converted to Jesus after hearing the preaching of the apostles. They spoke Greek and were being neglected because more attention was being placed on the naturalized, ★ *Hebrews,* or the Hebrew-speaking widows. They may have been speaking Aramaic, which was a dialect of Hebrew. Widows were under special protection by the Law of Moses:

And the Levite, (because he hath no part nor inheritance with thee,) and the stranger, and the fatherless, and the widow, which are within thy gates, shall come, and shall eat and be satisfied; that the Lord thy God may bless thee in all the work of thine hand which thou doest. (Deut.14:29)

When thou cuttest down thine harvest in thy field, and hast forgot a sheaf in the field, thou shalt not go again to fetch it: it shall be for the stranger, for the fatherless, and for the widow: that the Lord thy God may bless thee in all the work of thine hands. **(Deut.24:19)**

When thou hast made an end of tithing all the tithes of thine increase the third year, which is the year of tithing, and hast given it unto the Levite, the stranger, the fatherless, and the widow, that they may eat within thy gates, and be filled. **(Deut.26:12)**

On the contrary, the religious leaders of Israel were taking advantage of the widows during Jesus' ministry:

And he said unto them in his doctrine, Beware of the scribes, which love to go in long clothing, and love salutations in the marketplaces, And the chief seats in the synagogues, and the uppermost rooms at feasts: Which devour widows' houses, and for a pretence make long prayers: these shall receive greater damnation. **(Mark 12:38-40)**

Widows became a special concern of the early church:

Pure religion and undefiled before God and the Father is this, To visit the fatherless and widows in their affliction, and to keep himself unspotted from the world. **(James 1:27)**

★ *(It is important to know where we get the word "disciple." The actual word disciple comes from the Latin word, "discere," which means to learn. The Greek word for disciple here is "mathetes," which means pupil or learner. They all come from the Jewish background of being a Hebrew, "talmid," or a student of a rabbi. The Greek word "mathetes" is found 157 times in Matthew, Mark, and Luke. It is found 78 times in the gospel of John. In the book of Acts we find it 28 times. The word is not used in the Epistles or the book of the Revelation. The term is only found in the historical books of the New Testament. The term gave way to saints and brethren in the rest of the New Testament.)*

* *(The word Hebrew is first found in **Genesis 14:13**, when Abraham is called a Hebrew.)*

"Then the twelve called the multitude of the disciples unto them, and said, It is not reason that we should leave the word of God, and serve tables." - It was not pleasing for the apostles of Jesus to leave the study of God's Word to *serve,* or the Greek, *diakoneo,* the needs of the widows or the church. The Greek word is where we get the word *deacon.*

"Wherefore, brethren, look ye out among you seven men of honest report, full of the Holy Ghost and wisdom, whom we may appoint over this business." - The number of servants was *three* in each Jewish synagogue who were to take care of the poor and the needy. Because the number of Messianic believers had increased so much, the apostles increased it to *seven.* If there is a hidden meaning to the number *seven,* no one knows for sure. Several qualifications are listed within the pericope of the text:

* ***They had to be men of honest reputation***
* ***They had to be controlled by the Holy Ghost***
* ***They had to be full of wisdom***

"But we will give ourselves continually to prayer, and to the ministry of the word." - While the physical needs would be taken care of by the seven whom the apostles chose, the apostles would continue to pray for the spiritual needs of the church and teach the Word of God. This may sound simple, but the apostles were taught how to explain the Old Testament from their Master and Lord. They knew how to feed the sheep, and that was the top priority. If every local church followed this pattern, what a difference it would make in our communities.

"And the saying pleased the whole multitude: and they chose Stephen, a man full of faith and of the Holy Ghost, and Philip, and Prochorus, and Nicanor, and Timon, and Parmenas, and Nicolas a proselyte of Antioch: Whom they set before the apostles: and when they had prayed, they laid their hands on them." - After the multitude had agreed with the apostles, the first deacon chosen was *Stephen* because he was a *man of faith and filled with the Holy Ghost*, which we could assume was the spiritual condition of all seven men. We would later see *Philip* in **Acts 8:26-40** leading the Ethiopian eunuch to Christ and again in Caesarea, where he had four daughters that prophesied. **(Acts 21:8-9)** It is recorded in history that the deacon *Prochorus* is identified as a scribe to the apostle John on the Isle of Patmos. It is recorded that *Nicanor* was born in Thessaloniki, Greece, and died from martyrdom in 76AD. The deacon *Timon* later served as Bishop in Bosra, Syria, and was killed by being thrown into a burning furnace. *Parmenas* would later serve as a Bishop in Asia Minor and lived to 98AD, where he suffered martyrdom. *Nicolas,* from Antioch, was the only Gentile proselyte that was chosen. All of these men had Greek names and were chosen so they could communicate well the needs of the Grecian Jewish widows.

The *laying on of hands* as a way of being divinely appointed goes back to Moses appointing Joshua:

> ***And Moses did as the Lord commanded him: and he took Joshua, and set him before Eleazar the priest, and before all the congregation: And <u>he laid his hands upon him</u>, and gave him a charge, as the Lord commanded by the hand of Moses.* (Numbers 27:22-23)**

The Bible does not teach a democratic congregational rule of government in the local church. It teaches that the spiritual leaders of the church should make the decisions.

"And the word of God increased; and the number of the disciples multiplied in Jerusalem greatly; and a great company of the priests were obedient to the faith." - Because peace was restored and the apostles were now free to study the Word, *the disciples multiplied in Jerusalem greatly*. Amazing things can happen when the church is operating by the pattern that God laid down in the scriptures. *A great company of the priests were obedient to the faith* that the apostles were preaching. It means that priests were being added one after the other. These were Sadducees who had previously been outside the faith. This is an astounding new statement that is not found until now. We need to make the connection with what Jesus cried from the tree:

> ***Then said Jesus, Father, forgive them; for they know not what they do.* (Luke 23:34)**

Some of the very same priests who were responsible for the crucifixion of Christ were later converted to Christ! What a thought!

THE THIRD PERSECUTION

Acts 6:8-7:1 - *And Stephen, full of faith and power, did great wonders and miracles among the people. Then there arose certain of the synagogue, which is called the synagogue of the Libertines, and Cyrenians, and Alexandrians, and of them of Cilicia and of Asia, disputing with Stephen. And they were not able to resist the wisdom and the spirit by which he spake. Then they suborned men, which said, We have heard him speak blasphemous words against Moses, and against God. And they stirred up the people, and the elders, and the scribes, and came upon him, and caught him, and brought him to the council, And set up false witnesses, which said, This man ceaseth not to speak blasphemous words against this holy place, and the law: For we have heard him say, that this Jesus of Nazareth shall destroy this place, and shall change the customs which Moses delivered us. And all that sat in the council, looking stedfastly on him, saw his face as it had been the face of an angel. Then said the high priest, Are these things so?*

By the authority of the apostles, *Stephen also performed great wonders and miracles among the people.* His ministry was not limited to waiting on tables. The book of Acts records primarily the ministries of Peter and Paul, but Stephen is the link between the two apostles. Stephen was chosen by Peter, and Paul would consent to Stephen's death.

"Then there arose certain of the synagogue, which is called the synagogue of the Libertines, and Cyrenians, and Alexandrians, and of them of Cilicia and of Asia, disputing with Stephen." - Opposition arose from members of different synagogues. Jewish sources say that there were hundreds of synagogues in Jerusalem during the Second Temple period that were built by Jews coming from various locations in the * *Diaspora*. Stephen was also from the Diaspora. Luke only mentions five synagogues by name who were opposing Stephen:

* *Libertines - Former Jewish slaves of Rome*
* *Cyrenians - Jews from North Africa*
* *Alexandrians - Jews from Egypt*
* *Cilicia - Jews who came from Asia Minor (Turkey)*
* *Asia - Jews from other parts of Asia Minor*

* *(The Diaspora was the name given to the Jews who had been dispersed from their homeland into various parts of the Roman world. Conquering nations like the Egyptians, the Assyrians, the Persians, the Greeks, and the Romans had caused multitudes of Jews to be expelled from Israel.)*

Paul was from the area of Cilicia, so he was most likely opposing what Stephen had said as well.

"And they were not able to resist the wisdom and the spirit by which he spake" - The *wisdom and spirit* of Stephen were too powerful for their oppositions. This is what led to the third persecution of the church and the first major scattering of the Jewish believers.

"Then they suborned men, which said, We have heard him speak blasphemous words against Moses, and against God." - The religious leaders of the synagogues initiated by the Pharisees hired men to become false witnesses. They charged Stephen

with speaking blasphemy against the Law of *Moses* and the *God of Israel* because he preached against the Temple.

"And they stirred up the people, and the elders, and the scribes, and came upon him, and caught him, and brought him to the council, And set up false witnesses, which said, This man ceaseth not to speak blasphemous words against this holy place, and the law:" - These *false witnesses* phrased their accusations in a way that stirred up both the Sadducees and the Pharisees. Stephen was continuing to preach what the apostle Peter had told them about the *holy place* that was to be destroyed. The Sadducees were mere hired puppets of Rome and were afraid of losing their positions in the Temple. Stephen was repeating the same message of Jesus:

> *And Jesus went out, and departed from the temple: and his disciples came to him for to shew him the buildings of the temple. And Jesus said unto them, See ye not all these things? verily I say unto you, There shall not be left here one stone upon another, that shall not be thrown down.* **(Matthew 24:1-2)**

Stephen preached the grace of God through Jesus Christ. Now a person was saved by the finished work of his/her Messiah, not the works of the Law. This angered the Pharisees who were filled with self-righteousness and believed they were children of God by keeping their man-made, religious traditions and by honoring the Jewish Feasts written in **Leviticus 23**.

"For we have heard him say, that this Jesus of Nazareth shall destroy this place, and shall change the customs which Moses delivered us." - Probably Stephen was preaching about the death of *Jesus of Nazareth*, which would have superseded their

Rabbinical Judaism understanding of Jesus. *Jesus of Nazareth* was the Messiah, and the nation had committed the unpardonable sin by rejecting Him. To the religious council Jesus of Nazareth was only a carpenter, and *their understanding* of the long-awaited Messiah was not one of dying on a tree. They only believed in one coming of a ruling, reigning Messiah.

"And all that sat in the council, looking stedfastly on him, saw his face as it had been the face of an angel" - Although Stephen was being charged by false witnesses, he didn't show any kind of anger or uneasiness on his face. His face shined like an *angel*, or with the ★ *Shechinah* glory of God!

★ *(The Shechinah is a transliteration of the Hebrew words for the dwelling or settling of the divine presence of God.)*

"Then said the high priest, Are these things so?" - Are you guilty Stephen, or not? This gives Stephen the opportunity to give the longest sermon recorded in the book of Acts. Because of the pressure that was placed upon Stephen and the urgency of the moment, he rounded some years off and gave some general overviews and a panorama of some of the history of God dealing with Israel. The primary point that Stephen will be making is that God has dealt with Israel before outside the Temple and even outside the Land itself. He will reiterate to the religious rulers that Jesus is the One Moses wrote about in a different way. Stephen would be trying to help them see that the Law of Moses was giving way to the New Covenant. Through the inspiration of the Holy Spirit, Luke records the sermon the way Stephen presented it. His sermon would be the message that would result in the dispersion of the believing Jews and the advancement of the glorious gospel of Christ.

CHAPTER SEVEN

GOD'S PROMISE TO ABRAHAM

Acts 7:2-5 - *And he said, Men, brethren, and fathers, hearken; The God of glory appeared unto our father Abraham, when he was in Mesopotamia, before he dwelt in Charran, And said unto him, Get thee out of thy country, and from thy kindred, and come into the land which I shall shew thee. Then came he out of the land of the Chaldaeans, and dwelt in Charran: and from thence, when his father was dead, he removed him into this land, wherein ye now dwell. And he gave him none inheritance in it, no, not so much as to set his foot on: yet he promised that he would give it to him for a possession, and to his seed after him, when as yet he had no child.*

Stephen is saying that the calling of Abraham was not confined to the Land of Israel or the Temple. The God of Israel was greater than any particular location. God appeared to Abraham in Mesopotamia even before he dwelt in *Charran*, or *Haran*. **(Genesis 11:31-32)** The fact that Abraham was a

Syrian **(Deut.26:5)** may also be alluding to the gospel going out to the Gentiles, and Abraham was called the father of *all* of the believers. **(Galatians 3:7)** Without any outward evidence, Abraham believed God even though he had no land or a child. What makes the calling of Abraham even more confusing for the Jewish council is that at that time, he dwelt in the land of religious idols.

> *And Joshua said unto all the people, Thus saith the Lord God of Israel, Your fathers dwelt on the other side of the flood in old time, even Terah, the father of Abraham, and the father of Nachor: and they served other gods.* **(Joshua 24:2)**

The Prophecy and Covenant to Abraham

Acts 7:6-8 - *And God spake on this wise, That his seed should sojourn in a strange land; and that they should bring them into bondage, and entreat them evil four hundred years. And the nation to whom they shall be in bondage will I judge, said God: and after that shall they come forth, and serve me in this place. And he gave him the covenant of circumcision: and so Abraham begat Isaac, and circumcised him the eighth day; and Isaac begat Jacob; and Jacob begat the twelve patriarchs.*

The promise that God gave to Abraham would not be easy or without troubles for his descendants. God gave Abraham the prophecy of *four hundred years of bondage*. Stephen is quoting from **Genesis 15:13**. We know from the account in **Exodus 12:40** and **Galatians 3:17,** the exact years were *four hundred and thirty years.* Abraham's descendants would be in bondage and God would judge the nation of Egypt by sending ten plagues. **(Exodus 7-10)** The religious rulers to whom Stephen was speaking were now living in *the place,* or the land that God promised to Abraham. God knows how to protect and care for His people, and that they were living in the appointed time when their promised Messiah had been in their midst.

God gave the covenant of *circumcision* to Abraham that was handed down to His children and the * *twelve patriarchs* of Israel. *Circumcision* became the sign of the covenant of Israel.

* *(Reuben, Simeon, Judah, Issachar, Zebulun, Benjamin, Dan, Naphtali, Gad, Asher, Ephraim and Manasseh)*

God's Faithfulness Through Joseph

Acts 7:9-16 - *And the patriarchs, moved with envy, sold Joseph into Egypt: but God was with him, And delivered him out of all his afflictions, and gave him favour and wisdom in the sight of Pharaoh king of Egypt; and he made him governor over Egypt and all his house. Now there came a dearth over all the land of Egypt and Chanaan, and great affliction: and our fathers found no sustenance. But when Jacob heard that there was corn in Egypt, he sent out our fathers first. And at the second time Joseph was made known to his brethren; and Joseph's kindred was made known unto Pharaoh. Then sent Joseph, and* *called his father Jacob to him, and all his kindred, threescore and fifteen souls. So Jacob went down into Egypt, and died, he, and * our fathers, And were carried over into Sychem, and laid in the sepulchre that Abraham bought for a sum of money of the sons of Emmor the father of Sychem.*

Before there was a Temple, God's presence was with *Joseph* all the time, for he was a beautiful Old Testament picture of the life of Christ. **(Genesis 37-50)** Just as the *patriarchs* were *moved with envy* and rejected *Joseph*, the Jewish leaders were envious of Christ and rejected Him. Just as *Joseph* was eventually raised up and exalted to provide for His own brothers, Jesus suffered death and was then exalted to provide eternal salvation for all who would embrace Him.

"laid in the sepulchre that Abraham bought for a sum of money of the sons of Emmor the father of Sychem." - Abraham purchased this cave in the field of *Machpelah* from *Ephron* with 400 shekels of silver. **(Genesis 23:13-20)** In the passing of 80 years, the owner's name had changed, and Jacob purchased the land from *Emmor*, or *Hamor*, who was the father of *Shechem*. **(Genesis 33:19)**

* *(It is commonly believed among the Jews that the bones of all 12 patriarchs, as well as those of Jacob, were carried out of Egypt into Canaan. The bones of important people in the history of Israel were very important. Notice the bones of Joseph are connected to his great faith and would be carried by the children of Israel when they entered into the Promised Land.* **Genesis 50:24-25, Hebrews 11:22***)*

Three things about Stephen's sermon so far regarding the patriarchs of Israel:

- *God began the nation of Israel with a covenant*
- *God's revelation was given outside and inside the land*
- *God used a rejected Joseph akin to the rejected Messiah*

STEPHEN CONTINUES WITH THE LIFE OF MOSES

Acts 7:17-22 - *But when the time of the promise drew nigh, which God had sworn to Abraham, the people grew and multiplied in Egypt, Till another king arose, which knew not Joseph. The same dealt subtilly with our kindred, and evil entreated our fathers, so that they cast out their young children, to the end they might not live. In which time Moses was born, and was exceeding fair, and nourished up in his father's house three months: And when he was cast out, Pharaoh's daughter took him up, and nourished him for her own son. And Moses was learned in all the wisdom of the Egyptians, and was mighty in words and in deeds.*

This long, but powerful sermon of Stephen continues with the recount of Moses. We must keep in mind that the accusations the religious rulers had against Stephen were that he was *speaking blasphemous words against this holy place, and the law*. Moses represented the law, and Stephen is going to let the Jewish establishment know that Jesus of Nazareth is the One Moses wrote about.

While the Israelites were in bondage down in the land of Egypt, *another* Pharaoh arose who *did not know about Joseph*, and thus oppressed Joseph's people. As the time began to be fulfilled concerning what God had spoken to Abraham about, God started working.

"The same dealt subtilly with our kindred, and evil entreated our fathers, so that they cast out their young children, to the end they might not live." – In a *crafty* and evil way the new Pharaoh thought of a way to stop the Israelites from multiplying. He issued a decree that would kill the little children by ordering the Hebrews to cast their babies into the river. This is paralleled to when the wicked Herod the king killed the babies when Jesus the Messiah was born:

> *Then Herod, when he saw that he was mocked of the wise men, was exceeding wroth, and sent forth, and slew all the children that were in Bethlehem, and in all the coasts thereof, from two years old and under, according to the time which he had diligently inquired of the wise men.* **(Matthew 2:16)**

"In which time Moses was born, and was exceeding fair, and nourished up in his father's house three months: And when he was cast out, Pharaoh's daughter took him up, and nourished him for her own son." – At this crucial point in the history of the Jewish people, Moses was born in the plan of God. His parents saw that he was a beautiful child, and their faith saw that God would preserve him and use him to help His people. Moses' parents are considered to be heroes of faith. They placed the baby Moses in an *ark of bulrushes*, knowing that God would protect him:

> *And when she could not longer hide him, she took for him an ark of bulrushes, and daubed it with slime*

and with pitch, and put the child therein; and she laid it in the flags by the river's brink. (**Exodus 2:3**)

By faith Moses, when he was born, was hid three months of his parents, because they saw he was a proper child; and they were not afraid of the king's commandment. (**Hebrews 11:23**)

"And when he was cast out, Pharaoh's daughter took him up, and nourished him for her own son. And Moses was learned in all the wisdom of the Egyptians, and was mighty in words and in deeds." - To protect Moses until his appointed time, God orchestrated the current of the Nile River to guide the baby Moses to *Pharaoh's daughter.* Moses was her legal son. Moses would have been taught science, astronomy, medicine, and mathematics. His *wisdom* helped him to become *mighty in words and deeds.*

ISRAEL REJECTED MOSES

Acts 7:23-29 - *And when he was full forty years old, it came into his heart to visit his brethren the children of Israel. And seeing one of them suffer wrong, he defended him, and avenged him that was oppressed, and smote the Egyptian: For he supposed his brethren would have understood how that God by his hand would deliver them: but they understood not. And the next day he shewed himself unto them as they strove, and would have set them at one again, saying, Sirs, ye are brethren; why do ye wrong one to another? But he that did his neighbour wrong thrust*

> *him away, saying, Who made thee a ruler and a judge over us? Wilt thou kill me, as thou diddest the Egyptian yesterday? Then fled Moses at this saying, and was a stranger in the land of Madian, where he begat two sons.*

When Moses became 40 *years of age, God put into the heart of Moses* to be identified with his people. When he saw an Egyptian mistreating a Jew, he stepped in and killed the Egyptian. Moses assumed that the Jews would realize that the God of Israel had sent him, but they did not. When he tried to bring peace between two Jews who were fighting, their rejection came in the form of two questions; *Who made thee a ruler and a judge over us? Wilt thou kill me, as thou diddest the Egyptian yesterday?* This made Moses a sojourner in the land of ✶ *Midian* for the next 40 years, and there he had *two sons* by his wife *Zipporah.* **(Exodus 2:21)**

✶ *(The land of Midian was on the eastern side of the Red Sea, present-day Gulf of Aqaba, in the northwestern part of Arabia. The history of the Midianites plays a very unusual part in the history of Israel. In* **Genesis 25:1-2**, *one of the wives of Abraham was Keturah. They had six sons, and one of them was Midian. The descendants were called Midianites and lived in what is today southwest Arabia. Moses married a Midianite woman named Zipporah and they had two sons, Eliezer and Gershom. That would make Mose's father-in-law, Jethro, a Midianite. The Midianites were Arabs, and at the time of Moses they worshipped the God of Abraham. In the famous biblical movie, "The Ten Commandments," the person who is portraying Jethro says that their father was Ishmael, but that is incorrect, as it was Midian.)*

MOSES AT THE BURNING BUSH

Acts 7:30-34 - *And when forty years were expired, there appeared to him in the wilderness of mount * Sina an angel of the Lord in a flame of fire in a bush. When Moses saw it, he wondered at the sight: and as he drew near to behold it, the voice of the* LORD *came unto him, Saying, I am the God of thy fathers, the God of Abraham, and the God of Isaac, and the God of Jacob. Then Moses trembled, and durst not behold. Then said the Lord to him, Put off thy shoes from thy feet: for the place where thou standest is holy ground. I have seen, I have seen the affliction of my people which is in Egypt, and I have heard their groaning, and am come down to deliver them. And now come, I will send thee into Egypt.*

Stephen is again preaching to the unbelieving Jewish establishment that God can reveal Himself however and wherever He chooses by referring to the call of Moses in **Exodus 2:2-6.** God appeared to Moses by using an *angel of the Lord in a flaming fire in a bush*. This happened while Moses was in the land of Midian! Moses became the *redeemer* of those who had *rejected* him, just as Jesus the Messiah. The greatest leader in the Old Testament received his call from God *outside* of the Land of Israel.

* *(Many Jews have tried to say for centuries that Mount Sinai was in the lower parts of Israel, at Saint Catherine's Monastery. This place only dates back to 565AD. The real Mount Sinai was discovered in Arabia in 1998, which was the land of Midian in Moses' time.*

The apostle Paul even mentions Mount Sinai being in Arabia in **Galatians 4:25.***)*

MOSES LEADS THE ISRAELITES OUT OF BONDAGE

> **Acts 7:35-37** - *This Moses whom they refused, saying, Who made thee a ruler and a judge? the same did God send to be a ruler and a deliverer by the hand of the angel which appeared to him in the bush. He brought them out, after that he had shewed wonders and signs in the land of Egypt, and in the Red sea, and in the wilderness forty years. This is that Moses, which said unto the children of Israel, A prophet shall the Lord your God raise up unto you of your brethren, like unto me; him shall ye hear.*

Even though they rejected Moses, he is the one God chose to lead the children of Israel out of Egyptian bondage. Then Stephen quotes from **Deuteronomy 18:15**:

> **The Lord thy God will raise up unto thee a Prophet from the midst of thee, of thy brethren, like unto me; unto him ye shall hearken.**

When Jesus fed the multitude in Galilee, many of the people thought that Jesus was *that Prophet*:

> **Then those men, when they had seen the miracle that Jesus did, said, This is of a truth that prophet that should come into the world. (John 6:14)**

Stephen is telling the religious leaders that *Yeshua* is that *Prophet* whom God has raised up *in their midst, of thy brethren like unto Moses*. Of course Jesus the Son of God was much greater than Moses, but He was a *Prophet-like* figure. **(Hebrews 3:1-6, John 5:46)**

The leaders of Israel were supposed to be leading the Jewish people to their Messiah, not just holding a position of authority. They needed to *hearken* to what Jesus said and to what Stephen is saying about Jesus. Every individual needs to pay close attention to the words of Christ and accept Him as his/her *personal* Savior. A rejection of Jesus as the Son of God will result in eternal damnation. The Heavenly Father did everything He could do to provide salvation for the world. Jesus died on a tree for the sins of the world, and He is only asking us to turn from our sins and receive Him into our hearts and lives. **(I John 2:2)** He is the only way to heaven, and His words are superior to any prophet or any one else.

> *Jesus saith unto him, I am the way, the truth, and the life: no man cometh unto the Father, but by me.* **(John 14:6)**

ISRAEL REJECTS MOSES AGAIN

Acts 7:38-41 - *This is he, that was in the church in the wilderness with the angel which spake to him in the mount Sina, and with our fathers: who received the lively oracles to give unto us: To whom our fathers would not obey, but thrust him from them, and in their hearts turned back again into Egypt, Saying*

> *unto Aaron, Make us gods to go before us: for as for this Moses, which brought us out of the land of Egypt, we wot not what is become of him. And they made a calf in those days, and offered sacrifice unto the idol, and rejoiced in the works of their own hands.*

The Greek word *ekklesia* is used here for the *church* and is not referring to the New Testament church. It is used in the Greek translation to refer to the *congregation of Israel*. Interestingly enough, it shows that the word for church does not mean a denomination or building, it is *the called out people*.

God spoke to Moses and gave him the *lively oracles*, or the divine declarations and statements. Israel rejected Moses again and built their own man-made religious idol, *a golden calf*. They not only refused God's commandments, but they offered sacrifices to pagan gods. What Stephen is saying is that just as the children of Israel worshipped false gods, the religious leaders in Jerusalem had created their own false, religious system. Stephen wasn't preaching against the Temple, but the man-made traditions that had superseded the commandments of the God of Israel.

God Responds to Israel's Rejection of Moses

> **Acts 7:42-43** - *Then God turned, and gave them up to worship the host of heaven; as it is written in the book of the prophets, O ye house of Israel, have ye offered to me slain beasts and sacrifices by the space of forty years in the wilderness? Yea, ye took up the tabernacle of Moloch, and the star of your god*

Remphan, figures which ye made to worship them: and I will carry you away beyond Babylon.

The phrase *gave them up* means that God turned them over to their own evil ways to receive punishment. This phrase is also used in **Romans 1:24, 28**, where God *gives up* on the men and women who sexually pervert their own bodies. It is called *reprobation* when people call evil good, and good evil. We need to ponder the question, has God *given up* on many people in our world today?

Stephen is quoting from the prophet Amos, and uses the word *Babylon* for *Damascus*. **Amos 5:25-27**:

Have ye offered unto me sacrifices and offerings in the wilderness forty years, O house of Israel? But ye have borne the tabernacle of your Moloch and Chiun your images, the star of your god, which ye made to yourselves. Therefore will I cause you to go into captivity beyond Damascus, saith the LORD, whose name is The God of hosts.

What started with the golden calf resulted in Israel of old worshipping the host of heaven. **(Deut.17:3, 2 Kings 17:16-17, 21:3-6, 23:5, 2 Chron.33:3-7, Jere.8:2, 19:13)**

ISRAEL HAD THE TABERNACLE

Acts 7:44-45 - *Our fathers had the tabernacle of witness in the wilderness, as he had appointed, speaking unto Moses, that he should make it according to the fashion that he had seen. Which also* *our fathers that came after brought in with Jesus into the possession of the Gentiles, whom God drave out before the face of our fathers, unto the days of David;*

Stephen now moves from the rejection of Moses to *the tabernacle*. Even though Israel had the *tabernacle of witness in the wilderness*, it still rejected God and His message. The *tabernacle* was built by God's design *outside* of the Land of Israel, showing again that God was not limited to the Temple in Jerusalem.

Notice the word *Jesus* in this section is the Greek, *Iesous*, and is referring to *Yehoshua*, or *Joshua* of the Old Testament. Because their names are the same, the KJV translators left it *Jesus*. *Joshua* led the Israelites into the same Land where the religious leaders were living now. Stephen is reminding them that they are enjoying the place that was once *possessed by the Gentiles*:

And Joshua said, Hereby ye shall know that the living God is among you, and that he will without fail drive out from before you the Canaanites, and the Hittites, and the Hivites, and the Perizzites, and the Girgashites, and the Amorites, and the Jebusites. **(Joshua 3:10)**

The transition from the tabernacle to the Temple started with David.

ISRAEL HAD THE TEMPLE

Acts 7:46-51 - *Who found favour before God, and desired to find a tabernacle for the God of Jacob.*

But Solomon built him an house. Howbeit the most High dwelleth not in temples made with hands; as saith the prophet, Heaven is my throne, and earth is my footstool: what house will ye build me? saith the Lord: or what is the place of my rest? Hath not my hand made all these things? Ye stiffnecked and uncircumcised in heart and ears, ye do always resist the Holy Ghost: as your fathers did, so do ye.

It was David's son, *Solomon*, who finally was commanded to build the Temple for the God of Israel. God's presence was in the tabernacle and the Temple, but His greatness was certainly not limited to a *house made with hands*. Stephen is quoting from **Isaiah 66:1-2**:

Thus saith the L<small>ORD</small>, The heaven is my throne, and the earth is my footstool: where is the house that ye build unto me? and where is the place of my rest? For all those things hath mine hand made, and all those things have been, saith the L<small>ORD</small>: but to this man will I look, even to him that is poor and of a contrite spirit, and trembleth at my word.

The point that Stephen is making is that even though Israel had the Temple in Jerusalem, it still had not followed the God of Israel. For if it had been following God, it would have known its Messiah when He came. The people were not worshipping idols of stone anymore, but their sins were *spiritual* and deep-seated self-righteousness, and they were ★ limiting God's presence again to the Temple. The new community of believers was about to leave Israel and go into the Roman world. Even the apostles did not fully understand this until **Acts 10**.

* *(Many Christians today are guilty of the same sins of Israel in the time of Stephen. They substitute attending a church building for having God in their daily lives. The worst form of hypocrisy is to sing hymns and spiritual songs and look the part of a Christian and then serve the world through the week.)*

"Ye stiffnecked and uncircumcised in heart and ears, ye do always resist the Holy Ghost: as your fathers did, so do ye." - Stephen uses the words *stiffnecked* from **Exodus 32:9**, and *uncircumcised in heart* from **Jeremiah 9:26**. Almost 20 times in the Old Testament God uses the word *stiffnecked*. Stephen was saying that the hearts of the unbelieving Jewish leaders were no better than the *uncircumcised* Gentiles.

"ye do always * resist the Holy Ghost: as your fathers did, so do ye." - The Jewish people always *resisted the Holy Ghost*, even as their forefathers did. **(Isaiah 63:10)** They not only *resisted the Holy Ghost* when they crucified Jesus, they were *resisting* Him now through the message of Stephen.

* *(The erroneous doctrine of Calvinism teaches that those whom God has elected to be saved cannot resist the Holy Spirit. This is just one of the passages that explains that theory away.)*

Stephen's Last Accusation

> **Acts 7:52-53 - *Which of the prophets have not your fathers persecuted? and they have slain them which shewed before of the coming of the Just One; of whom ye have been now the betrayers and murderers: Who***

have received the law by the disposition of angels, and have not kept it.

Stephen's last accusation against the Sanhedrin is that they had been guilty of the same sins of their forefathers, but they were even worse. The *prophets* of old had told them that the *Just One* was coming, and their forefathers slew the *prophets*. And now, you (Sanhedrin) have *betrayed and murdered* your Messiah. God had given the law and they had *not kept it*. We must keep in mind that the religious establishment prided themselves in keeping the law. They believed that the world should come to them for salvation. However, God was going to send the gospel into the world primarily through the Gentiles. This generation has been guilty of the unpardonable sin as Jesus mentions in **Matthew 12**, and the old wine skin traditions of old Judaism could not hold the new wine of God's kingdom:

> ***No man also seweth a piece of new cloth on an old garment: else the new piece that filled it up taketh away from the old, and the rent is made worse. And no man putteth new wine into old bottles: else the new wine doth burst the bottles, and the wine is spilled, and the bottles will be marred: but new wine must be put into new bottles.* (Mark 2:21-22)**

"*Who have received the law by the disposition of angels, and have not kept it.*" - God gave the law to Moses by means of *angels*. **(Acts 7:53, Galatians 3:19, Hebrews 2:2)**

They Evaluate Stephen's Sermon

Acts 7:54 - *When they heard these things, they were cut to the heart, and they gnashed on him with their teeth.*

It's interesting here that the Bible says they were *cut to the heart* as Luke describes in **Acts 5:33**. They *gnashed on him with their teeth.* Jesus used these words to describe hell itself and told a group of the leaders that they were children of the devil:

> *But the children of the kingdom shall be cast out into outer darkness: there shall be weeping and gnashing of teeth.* **(Matthew 8:12)**

> *Ye are of your father the devil, and the lusts of your father ye will do. He was a murderer from the beginning, and abode not in the truth, because there is no truth in him. When he speaketh a lie, he speaketh of his own: for he is a liar, and the father of it.* **(John 8:44)**

The Vision of Stephen

Acts 7:55-56 - *But he, being full of the Holy Ghost, looked up stedfastly into heaven, and saw the glory of God, and Jesus standing on the right hand of God, And said, Behold, I see the heavens opened, and the Son of man standing on the right hand of God.*

While the religious authorities were staring at Stephen, he was *looking up stedfastly into heaven*. While they were making noises with their teeth, Stephen was in perfect peace. The source of his peace was that he was *full of the Holy Ghost*, or being controlled by the Holy Ghost.

"Jesus standing on the right hand of God, And said, Behold, I see the heavens opened, and the Son of man standing on the right hand of God." - This is a very powerful picture of Jesus *standing*, not sitting, *on the right hand of God*. **(Psalm 110:1, Matthew 26:64, Colossians 3:1)** The image of Jesus sitting emphasizes that His work of providing salvation and sacrifice is a finished work. However, the image of Jesus standing shows His continued work as our intercessor and sustainer. At the martyrdom of the very first believer in the early church, Jesus chose to *stand* with Stephen. Stephen had confessed Christ before men, and now Jesus was confessing Stephen before the Father. **(Matthew 10:32)**

"and the Son of man standing on the right hand of God." - This is the first time that anyone called Israel's Messiah the *Son of man* other than Jesus Himself. **(John 3:13)** After the work of salvation was completed for humanity, Jesus is in heaven still in the form of the *Son of man*! This would also be the last time the title *Son of man* would be used until the apostle John saw the vision of the glorified Christ in **Revelation 1:13**:

> *And in the midst of the seven candlesticks one like unto the Son of man, clothed with a garment down to the foot, and girt about the paps with a golden girdle.*

THE STONING OF STEPHEN

> **Acts 7:57-60 -** *Then they cried out with a loud voice, and stopped their ears, and ran upon him with one accord, And cast him out of the city, and stoned him: and the witnesses laid down their clothes at a young man's feet, whose name was Saul. And they stoned Stephen, calling upon God, and saying, Lord Jesus, receive my spirit. And he kneeled down, and cried with a loud voice, Lord, lay not this sin to their charge. And when he had said this, he fell asleep.*

After Stephen declared with his mouth that he saw the crucified Jesus standing at the right hand of God, the Sanhedrin acted quickly and violently. It is interesting that when Jesus declared that he would sit at the right hand of God, they had the same reaction:

> *Jesus saith unto him, Thou hast said: nevertheless I say unto you, Hereafter shall ye see the Son of man sitting on the right hand of power, and coming in the clouds of heaven. Then the high priest rent his clothes, saying, He hath spoken blasphemy; what further need have we of witnesses? behold, now ye have heard his blasphemy. What think ye? They answered and said, He is guilty of death.* **(Matthew 26:64-66)**

The stoning of Stephen is a reminder of what Jesus prophesied would happen:

They shall put you out of the synagogues: yea, the time cometh, that whosoever killeth you will think that he doeth God service. **(John 16:2)**

"stopped their ears, and ran upon him with one accord" - They put their hands over their ears and rushed toward Stephen. The same wording here is also used after Jesus cast the demons out of the maniac of Gadara, and the swine *ran violently* down the hill and into the lake in **Luke 8:33**.

"And cast him out of the city, and stoned him" - The Sanhedrin had the authority to perform capital punishment when the offense pertained to the Temple. However, a mob regards no law. The false witnesses would have been the first ones to cast a stone at Stephen.

The hands of the witnesses shall be first upon him to put him to death, and afterward the hands of all the people. So thou shalt put the evil away from among you. **(Deut.17:7)**

"and the witnesses laid down their clothes at a young man's feet, whose name was Saul." - It wasn't the clothes of Stephen, but the *clothes of the false witnesses*. Here Luke uses the Roman name *Saul*, who would later become *Paul*. Saul had approved of the execution, and this would be an arrow of conviction that would haunt Saul for years to come.

"And they stoned Stephen, calling upon God, and saying, Lord Jesus, receive my spirit." - Because Stephen saw Jesus, he called out *Lord Jesus, receive my spirit!* No purgatory, no soul sleep, Stephen was committing his spirit into the hands of the

Lord Jesus. *"To be absent from the body is to be present with the Lord."* **(2 Cor.5:8)**

"And he kneeled down, and cried with a loud voice, Lord, lay not this sin to their charge. And when he had said this, he fell asleep." - There is a parallel to Stephen's dying words and to the dying words of Christ on the tree:

> *Then said Jesus, Father, forgive them; for they know not what they do. And they parted his raiment, and cast lots.* **(Luke 23:34)**

No doubt his words touched the heart of Saul. The prayer of Stephen was the stepping stone for the apostle Paul. Stephen's body fell asleep and his spirit went to heaven. *Sleep* is a euphemism for death in the Bible. The three stages were:

* *Stephen kneeled down*
* *Stephen cried with a loud voice*
* *Stephen fell asleep*

The lesson for all of us is that we can be greatly used by God, even in our dying moments if we are filled with the Holy Spirit!

CHAPTER EIGHT

A Scattering of The Jewish Believers

Acts 8:1-4 - *And Saul was consenting unto his death. And at that time there was a great persecution against the church which was at Jerusalem; and they were all scattered abroad throughout the regions of Judaea and Samaria, except the apostles. And devout men carried Stephen to his burial, and made great lamentation over him. As for Saul, he made havock of the church, entering into every house, and haling men and women committed them to prison. Therefore they that were scattered abroad went every where preaching the word.*

Being from one of the synagogues that disputed with Stephen **(Acts 6:9),** Saul took pleasure in the stoning of Stephen. The day that Stephen was stoned there arose a *great persecution* because the first church of the Jewish believers was *in Jerusalem*. This persecution came from both the Sadducees and the Pharisees.

As a result of this persecution, the Jewish believers in Jesus were ★ *scattered abroad throughout the regions of Judaea and Samaria.* This scattering of the Messianic Jews was one of God's ways to remove them from the coming destruction upon Jerusalem and to *preach the gospel everywhere.* They were scattered like grain and the gospel seed was sown. Praise God! The apostles stayed in Jerusalem for now to shepherd the reduced flock.

★ *(As we study Jewish history long with the Bible, there were four major scatterings of the Jewish believers:*

1) The stoning of Stephen
2) The death of James, the half brother of Jesus, in 62AD
3) The destruction of the Temple in Jerusalem in 70AD
4) The Bar Kokhba Revolt in 132AD

It was also the scattering of the Jews that created the need for the first writings of the New Testament. There was no longer a central unified body of Jewish believers led by the apostles. It takes everyday common people to spread the gospel, such as you and me. They would need inspired writings by the apostles to help them proclaim the King Messiah to the places where they traveled. Books like the *Gospel of Matthew* were written first in about ★ 37AD to Jewish believers. Other sources that were written as a result of the dispersion were *James, I Peter, II Peter,* and *Jude.*

★ *(Most commentaries date Matthew's Gospel to 50-60AD. Matthew wrote his gospel in 37AD in Hebrew first, then later translated into Greek.)*

"And devout men carried Stephen to his burial, and made great lamentation over him." – Scholars disagree if these devout men were believers or religious Jews who were not members of the Sanhedrin who opposed the stoning of Stephen. Because of the way the Greek word, *eulabes*, is used most of the time to refer to religious Jews, these men were probably not believers. According to Jewish law, anyone who died a criminal's death was to be buried without *lamentation*. These men were so *devout* that they believed Stephen deserved a funeral of honor. One would like to think that these men were not true enemies of Christ and became some of His followers.

"As for Saul, he made havock of the church, entering into every house, and haling men and women committed them to prison" - The man who would later write most of the books of the New Testament and become one of the greatest Christians who ever lived had tried to destroy the church. No wonder he considered himself to be the chief of sinners. **(Acts 26:11, I Cor.15:9, I Tim. 1:15, Phil.3:6)** There was no such thing as church buildings in those days, so Saul had the *men and the women* taken out of the houses and *committed them to prison*. The good news is that the stoning of Stephen did not silence the gospel. It caused the gospel of Christ to spread. This leads us into the gospel going to the Samaritans as the Lord Jesus had said in **Acts 1:8**.

PHILIP BRINGS THE GOSPEL TO THE SAMARITANS

Acts 8:5-8 - *Then Philip went down to the city of Samaria, and preached Christ unto them. And the people with one accord gave heed unto those things which Philip spake, hearing and seeing the miracles which he did. For unclean spirits, crying with loud voice, came out of many that were possessed with* *them: and many taken with palsies, and that were lame, were healed. And there was great joy in that city.*

This is *Philip,* the deacon, **Acts 6:5**, not Philip, the apostle of **Mark 3:18**. He *went down to the city of* * *Samaria* from Jerusalem. Writing from a Jewish perspective, Luke is letting us know that no matter what direction one went from the high elevation of Jerusalem, he/she had to go *down*. We do not know for sure, but it is believed that *the city of Samaria* was the primary city of *Shechem*, known as *Nablus* today.

* *(It is important to connect the animosity the Jews had toward the Samaritans. About 750 years before this time, the Assyrians conquered this area and northern Israel. They deported all of the wealthy and middle-class Jews from the area. Then they moved in a pagan population from afar and intermarried with the lower class Jews in northern Israel. The religious Jews considered the Samaritans half-breeds who had corrupted the worship of the God of Israel.* **(II Kings 17:24-33)** *The ministry of Jesus to the Samaritan woman in* **John 4** *is one of the great chapters in the four gospels, and it is a foreshadowing of the gospel going to the Samaritans. Jesus also gave the story of the Good Samaritan in* **Luke 10:25-37** *to show that the Jews should not be prejudice toward their neighbors.)*

"hearing and seeing the miracles which he did. For unclean spirits, crying with loud voice, came out of many that were possessed with them: and many taken with palsies, and that were lame, were healed" - Philip's ability to perform supernatural miracles was a result of the laying on of hands by the apostles. Here is a Hellenized Jew having tremendous success in Samaria. The most important thing Philip did was that he *preached Christ unto them*. The miracles authenticated the gospel message.

"And there was great joy in that city." - The *joy* in Samaria contrasted the great pain and sorrow in Jerusalem. When the gospel of Christ is preached in the power of the Holy Spirit, it always brings *joy*. Hallelujah!

SIMON THE SORCERER

> **Acts 8:9-13 - *But there was a certain man, called Simon, which beforetime in the same city used sorcery, and bewitched the people of Samaria, giving out that himself was some great one: To whom they all gave heed, from the least to the greatest, saying, This man is the great power of God. And to him they had regard, because that of long time he had bewitched them with sorceries. But when they believed Philip preaching the things concerning the kingdom of God, and the name of Jesus Christ, they were baptized, both men and women. Then Simon himself believed also: and when he was baptized, he continued with Philip, and wondered, beholding the miracles and signs which were done.***

Here we have a very bizarre passage of scripture where a man called *Simon* used *sorcery to bewitch the people of Samaria*. Not only did he have fame, the people all said that *this man is the great power of God*. He was a man who dealt with the occult and magic. Whatever power he may have had came from Satan, not God. He was preying on the ignorance and superstitions of the people.

"But when they believed Philip preaching the things concerning the kingdom of God, and the name of Jesus Christ, they were baptized, both men and women." - When the people heard and felt the power of God through the *preaching of Philip concerning the kingdom of God, and the name of Jesus Christ, the men and the women were baptized*. The people proclaimed their faith by being identified with Jesus through water baptism. The attention shifted from Simon, the magician, to Philip, who was representing the true God.

"Then Simon himself believed also: and when he was baptized, he continued with Philip, and wondered, beholding the miracles and signs which were done." - Even Simon was convinced by Philip's preaching and miracles and made a profession of faith and was also baptized. It seems as though Simon was a real convert, but his conduct will prove something different.

The Samaritans Receive the Holy Spirit

Acts 8:14-17 - Now when the apostles which were at Jerusalem heard that Samaria had received the word of God, they sent unto them Peter and John: Who, when they were come down, prayed for them, that they might receive the Holy Ghost: (For as yet he was fallen upon none of them: only they were baptized in the name of the Lord Jesus.) Then laid they their hands on them, and they received the Holy Ghost.

Here is another ⋆ problematic passage when we do not understand the transitional importance. The Samaritans had heard the message from Philip and believed, and were *baptized in the name of the Lord Jesus*, but they did not know about the Holy Spirit. This would require the church in Jerusalem to authenticate the church in Samaria. So *they sent unto them Peter and John*. Peter had been given the keys to the kingdom **(Matthew 16:19)** and John who had previously wanted the Samaritans destroyed. **(Luke 9:54)** Interestingly, this is the last time John is mentioned in the book of Acts.

⋆ *(This passage is used by some denominational churches to say that people can be saved without the baptism of the Holy Spirit. They try to build a doctrine that salvation is separate from receiving the baptism of the Holy Spirit.)*

The problem with the Samaritans is that they had been baptized in water but not baptized in the Holy Spirit, which is the way anyone must enter into the body of Christ. **(I Cor. 12:13)** At this transitional moment the Holy Spirit had been given to believing Jews, but not the Samaritans. It was up to Peter to authorize any new group to be a part of the church. There were three primary groups of people in the New Testament:

⋆ *Jews – Samaritans - Gentiles*

Once Peter opened the door to any new group, then the door stayed open. In **Acts 2**, Peter opened the door for the Jews. In **Acts 8**, Peter opens the door to the Samaritans. In **Acts 10**, Peter will open the door to the Gentiles. It is very important that we understand this!

"Then laid they their hands on them, and they received the Holy Ghost." - The *laying on of hands to receive the Holy Spirit* had to be done by the Jewish apostles from Jerusalem, not Philip. The scripture does not say, but they may have spoken in tongues, or languages such as Hebrew or Aramaic, to show that they had entered into the body of the Messiah. No longer was there a rival between the Jews and Samaritans.

In **Acts 2**, water baptism followed Spirit baptism, and in **Acts 8,** water baptism preceded the Spirit baptism. This is why it is so dangerous to build a doctrine on historical events in the book of Acts. We must understand the context and the timing of the groups of people who are receiving the Holy Spirit.

SIMON'S SELFISH AND GREEDY REQUEST

Acts 8:18-19 - *And when Simon saw that through laying on of the apostles' hands the Holy Ghost was given, he offered them money, Saying, Give me also this power, that on whomsoever I lay hands, he may receive the Holy Ghost.*

Simon noticed something that he had never seen before and something that made a huge impression on him. When he saw the *apostles lay hands on the Samaritans* and they received the *Holy Ghost*, he thought that enough *money* would buy this supernatural gift. Simon thought that the Holy Spirit could be bought or sold. Simon wanted to pull a religious business deal so he could do what the apostles were doing. The word

★ *simony*, or the act of buying and selling sacred things, comes from the man Simon.

★ *(Before the founding of the Catholic Church in the 4th century, the clergy was not considered a profession, but a calling by God. Over the centuries, and even in the Protestant Churches, money has come into the local church to the point that there is no difference between sacred things and the business of the world. The Holy Spirit has been grieved in the local church by thinking that God's power can be bought by money. One solution is to keep our focus on the Lord Jesus Christ and see how He lived among the common people. Jesus taught more on the warnings about money than he did heaven or hell. Jesus taught us that God's kingdom is holy and sacred!)*

PETER REBUKES SIMON

Acts 8:20-23 - But Peter said unto him, Thy money perish with thee, because thou hast thought that the gift of God may be purchased with money. Thou hast neither part nor lot in this matter: for thy heart is not right in the sight of God. Repent therefore of this thy wickedness, and pray God, if perhaps the thought of thine heart may be forgiven thee. For I perceive that thou art in the gall of bitterness, and in the bond of iniquity.

God's gifts cannot be purchased with filthy lucre. Read these words in **Isaiah 55:1**:

Ho, every one that thirsteth, come ye to the waters, and he that hath no money; come ye, buy, and eat;

yea, come, buy wine and milk without money and without price.

Simon's view of the Holy Spirit that was being given through the apostles to the Samaritans was materialistic. Peter's rebuke of Simon was strong when he said, *"Thy money perish with thee."* This implies that Simon was not saved when he heard the preaching of Philip. He just made a profession of faith.

"Thou hast neither part nor lot in this matter: for thy heart is not right in the sight of God." – This tells us again that Simon was not a true convert at this point. People may be intellectually moved, and they may even adopt some ethical morals and join a local church. These things have never converted anyone to Christ. Salvation is a regeneration of a person, not just a reformation.

"Repent therefore of this thy wickedness, and pray God, if perhaps the thought of thine heart may be forgiven thee. For I perceive that thou art in the gall of bitterness, and in the bond of iniquity." – Simon had been a proud individual, and he wanted to look good in the eyes of others. Peter knew what was in his heart. Peter commands Simon to *repent* of trying to purchase God's gifts with money. It's interesting that when the word *gall* is used in the Hebrew, it is *rosh*, and means poison. **(Deut.29:18)** Simon had professed Christ and had been water baptized, but his heart was still filled with poison.

Simon's Reply and the Gospel Continued

> **Acts 8:24-25 - *Then answered Simon, and said, Pray ye to the Lord for me, that none of these things which ye have spoken come upon me. And they, when they had testified and preached the word of the Lord, returned to Jerusalem, and preached the gospel in many villages of the Samaritans.***

Because Simon asked Peter to *pray to the Lord* for him gives us some hope that maybe Simon finally had Christ in his heart. The text does not give us a definite answer. This author believes that because Peter was the head of the apostles, and because he had the keys to the kingdom, Simon learned a great lesson and became a true follower of our dear Lord. Scholars have debated Simon's conversion for centuries.

"And they, when they had testified and preached the word of the Lord, returned to Jerusalem, and preached the gospel in many villages of the Samaritans." - Now that the kingdom had been opened to the Samaritans, the door remained open. *Now*, whenever a Samaritan trusted in Christ, they received the Holy Spirit. In the gospel accounts Jesus had told the disciples not to go to the Samaritans, but now the time had come for them to hear the gospel and be a part of the body of Christ. This is another example of our need to rightly divide God's Word *dispensationally*.

> *These twelve Jesus sent forth, and commanded them, saying, Go not into the way of the Gentiles, and into any city of the Samaritans enter ye not: But go rather*

to the lost sheep of the house of Israel. (Matthew 10:5-6)

Philip and the Ethiopian Eunuch

Acts 8:26-28 - *And the angel of the Lord spake unto Philip, saying, Arise, and go toward the south unto the way that goeth down from Jerusalem unto Gaza, which is desert. And he arose and went: and, behold, a man of Ethiopia, an eunuch of great authority under Candace queen of the Ethiopians, who had the charge of all her treasure, and had come to Jerusalem for to worship, Was returning, and sitting in his chariot read Esaias the prophet.*

Just because someone has great success in a certain area of ministry doesn't mean that God will not change the direction. Many preachers would have stayed in Samaria, but Philip was called by God to leave Samaria and *go toward the south unto the way that goeth down from Jerusalem to Gaza*. It was about 95 miles from Samaria to Gaza. It's best to be in the *desert* when God calls than to stay in Samaria where ministry seems to be prospering. Philip was called to leave Samaria and go southward to a *desert road* that connected to the Via Maris, the major trade route that ran from Egypt to Mesopotamia. God knew exactly where the *man of Ethiopia* was and that he was seeking biblical truth. God knew he was trying to find answers from *Esaias the prophet*. Not everyone was wealthy enough to have a scroll that contained the sacred scriptures, so this eunuch must have been a man of prominence. He was either a Jew from Ethiopia who had been to *Jerusalem to worship*, or he was a Gentile who had been converted to Judaism. He was a ★ *eunuch of great authority under* ★ *Candace queen of the Ethiopians*. There is an interesting passage in the Torah concerning eunuchs:

> **He that is wounded in the stones, or hath his privy member cut off, shall not enter into the congregation of the Lord. (Deuteronomy 23:1)**

A eunuch could not be a member of the congregation of Israel, but he could be a *"proselyte of the gate."* However, there will be a great blessing for eunuchs in the Messianic Kingdom:

> **Neither let the son of the stranger, that hath joined himself to the LORD, speak, saying, The LORD hath utterly separated me from his people: neither let the eunuch say, Behold, I am a dry tree. For thus saith the LORD unto the eunuchs that keep my sabbaths, and choose the things that please me, and take hold of my covenant; Even unto them will I give in mine house and within my walls a place and a name better than of sons and of daughters: I will give them an everlasting name, that shall not be cut off. (Isaiah 56:3-5)**

★ *(A eunuch was castrated at a young age in order to serve as a male court official to help them act appropriately around the queen of Ethiopia, or the land of Kush in Africa.)*

★ *(Candace is the Latin and Greek form of her name. She has been identified as Queen Amanitaraqide, who was the Kandake in the Kingdom of Kush during the years of 21-41AD.)*

The Holy Spirit Tells Philip to Join the Chariot

Acts 8:29-31 - Then the Spirit said unto Philip, Go near, and join thyself to this chariot. And Philip ran thither to him, and heard him read the prophet Esaias, and said, Understandest thou what thou readest? And he said, How can I, except some man should guide me? And he desired Philip that he would come up and sit with him.

Philip was being so controlled by the Holy Spirit that the social standing of anyone did not matter. God gave him the courage and the compassion. This eunuch was probably being escorted back and forth from Ethiopia to Jerusalem on a *chariot*. Philip did not come to the chariot reluctantly, but *he ran thither to him*. It was a common practice in ancient times to read the scriptures *out loud*. Philip heard the eunuch reading from the *prophet* * *Esaias*. It was good that the Ethiopian eunuch was reading the sacred scriptures, but he did not *understand what he was reading*. God had called Philip to this road, to this chariot, to this eunuch, to help one man *understand* the person that Isaiah was writing about. Wow! This eunuch was seeking the Lord so much that he invited Philip to *come up and sit with him* in the chariot.

* *(Esaias is a Greek form of the Latin/English name Isaiah. The original Hebrew name is Yeshayahu, which means, "Yah is Salvation.")*

Philip Preached Unto Him Jesus

> **Acts 8:32-35** - *The place of the scripture which he read was this, He was led as a sheep to the slaughter; and like a lamb dumb before his shearer, so opened he not his mouth: In his humiliation his judgment was taken away: and who shall declare his generation? for his life is taken from the earth. And the eunuch answered Philip, and said, I pray thee, of whom speaketh the prophet this? of himself, or of some other man? Then Philip opened his mouth, and began at the same scripture, and preached unto him Jesus.*

This is such a powerful connection to the Old Testament describing Jesus as the One Isaiah wrote about. Many Jews have been converted by reading this one passage. It is a literal prophecy with a literal fulfillment:

> *He was oppressed, and he was afflicted, yet he opened not his mouth: he is brought as a lamb to the slaughter, and as a sheep before her shearers is dumb, so he openeth not his mouth. He was taken from prison and from judgment: and who shall declare his generation? for he was cut off out of the land of the living: for the transgression of my people was he stricken.* **(Isaiah 53:7-8)**

"*And the eunuch answered Philip, and said, I pray thee, of whom speaketh the prophet this? of himself, or of some other man?*" - Many Jews today think that Isaiah was writing about the sufferings of the nation of Israel. Possibly this was the reason why the eunuch did not understand the passage. He may have been told there would be only one coming of Israel's ruling and reigning Messiah. A *Suffering Messiah* was not part of Jewish theology, and this was part of the gospel that God had called His servants such as Philip to preach.

"Then Philip opened his mouth, and began at the same scripture, and preached unto him Jesus." - Philip may have used other scriptures, but he *began using the same scripture in Isaiah*. Philip had been preaching Christ to the Samaritans **Acts 8:5**, and now he is preaching Christ to this Ethiopian eunuch. There is a great lesson for all of us here. All scripture is pointing us to Christ. There are many churches and people who get lost along the way and focus on moral ethics, church government, testimonies, ordinances, and end-time prophecy, and lose sight of the Christ of the Bible. The Christian life is supposed to revolve around our relationship with Jesus the Son of God!

THE ETHIOPIAN EUNUCH BELIEVES AND IS BAPTIZED

Acts 8:36-38 - *And as they went on their way, they came unto a certain water: and the eunuch said, See, here is water; what doth hinder me to be baptized? And Philip said, If thou believest with all thine heart, thou mayest. And he answered and said, I believe that Jesus Christ is the Son of God. And he commanded the chariot to stand still: and they went down both into the water, both Philip and the eunuch; and he baptized him.*

This is a beautiful ending to a very unusual passage of scripture. Notice several important points about the Ethiopian eunuch:

- *He believed what Philip told him about Isaiah's writings*
- *He believed that Jesus was Israel's Messiah*
- *He believed that Jesus was the Son of God*
- *He wanted to be identified with Jesus by water baptism*
- *He was immersed to be identified with the death, burial, and resurrection of Jesus*

"*If thou believest with all thine heart, thou mayest*" - Biblical salvation is not just believing *about Jesus* intellectually, but believing *in Jesus* with our *hearts*. The very fact that the Ethiopian eunuch desired to be water baptized shows that he may have been a Jew who had seen and heard about water baptism in Jerusalem. Philip may have explained to him, or the Holy Spirit revealed to him, the difference between believer's baptism and the water purification rituals of the Jews.

PHILIP'S MYSTERIOUS DEPARTURE

Acts 8:39-40 - *And when they were come up out of the water, the Spirit of the Lord caught away Philip, that the eunuch saw him no more: and he went on his way rejoicing. But Philip was found at Azotus: and passing through he preached in all the cities, till he came to Caesarea.*

The Greek word that Luke uses for *caught away* is *harpazo*, and it means *to snatch up*. This is the very same word that Paul used in **I Thess.4:17** for *caught up*, referring to the rapture of the church. Philip was raptured, not to heaven, but away from the Ethiopian eunuch to *Azotus*, or *Ashdod*, about 40 miles north of where they were. No doubt the Ethiopian eunuch went back to his home country *rejoicing* and helped to bring ★ many to the gospel. There are three instances in the New Testament of mysterious and fast change of geographical locations:

> ★ *John 6:15-21* – (The disciples immediately came to its destination)
> ★ *Acts 8:39* – (The catching away of Philip)
> ★ *I Thess. 4:15-18* – (The catching away of the saints)

★ *(The Coptic Orthodox Christians make up almost 20 percent of the Egyptian population today and has a large population in Sudan and Libya. They trace their heritage to this Ethiopian eunuch and also from Mark, who preached in Alexandria.)*

"But Philip was found at Azotus: and passing through he preached in all the cities, till he came to Caesarea." – Not only did Philip preach in Samaria, but he also went into the Gentile city of *Caesarea*. *Azotus*, or *Ashdod*, was a seaport on the Mediterranean Sea close to *Caesarea*. *Caesarea* was a major city that replaced Jerusalem as a civil and military capital. We will find Philip living in *Caesarea* in **Acts 21:8**. The impact that Philip had in spreading the message of Christ was enormous and paved the way for the door to officially open to the Gentiles in **Acts 10**.

CHAPTER NINE

THE CONVERSION OF SAUL OF TARSUS

Acts 9:1-2 - *And Saul, yet breathing out threatenings and slaughter against the disciples of the Lord, went unto the high priest, And desired of him letters to Damascus to the synagogues, that if he found any of this way, whether they were men or women, he might bring them bound unto Jerusalem.*

"And Saul" - Before we get into the text, it is important that we give some background to this important person who became the writer of at least 13 books of the New Testament. The Book of Hebrews is uncertain. According to tradition, Saul's parents came from the Upper Galilee and fled to Tarsus in the early first century AD. Saul was brought up a Pharisee:

> *Circumcised the eighth day, of the stock of Israel, of the tribe of Benjamin, an Hebrew of the Hebrews; as touching the law, a Pharisee.* **(Philippians 3:5)**
>
> *And profited in the Jews' religion above many my equals in mine own nation, being more exceedingly*

***zealous of the traditions of my fathers.* (Galatians 1:14)**

The Bible, Jewish customs, and traditions give us some insight about *Saul,* who later became known as *Paul:*

* ***He began to study the scriptures at the age of five***
* ***He began to study rabbinic traditions at the age of ten***
* ***He learned a manual trade at the age of 12 (tentmaking)***
* ***He had his bar mitzvah at the age of 13***
* ***He was later sent to study at the feet of Gamaliel (Acts 22:3)***
* ***He had a sister who lived in Jerusalem (Acts 23:16)***
* ***He was a Roman citizen (Acts 16:37-38, 22:25-29)***
* ***He learned four languages: Hebrew, Aramaic, Greek, and Latin***

Of course we do not know what *Saul* looked like, but an old apocryphal book from the first century described him as follows:

"A man of moderate stature, with crisp hair, crooked legs, blue eyes, large knit brows, and long nose, at times looking like a man, at times like an angel."

"And Saul, yet breathing out threatenings and slaughter against the disciples of the Lord, went unto the high priest, And desired of him letters to Damascus to the synagogues" - The very breath of Saul had become the *threatenings and slaughter against the disciples of the Lord.* The high priest was probably ★ *Joseph Caiaphas.* How could the high priest in Jerusalem give Saul authority over Jews living in far away *Damascus?* Because Damascus was being ruled at this time by *Aretas IV,* the king of the Nabateans (9BC-40AD), and was under Roman authority that had granted jurisdiction over the Jews to the high priest and Sanhedrin in Jerusalem. Notice that the letters were to be sent to the *synagogues* hoping to receive their support. Many of the Jewish believers in Jerusalem had fled to *Damascus*. *Damascus* was one of the ten cities of the *Decapolis* with a Jewish population of about 16,000. The distance from *Damascus* to Jerusalem was about 130 miles, about a six-day journey.

★ *(In 1990 an ossuary was found in Jerusalem with the inscription of Joseph Caiaphas. Inside were the remains of a 60 year-old man from the first century. Many Hebrew archaeologists believe this to be the same Caiaphas that is mentioned in the Bible.)*

"that if he found any of <u>this way</u>, whether they were men or women, he might bring them bound unto Jerusalem." – This is a very important and overlooked verse in the New Testament. The very first name for the new believers in Jesus as their Messiah was people of *the way*, not Christianity, Messianism, or Jewish believers. This phrase is found six times in the book of Acts. **(Acts 9:2, 19:9, 19:23, 22:4, 24:14, 24:22)** Those first followers of Christ were not just giving a mental nod to a certain theology about Jesus of Nazareth, they were following a *new way* of life that Jesus had not only taught, but had made *the way*, or the Hebrew *derek*. *The way of the Nazarene* was their rule of life now. True followers of Christ are not characterized by the name of the church they attend, but how they live their lives each day. Following are two Old Testament passages to describe how the Jews lived out their new-found faith called *the way*:

> *The voice of him that crieth in the wilderness, Prepare ye the way of the Lord, make straight in the desert a highway for our God.* **(Isaiah 40:3)**
>
> *For the Lord knoweth the way of the righteous: but the way of the ungodly shall perish.* **(Psalm 1:6)**

It's important to notice that both *men and women* were included in the persecution. Little did Saul know that the Almighty God, the crucified and risen Lord Jesus Christ, was about to intervene.

Saul Meets Jesus on the Damascus Road

> **Acts 9:3-6** - *And as he journeyed, he came near Damascus: and suddenly there shined round about him a light from heaven: And he fell to the earth, and heard a voice saying unto him, Saul, Saul, why persecutest thou me? And he said, Who art thou, Lord? And the Lord said, I am Jesus whom thou persecutest: it is hard for thee to kick against the pricks. And he trembling and astonished said, Lord, what wilt thou have me to do? And the Lord said unto him, Arise, and go into the city, and it shall be told thee what thou must do.*

The Shechinah glory of the Lord from *heaven shined*, or flashed like lightning around Saul. This revelation at noonday **(Acts 22:6)** made Saul *fall to the earth*, and then he heard the voice from heaven. The text does not tell us if Saul was riding a horse or not, but most likely he was. *Saul, Saul, or Shaul,*

ACTS

Shaul, why persecutest thou me? We know that Jesus spoke to Saul in the Hebrew language:

And when we were all fallen to the earth, I heard a voice speaking unto me, and saying in the Hebrew tongue, Saul, Saul, why persecutest thou me? it is hard for thee to kick against the pricks. (Acts 26:14)

Calling Saul's name twice was the way God called others in the Old Testament and the way Jesus called others in the four gospels:

* *Abraham, Abraham – Genesis 22:11*
* *Moses, Moses – Exodus 3:4*
* *Samuel, Samuel – I Samuel 3:10*
* *Martha, Martha – Luke 10:41*
* *Jerusalem, Jerusalem – Matthew 23:37*

Although Saul was persecuting the followers of the Lord, he was persecuting the Lord Himself! Saul thought that he was serving God by attacking these new people of *the way*, and he did not know that he was persecuting the King of heaven!

"And he said, Who art thou, Lord? And the Lord said, I am Jesus whom thou persecutest:" – Even though Saul did not know Jesus as Lord at this moment, he knew that he was hearing from the *Divine Lord*. Jesus identifies Himself as the One whose followers Saul is persecuting.

"it is hard for thee to kick against the pricks. And he trembling and astonished said, Lord, what wilt thou have me to do? And the Lord said unto him, Arise, and go into the city, and it shall be told thee what thou must do." – A *prick*, or *goad*, was a long, sharp stick used to get an ox going the way you wanted when plowing. Jesus knew that Saul could be valuable in His kingdom, so He was *goading* Saul in the right direction. However, Saul was kicking against the *goad,* and it was only increasing his pain. Jesus knew Saul's heart, and he knew that something was bothering his conscience on the inside. It may have started at the death of Stephen. The direction that Jesus gave Saul was one step at a time. The details would be given later. There are vital important questions for any of us to ask:

* *Who are you Jesus?*
* *Lord, what wilt thou have me to do?*

Saul Struck Blind on the Damascus Road

Acts 9:7-9 - *And the men which journeyed with him stood speechless, hearing a voice, but seeing no man. And Saul arose from the earth; and when his eyes were opened, he saw no man: but they led him by the hand, and brought him into Damascus. And he was three days without sight, and neither did eat nor drink.*

The men who were traveling with Saul heard *a voice,* but they neither saw Jesus, nor did they understand what Jesus said. The Shechinah glory of the Lord Jesus Christ had blinded Saul. He had been spiritually blinded and now he was physically blind. Not only was he physically blind, but Saul also didn't *eat or drink for three days.* Saul was on his way to Damascus to persecute the followers of Jesus, and now he will arrive as a believer in Jesus! Wow! Jesus was separating Saul for His divine purpose.

The Ministry of Ananias

Acts 9:10-12 - *And there was a certain disciple at Damascus, named Ananias; and to him said the Lord in a vision, Ananias. And he said, Behold, I am here, Lord. And the Lord said unto him, Arise, and go into the street which is called Straight, and inquire in the house of Judas for one called Saul, of Tarsus: for, behold, he prayeth, And hath seen in a vision a man named Ananias coming in, and putting his hand on him, that he might receive his sight.*

We know that *Ananias* was a devout man and had a good reputation from the Jews that dwelt in Damascus. **(Acts 22:12)** His Hebrew name was *Chananyah*, which means, *"Yehovah is gracious."* Evidently, *Ananias* was part of the believing Jews who had come to Damascus. He was not an apostle, or a man of great prominence, but God uses ordinary people for extraordinary purposes. God revealed in a vision to *Ananias* exactly what He wanted him to do and where He wanted him to go. *Ananias* would be given the divine call to fulfill the vision of Saul who had already received a changed heart. The vision of Ananias was very specific:

* *A specific street called Straight*
* *A specific house of Judas*
* *A specific man called Saul of Tarsus*
* *A specific thing that Saul was doing (praying)*
* *A specific vision that Saul had of Ananias*
* *A specific laying on of hands by Ananias*

Ananias Knew About Saul's Evil Ways

Acts 9:13-16 - *Then Ananias answered, Lord, I have heard by many of this man, how much evil he hath done to thy saints at Jerusalem: And here he hath authority from the chief priests to bind all that call on thy name. But the Lord said unto him, Go thy way: for he is a chosen vessel unto me, to bear my name before the Gentiles, and kings, and the children of Israel: For I will shew him how great things he must suffer for my name's sake.*

Saul's reputation as a persecutor of the church had spread as far as Damascus, probably by many who had fled Judea after the stoning of Stephen. As devout as Ananias was, he still could not understand why the Lord would send him to meet a man who had done much evil to the *saints* of God. He knew about the authority Saul had been given to bind and to bring back Jewish believers to Jerusalem. This is the first reference to the Jewish believers in Jesus as *saints*. This term would become the common designation of all believers in the New Testament.

"But the Lord said unto him, Go thy way: for he is a chosen vessel unto me, to bear my name before the Gentiles, and kings, and the children of Israel:" - Before Saul knew Jesus as Savior and Lord, He had been called from his mother's womb to be a *chosen vessel*. **(Galatians 1:15)** There were three elements to Saul's calling:

* *To bear God's name to the Gentiles*
* *To testify to kings (ultimately to Rome)*
* *To go to the children of Israel (Romans 1:16)*

"For I will shew him how great things he must suffer for my name's sake." - Saul had caused suffering among the followers of Christ, and his calling would also include great suffering. **(2 Corinthians 11:22-33)**

SAUL IS HEALED AND FILLED WITH THE HOLY SPIRIT

Acts 9:17-19 - *And Ananias went his way, and entered into the house; and putting his hands on him said, Brother Saul, the Lord, even Jesus, that appeared unto thee in the way as thou camest, hath sent me, that thou mightest receive thy sight, and be filled with the Holy Ghost. And immediately there fell from his eyes as it had been scales: and he received sight forthwith, and arose, and was baptized. And when he had received meat, he was strengthened. Then was Saul certain days with the disciples which were at Damascus.*

It's very interesting to see that not only did Ananias obey the Lord and put his hands on Saul, he called him *Brother Saul,* showing also that Ananias spoke in Hebrew. After the Lord told Ananias about Saul's divine and unique calling, he knew that Saul was now a brother in the Lord. We can see here also that ★ *Ananias* calls *Jesus the Lord*!

Luke, a physician, says that Saul's eyes felt as though *scales* were falling off, which was used in medical terms for skin falling off of the body. Saul not only received his sight, but this is the time when Saul was actually born again and received *the Holy Spirit.* As a Jew, Saul had been ritually immersed in Jerusalem to be identified with Judaism, but here he is immersed in water in Damascus to be identified with the death, burial, and resurrection of the Lord Jesus Christ. No doubt he had witnessed many of the thousands who had been immersed at the preaching of Peter in Jerusalem. **(Acts 2:41)**

"And when he had received meat, he was strengthened. Then was Saul certain days with the disciples which were at Damascus." - God was concerned about the spiritual and physical strength of Saul. Saul was now numbered among the *disciples of Jesus at Damascus*. The remarkable transformation had brought Saul to be accepted by the brothers and sisters he had been sent to persecute.

Saul's conversion reminds us that no one is outside of the reach of God's hand. Whatever has been in a person's past life can be used to mold him/her into a great vessel for God's kingdom. About 30 years later, Saul would say these words:

> *Who was before a blasphemer, and a persecutor, and injurious: but I obtained mercy, because I did it ignorantly in unbelief.* **(I Timothy 1:13)**
>
> *Howbeit for this cause I obtained mercy, that in me first Jesus Christ might shew forth all longsuffering, for a pattern to them which should hereafter believe on him to life everlasting.* **(I Timothy 1:16)**

* *(There is a strong tradition that Ananias was martyred in Beit Gubrin, about 33 miles southwest of Jerusalem. His tomb is located in Zoravar Church, in Yerevan, Armenia.)*

The Preaching of Saul

Acts 9:20-22 - *And straightway he preached Christ in the synagogues, that he is the Son of God. But all that heard him were amazed, and said; Is not this he that destroyed them which called on this name in Jerusalem, and came hither for that intent, that he might bring them bound unto the chief priests? But* ★ *Saul increased the more in strength, and confounded the Jews which dwelt at Damascus, proving that this is very Christ.*

This passage shows how quickly Saul started his ministry. He had left Jerusalem with letters addressed to the synagogues to persecute the believers in Jesus, and now Saul is in the synagogues proclaiming that *Jesus is the Son of God.* Wow! Through the teaching from the rabbi Gamaliel from the Old Testament and through his experience on the Damascus Road, Saul was now able to connect the scriptures. Saul could now explain to the people from the Holy Scriptures that Jesus was the One the prophets wrote about.

This is the only time that this title of Jesus being the Son of God is mentioned in the book of Acts. There would be much greater results in our preaching today, and we would feel God's presence more in our churches if we kept our focus on the deity of Christ:

But these are written, that ye might believe that Jesus is the Christ, the Son of God; and that believing ye might have life through his name. **(John 20:31)**

"*But all that heard him were amazed, and said; Is not this he that destroyed them which called on this name in Jerusalem, and came hither for that intent, that he might bring them bound unto the chief priests?*" - The people were beside themselves and astonished at the radical change that Christ had made in Saul. Saul would no longer be bringing believers to Jerusalem bound as prisoners, but he would be used by the Lord to enlarge the number of the believers in Damascus and throughout the Roman world. When people have a true conversion experience with the Lord Jesus Christ, there will be a change that people cannot understand. Saul would later write these words after he had lived them out himself:

Therefore if any man be in Christ, he is a new creature: old things are passed away; behold, all things are become new. **(2 Corinthians 5:17)**

"*But * Saul increased the more in strength, and confounded the Jews which dwelt at Damascus, proving that this is very Christ.*" - It is a great possibility that this is the time that Saul traveled into Arabia *(Nabatea)* as he mentions in **Galatians 1:17**:

Neither went I up to Jerusalem to them which were apostles before me; but I went into Arabia, and returned again unto Damascus.

The Unbelieving Jews Try to Kill Saul

Acts 9:23-25 - *And after that many days were fulfilled, the Jews took counsel to kill him: But their*

> *laying await was known of Saul. And they watched the gates day and night to kill him. Then the disciples took him by night, and let him down by the wall in a basket.*

This was only the beginning of the many things that Saul would suffer for the name of Jesus that was told to Ananias by Christ himself. **(Acts 9:16)** One has to wonder what was going on in the mind of Saul, as he had been a persecutor of the church and now he was the one being persecuted by the unbelieving Jews. Saul was going to learn that he would be protected until his ministry was complete. Not only were the unbelieving Jews watching day and night to kill Saul, the conspiracy included the ethnarch *Aretas IV* who appointed some of them as guards of the city gates:

> *In Damascus the governor under Aretas the king kept the city of the Damascenes with a garrison, desirous to apprehend me.* **(2 Corinthians 11:32)**

"Then the disciples took him by night, and let him down by the wall in a basket." - Saul's ministry had already been fruitful and multiplied the disciples for the Lord. They took Saul and placed him in a large basket, probably made out of plaited reeds, and let him down the wall at night. The inside of the wall allowed them to rescue Saul through a window into a home. We are reminded of a similar escape of *Rahab and the spies* in **Joshua 2:15**.

> *And through a window in a basket was I let down by the wall, and escaped his hands.* **(2 Corinthians 11:33)**

Barnabas Stands Up For Saul in Jerusalem

Acts 9:26-30 - *And when Saul was come to Jerusalem, he assayed to join himself to the disciples: but they were all afraid of him, and believed not that he was a disciple. But Barnabas took him, and brought him to the apostles, and declared unto them how he had seen the Lord in the way, and that he had spoken to him, and how he had preached boldly at Damascus in the name of Jesus. And he was with them coming in and going out at Jerusalem. And he spake boldly in the name of the Lord Jesus, and disputed against the Grecians: but they went about to slay him. Which when the brethren knew, they brought him down to Caesarea, and sent him forth to Tarsus.*

This was the first time that Saul had returned to Jerusalem since his conversion to Christ. It's understandable why the followers of Christ in Jerusalem were *afraid* of Saul. Perhaps they thought that Saul was planted by the Sanhedrin to persecute them again. This period is described in **Galatians 1:18-20.** But *Barnabas* brought Saul to the *apostles* (Peter and James) and declared four things about Saul:

* *Saul had seen the Lord in the way*
* *The Lord had spoken to Saul*
* *Saul had been preaching boldly in Damascus in the name of Jesus*
* *The Grecian (Hellenized) Jews tried to kill Saul*

According to **Galatians 1:18**, Saul abode 15 days in the house with Peter.

"Which when the brethren knew, they brought him down to Caesarea, and sent him forth to Tarsus." - Barnabas, being a man full of the Holy Spirit, had convinced the apostles and the disciples in Jerusalem that Saul was truly a chosen vessel of God. While *Caesarea* was over 75 miles northwest of Jerusalem on the Mediterranean coast, it was still *going down* from the mountains of Judea. From the seaport in Caesarea Saul sailed by ship to the important city of *Tarsus*, one of the great cities of the ancient world. This time period covers 8 to 12 years of Saul's life. God was preparing Saul for the rest of his life. During these years Saul went into other regions while not being seen in the regions of Judea:

Afterwards I came into the regions of Syria and Cilicia; And was unknown by face unto the churches of Judaea which were in Christ. (**Galatians 1:21-22**)

Notice the progression in the life of Saul:

* *Saul the persecutor*
* *Saul the blind*
* *Saul the convert*
* *Saul the preacher*

SAULS' CONVERSION BRINGS PEACE

Acts 9:31 - *Then had the churches rest throughout all Judaea and Galilee and Samaria, and were*

edified; and walking in the fear of the Lord, and in the comfort of the Holy Ghost, were multiplied.

The followers of the Lord Jesus had *multiplied* to the point that they had started small churches in ⋆ *Judea and* ⋆ *Galilee and Samaria*. In the midst of Roman oppression and Jewish persecution, the believers were still *edified, walked in the fear of the Lord, and in the comfort of the Holy Ghost*. They would later experience more persecution, but this peace that was brought about from Saul's conversion allowed the believers to multiply and the gospel to spread throughout the known world. There is no evil strong enough in the world to prevent God's children from enjoying His presence.

⋆ *(There is not much recorded about where these churches were, but according to archaeologists, there was a church of Jewish believers in an underground cave on Mount Zion in Jerusalem. Small churches were started in places such as the house of Simon Peter on the shores of Galilee, and other places where they knew Jesus the Son of God had been throughout His earthly ministry. Many of the synagogues became Messianic places of worship where later would be the sites of Byzantine churches from 330-1453AD.)*

SIMON PETER'S MINISTRY AT LYDDA

Acts 9:32-35 - *And it came to pass, as Peter passed throughout all quarters, he came down also to the saints which dwelt at Lydda. And there he found a certain man named Aeneas, which had kept his bed eight years, and was sick of the palsy. And Peter said unto him, Aeneas, Jesus Christ maketh thee whole:*

arise, and make thy bed. And he arose immediately. And all that dwelt at Lydda and Saron saw him, and turned to the Lord.

Peter's ministry now shifts away from Jerusalem approximately 35 miles to *Lydda*, the Greek name of the Hebrew town of *Lod*. Today it is just on the outskirts of the modern city of Tel Aviv, where the main *Ben Gurion Airport* is located in Israel. There were already *saints* living in *Lydda* probably as a result of the preaching of Philip throughout this region. **(Acts 8:40)** *Aeneas* may have already been a believer in Christ, but the text is not clear. He had been unable to walk for *eight years* because of the *palsy*, which was a medical term for *paralysis*.

"And Peter said unto him, Aeneas, Jesus Christ maketh thee whole: arise, and make thy bed. And he arose immediately." – Peter wanted *Aeneas* to know that the source of his healing would come immediately from the person of *Jesus Christ*. *Make thy bed,* or *spread your bed for yourself*, meant that he could now do for himself what others had been doing for him. No doubt Peter was imitating what Jesus told the paralytic in **Mark 2:10-12**:

> *But that ye may know that the Son of man hath power on earth to forgive sins, (he saith to the sick of the palsy,) I say unto thee, Arise, and take up thy bed, and go thy way into thine house. And immediately he arose, took up the bed, and went forth before them all; insomuch that they were all amazed, and glorified God, saying, We never saw it on this fashion.*

"And all that dwelt at Lydda and Saron saw him, and turned to the Lord." - This is referring to all of the Jews that dwelt in *Lydda* and the *Saron*, or the ★ *Plain of Sharon*, because the gospel had not been officially opened to the Gentiles at this moment. Most of the people who lived in the coastal plain were Gentiles, so the Jews who lived there turned to the Lord Jesus as their Messiah as a result of this miracle.

★ *(The Plain of Sharon is mentioned in I Chronicles 5:16, 27:29; Isaiah 33:9, 35:2, 65:10, including the famous reference to the enigmatic "Rose of Sharon" in Song of Songs 2:1.)*

Tabitha Dies in Joppa

Acts 9:36-38 - ***Now there was at Joppa a certain disciple named Tabitha, which by interpretation is called Dorcas: this woman was full of good works and almsdeeds which she did. And it came to pass in those days, that she was sick, and died: whom when they had washed, they laid her in an upper chamber. And forasmuch as Lydda was nigh to Joppa, and the disciples had heard that Peter was there, they sent unto him two men, desiring him that he would not delay to come to them.***

Tabitha is her Aramiac name, and *Dorcas* is her Greek name, which means, *gazelle*, a species of antelope that lives in Israel. Here is a woman *disciple* whose life is *full of good works* and giving to the poor.

Joppa was about ten miles northwest of Lydda.

"And it came to pass in those days, that she was sick, and died: whom when they had washed, they laid her in an upper chamber." – In Jerusalem a dead body had to be buried before sundown, but outside of the holy city a body was permitted to remain unburied for three days and nights. The healing of Aeneas in Lydda had caused such encouragement among the believing Jews that they sent *two men* for Peter to come immediately.

Tabitha is Raised From the Dead

Acts 9:39-43 - *Then Peter arose and went with them. When he was come, they brought him into the upper chamber: and all the widows stood by him weeping, and shewing the coats and garments which Dorcas made, while she was with them. But Peter put them all forth, and kneeled down, and prayed; and turning him to the body said, Tabitha, arise. And she opened her eyes: and when she saw Peter, she sat up. And he gave her his hand, and lifted her up, and when he had called the saints and widows, presented her alive. And it was known throughout all Joppa; and many believed in the Lord. And it came to pass, that he tarried many days in Joppa with one Simon a tanner.*

For the apostles to raise a dead person back to life was very unusual and remarkable at this point in the early church. What a touching scene for the *widows to show the coats and garments* (inner garments and outer tunics) that *Dorcas* had made for them while she was living.

"Tabitha, arise" - Peter was there when Jesus told the 12 year-old daughter of Jairus, *"Talitha Cumi,"* **(Mark 5:38-43)** and Peter probably said, *"Tabitha Cumi."*

"And she opened her eyes: and when she saw Peter, she sat up. And he gave her his hand, and lifted her up, and when he had called the saints and widows, presented her alive. And it was known throughout all Joppa; and many believed in the Lord." - This miracle was not done in secret; *Peter presented her alive*. Why didn't God raise Stephen from the dead? Why did He raise Tabitha? We cannot know the mind of the Lord, but this woman disciple had such influence that she was chosen to *be* a miracle in order to help others. The primary reason for the miracle was that *many believed in the Lord*. Hallelujah!

"And it came to pass, that he tarried many days in Joppa with one Simon a tanner." - This is an amazing statement because religious Jews were not allowed to live within 75 feet of the house of a tanner, because he worked with unclean carcasses of animals. **(Leviticus 11:39-40)** This tells us that Peter was becoming less concerned about the Jewish customs and traditions and more concerned about people. This also helped prepare Peter for what was about to happen in the following chapter. *Simon the tanner* must have been a believer in Jesus as the Messiah! Things were changing for Simon Peter and for the world.

CHAPTER TEN

CORNELIUS, THE ROMAN CENTURION

Acts 10:1-2 - *There was a certain man in Caesarea called Cornelius, a centurion of the band called the Italian band, A devout man, and one that feared God with all his house, which gave much alms to the people, and prayed to God alway.*

Here we find one of the most important chapters in the book of Acts, as well as the New Testament concerning Gentile Christianity. This chapter marks a major transition, and while it is rather lengthy, we would be wise to pay very close attention. God chose to use the Jewish Simon Peter and a very unlikely Roman centurion in a very pagan Roman city to officially launch the gospel to the Gentile world.

"There was a certain man in Caesarea called Cornelius, a centurion of the band called the Italian band," - ★ Caesarea was a very important seaport town on the Mediterranean Coast and the Roman headquarters during the early first century.

★ *(Caesarea was originally a small way-station called Strato's Tower. Herod the Great rebuilt it between the years 22-10BC. Drinking and bathing water was piped in using an enormous aqueduct that was built from the Carmel springs in the north, about 25 miles away. It was the headquarters of Pontius Pilate in Jesus' time, and a stone was discovered in 1961 with the name Pontus Pilate inscribed from the first century. Caesarea boasted of its market, bathhouses, wide streets, theatre, frescoes, and statues to honor Rome and Caesar Augustus. Herod built himself a palace that jutted out into the harbor. Gladiator and horse racing events were held each year in the hippodrome. The seaport was one of the largest in the Mediterranean world and one of the most beautiful. Herod designed a way to use volcanic ash and lime to build concrete breakwaters under the sea. He had the raw materials shipped in from hundreds of miles away from places such as Putoli, Italy, where the pozzolana ash was found. This was a feat that was unthinkable in that day. This author has been to Caesarea on countless occasions and found the city to hold a very important place in helping to ship the gospel of Christ to the known world. God used the Romans, and they didn't even know it.)*

* *Cornelius* was part of a *band*, or *cohort*, of 600 Italian Roman soldiers. Cornelius was a * *centurion* that led 100 of the soldiers. The *Italian band* was just one segment of the Roman army and represented those who were Italian nationally, and spoke Latin and possibly Greek.

* *(Cornelius was not the first Gentile to believe in the Jewish Christ. There were Gentiles like the Wise Men in* **Matthew 2**; *the Samaritan Woman in* **John 4**; *the Maniac of Gadara in* **Mark 5**; *and the Roman centurion in Capernaum in* **Luke 7**. *Many other Gentiles came to hear and to see Jesus in* **Matthew 4:25**. *Cornelius would be the first Gentile to make the promise of God to the Gentiles* <u>official</u>. **Isaiah 2:2-5; 26:5-8; 56:3-8; 60:3-5)**

*(It's interesting that Roman centurions are given a positive light in the New Testament. The Roman centurion in **Luke 7:1-10**; the believing centurion at the cross in **Mark 15:39**; Cornelius in **Acts 10**; and the centurion that befriended Paul in **Acts 27:43**.)*

"A devout man, and one that feared God with all his house, which gave much alms to the people, and prayed to God alway." - A typical Roman centurion was exposed to the worship of gods, such as Jupiter, Augustus, Mars, and Venus, etc., but Cornelius believed in the God of Israel and would have been called a *God-fearer*. Yet he stopped short of becoming fully converted primarily because of the Jewish law of circumcision. Although he was not a part of mainstream Jewish life, Cornelius was serving God by *giving to the Jewish poor people and praying always*. While Cornelius was not yet fully *saved*, he was living in obedience to the light he had been given. There are four things about Cornelius that are worth remembering:

* *He was devout*
* *He feared God*
* *He gave generously to the poor*
* *He prayed always*

The Vision of Cornelius

Acts 10:3-6 - He saw in a vision evidently about the ninth hour of the day an angel of God coming in to him, and saying unto him, Cornelius. And when he looked on him, he was afraid, and said, What is it, Lord? And he said unto him, Thy prayers and

> *thine alms are come up for a memorial before God. And now send men to Joppa, and call for one Simon, whose surname is Peter: He lodgeth with one Simon a tanner, whose house is by the sea side: he shall tell thee what thou oughtest to do.*

The *ninth hour* was three o'clock in the afternoon, and Cornelius was praying. (**Acts 10:30**) The *angel of God* spoke to Cornelius personally and called him by name. Cornelius was *afraid* and recognized that the angel was a supernatural heavenly being. The angel told him that *his prayers and giving* had reached God in heaven for a *memorial*. The deeds of Cornelius were as a smoke of incense going up to heaven.

The *angel of God* told Cornelius to *send men to Joppa, and call for one Simon, whose surname is Peter*. This was necessary to distinguish Simon Peter from Simon the tanner. He was not to go himself, but to send men that were under his authority. Because of the heart of the Roman centurion Cornelius, an *angel* was sent to him, but it would be the Jewish preacher *Simon Peter* from Galilee who would tell him what to do.

The Obedience of Cornelius

> **Acts 10:7-8 –** *And when the angel which spake unto Cornelius was departed, he called two of his household servants, and a devout soldier of them that waited on him continually; And when he had declared all these things unto them, he sent them to Joppa.*

Apparently the faith of Cornelius had spread to his *household servants* and to some of his *soldiers*. A true believer in God will have an effect on those around him/her. After rehearsing all the things the angel had said, Cornelius sends the three to fetch Simon Peter.

Joppa was about 40 miles south of Caesarea.

THE VISION OF SIMON PETER

Acts 10:9-10 - *On the morrow, as they went on their journey, and drew nigh unto the city, Peter went up upon the housetop to pray about the sixth hour: And he became very hungry, and would have eaten: but while they made ready, he fell into a trance,*

God is spiritually working on *both* Cornelius and Peter while the two men are 40 miles apart. As the messengers were on their two-day journey, Peter was praying on the *housetop* at the sixth hour, or *twelve o'clock noon*. God used the physical *extreme hunger* of Peter to reveal what was about to happen spiritually that would change the course of history. Housetops in Israel were flat and used as a patio-like place, not just as a rooftop. Peter fell into a *trance*, from the Greek word *ekstasis*, where we get the English word *ecstasy*.

Acts 10:11-13 - *And saw heaven opened, and a certain vessel descending upon him, as it had been a great sheet knit at the four corners, and let down to the earth: Wherein were all manner of fourfooted beasts of the earth, and wild beasts, and creeping things, and fowls of the air. And there came a voice to him, Rise, Peter; kill, and eat.*

In his vision, Peter was surprised to see a huge linen cloth that was lowered to the earth by four cords to which the corners were fastened. The text does not tell us if an angel or anyone was holding the four corners, but the huge cloth was lowered to where Peter was.

"Wherein were all manner of fourfooted beasts of the earth, and wild beasts, and creeping things, and fowls of the air." - All manner means clean and unclean or kosher and non-kosher in the Jewish mind of Peter.

"And there came a voice to him, Rise, Peter; kill, and eat." - Not only did Peter see a vision, he heard a *voice* out of heaven. The *voice* was telling Peter *to kill and to eat* even the non-kosher animals, which went against Peter's belief as a law-abiding Jew. **(Lev.10:10, 20:25, Eze.4:14, Dan.1:8-12)**

PETER'S RESPONSE

Acts 10:14-16 - *But Peter said, Not so, Lord; for I have never eaten any thing that is common or unclean. And the voice spake unto him again the second time, What God hath cleansed, that call not thou common. This was done thrice: and the vessel was received up again into heaven.*

To prove how strong a religious Jew was in trying to keep the Law of Moses, Peter said, *"Not so, Lord; I have never eaten any thing that is common or unclean."* Peter was not as obedient as Cornelius. He told God, *"No."* God was going to shake Peter up and change the paradigms in his mind, just as He does with us many times. There are many believers today who are so legalistic that they will never reach their potential in God's service. While Peter was filled with the Holy Spirit, he was still Peter.

"And the voice spake unto him again the second time, What God hath cleansed, that call not thou common. This was done thrice: and the vessel was received up again into heaven." – God's responded to Peter with a deep emphasis by repeating the vision *three times*. In the original language what God told Peter was, *"You stop making common what God has cleansed."* Jesus had already predicted that He would remove the distinction between the clean and unclean food:

> *And Jesus said, Are ye also yet without understanding? Do not ye yet understand, that whatsoever entereth in at the mouth goeth into the belly, and is cast out into the draught? But those things which proceed out of the mouth come forth from the heart; and they defile the man. For out of the heart proceed evil thoughts, murders, adulteries, fornications, thefts, false witness, blasphemies: These are the things which defile a man: but to eat with unwashen hands defileth not a man.* **(Matthew 15:16-20)**

While there are still ★ Jewish and Gentile believers in Christ who will argue this point about clean and unclean foods, the apostle Paul reaffirmed this in **Romans 14:14**:

> *I know, and am persuaded by the Lord Jesus, that there is nothing unclean of itself: but to him that esteemeth any thing to be unclean, to him it is unclean.*

(Once in Israel, this author was working with a Jew who had been converted to Christ. This Jewish man would drink alcohol, had little respect for women, and would not talk very much about the deity of Yeshua. Yet he would not eat anything non-kosher and would judge us for eating a ham sandwich. The inconsistency is still very visible in many religious circles today. Because of the finished work of the Christ on the cross, a Gentile believer is free from the Law of Moses, which includes all 613 commandments. They are also free to keep parts of the Law if they decide to do so, provided they do not trust in it contributing to their justification before God. The second danger is expecting other believers to keep the same commandments they have decided to keep.)

The immediate context in the vision of Peter was referring to food, but the vision certainly had a deeper meaning, referring to the Gentiles. The food laws underscored Israel's separation from the Gentile nations, but God was showing Peter that a new era was about to begin. This is a perfect example of how we must read God's Holy Word in progression and rightly divide the Word of truth. (**2 Timothy 2:15**) God never changes in His character, but He worked in different ways throughout different periods of time.

THE MESSENGERS OF CORNELIUS

Acts 10:17-22 - *Now while Peter doubted in himself what this vision which he had seen should mean, behold, the men which were sent from Cornelius had made inquiry for Simon's house, and stood before the gate, And called, and asked whether Simon, which was surnamed Peter, were lodged there. While Peter thought on the vision, the Spirit said unto him,*

Behold, three men seek thee. Arise therefore, and get thee down, and go with them, doubting nothing: for I have sent them. Then Peter went down to the men which were sent unto him from Cornelius; and said, Behold, I am he whom ye seek: what is the cause wherefore ye are come? And they said, Cornelius the centurion, a just man, and one that feareth God, and of good report among all the nation of the Jews, was warned from God by an holy angel to send for thee into his house, and to hear words of thee.

When the vision had ended, Peter did not know what the vision meant. Now the *Spirit* would speak to Peter and use the Gentile messengers of Cornelius to help clarify his doubting mind. Here we have Roman soldiers coming to fetch the Jewish Peter to bring him to the devout centurion, Cornelius. Notice four ways that Cornelius is described:

* *A Centurion*
* *A Just man*
* *He feared God*
* *He had a good report among the nation of the Jews*

This chapter is such a turning point in salvation going to the Gentiles through the preaching of a Jewish man, several supernatural moments need to be mentioned again:

* *An angel came to Cornelius*
* *A voice from heaven spoke three times to Peter*
* *The Holy Spirit spoke to Peter*
* *It took two visions, one for Cornelius and one for Peter*

Peter Goes to Caesarea

Acts 10:23-24 - *Then called he them in, and lodged them. And on the morrow Peter went away with them, and certain brethren from Joppa accompanied him. And the morrow after they entered into Caesarea. And Cornelius waited for them, and he had called together his kinsmen and near friends.*

We can already see a change in the heart of Peter by having the Gentile visitors lodge in the house. The Holy Spirit watched over the house that night as Gentiles *with* Jews sat at a table together. According to **Acts 11:12**, there were six other brethren who went with Peter to Caesarea to serve as witnesses. Cornelius eagerly waited for Peter to enter into his house, and he even called his *relatives and friends* to come. Cornelius did not want to keep this history-changing moment all to himself. He knew that the vision he had from God would come to pass.

Peter Meets Cornelius

Acts 10:25-27 - *And as Peter was coming in, Cornelius met him, and fell down at his feet, and worshipped him. But Peter took him up, saying, Stand up; I myself also am a man. And as he talked with him, he went in, and found many that were come together.*

In Pharisaic Judaism it was unlawful for a Jew to enter into the house of a Gentile. Peter was beginning to grasp the vision that God gave to him about the clean and unclean. The devout Gentile, Cornelius, *fell down at his feet and worshipped him.* We must try to wrap our thoughts around the fact that here is a common Jewish fisherman from Galilee, who has been looked down upon by the religious Jews, and now God has raised him to a place of such importance that Cornelius kneels down at his feet while many other Gentiles in the house were watching. God had not only taught Peter how to be a leader, but He also taught him the importance of humility. Peter took Cornelius and told him to *Stand up; I myself also am a man.* As great as Peter was, he knew that no man was holy and righteous enough within himself to be worshipped. As the scriptures say, **"There is none righteous, no not one." (Psalm 14:1-3, Romans 3:10)** Our Catholic friends teach that Peter was the *"first pope."* That is not only ridiculous, it goes against the teachings of the Holy Bible. We are also reminded of the apostle John falling down before the angel and what the angel told John:

> *And I John saw these things, and heard them. And when I had heard and seen, I fell down to worship before the feet of the angel which shewed me these things. Then saith he unto me, See thou do it not: for I am thy fellowservant, and of thy brethren the prophets, and of them which keep the sayings of this book: worship God.* **(Revelation 22:8-9)**

Peter's Explanation & Question

Acts 10:28-29 - *And he said unto them, Ye know how that it is an unlawful thing for a man that is a Jew to keep company, or come unto one of another nation; but God hath shewed me that I should not call any man common or unclean. Therefore came I unto you without gainsaying, as soon as I was sent for: I ask therefore for what intent ye have sent for me?*

We can begin to see that this all-important chapter not only reveals the conversion of the Gentile Cornelius, but a conversion of the Jewish Simon Peter. Here Peter is explaining to Cornelius that the vision he had was clearly not just referring to food, but to Gentile people. If Peter had not received the vision, he never would have entered into the house of a Gentile.

"I ask therefore for what intent ye have sent for me?" - Cornelius was obeying the vision that he had been given in **vs. 3-8.** Even if Peter had thoughts about why Cornelius had called for him, it was still such a life-changing and history-changing moment for the kingdom of God that Peter simply asked, *"Why did you send for me?"*

The Response of Cornelius

Acts 10:30-33 - *And Cornelius said, Four days ago I was fasting until this hour; and at the ninth hour I prayed in my house, and, behold, a man stood before me in bright clothing, And said, Cornelius, thy prayer* *is heard, and thine alms are had in remembrance in the sight of God. Send therefore to Joppa, and call hither Simon, whose surname is Peter; he is lodged in the house of one Simon a tanner by the sea side: who, when he cometh, shall speak unto thee. Immediately therefore I sent to thee; and thou hast well done that thou art come. Now therefore are we all here present before God, to hear all things that are commanded thee of God.*

We do not know what Cornelius' prayer was, but God knew his thoughts and his heart. The answer to his prayer would come through the sending of Peter to his house and the message that Peter would give. This shows that even if someone has not been born again, God knows if he/she has a heart to receive the gospel. People may live in an isolated part of the planet, but God can and does make Himself known to all who desire to know Him. God had prepared the heart of Cornelius and of the fisherman Simon Peter. This house meeting in Caesarea was all orchestrated by heaven! We all need to learn how to prepare ourselves to hear God's message, and the preacher needs to prepare himself. Notice that the military term *commanded* is used here by Cornelius when he was ready to hear what Peter had to say.

Peter Uses the Keys of the Kingdom Twice

Acts 10:34-43 - *Then Peter opened his mouth, and said, Of a truth I perceive that God is no respecter of persons: But in every nation he that feareth him,* *and worketh righteousness, is accepted with him. The word which God sent unto the children of Israel, preaching peace by Jesus Christ: (he is Lord of all:) That word, I say, ye know, which was published throughout all Judaea, and began from Galilee, after the baptism which John preached; How God anointed Jesus of Nazareth with the Holy Ghost and with power: who went about doing good, and healing all that were oppressed of the devil; for God was with him. And we are witnesses of all things which he did both in the land of the Jews, and in Jerusalem; whom they slew and hanged on a tree: Him God raised up the third day, and shewed him openly; Not to all the people, but unto witnesses chosen before God, even to us, who did eat and drink with him after he rose from the dead. And he commanded us to preach unto the people, and to testify that it is he which was ordained of God to be the Judge of quick and dead. To him give all the prophets witness, that through his name whosoever believeth in him shall receive remission of sins.*

"*Then Peter opened his mouth, and said, Of a truth I perceive that God is no respecter of persons: But in every nation he that feareth him, and worketh righteousness, is accepted with him. The word which God sent unto the children of Israel, preaching peace by Jesus Christ: (he is Lord of all:)*" – In chapter two Peter used the keys the first time to the Jews, and here he uses the keys the second time to officially open the door to the Gentiles. To help us understand what a transitional passage this is, let's review a few customs that the Jews practiced concerning Gentiles:

- *The Jews thought that God did show respect to the Jews*
- *The Jews thought that God hated the Gentiles*
- *The Jews thanked God that they were not Gentiles*
- *The Jews would not help a Gentile woman give birth*
- *The Jews would have a funeral if a Jew married a Gentile*
- *The Jews would close the door in the face of a Gentile*

All of this was about to change, and Christianity would be the very first so-called religion to disregard race and cultural limitations. What was about to happen in the house of the Gentile Cornelius was revealing the heart of God:

Wherefore now let the fear of the Lord be upon you; take heed and do it: for there is no iniquity with the Lord our God, nor respect of persons, nor taking of gifts. **(2 Chronicles 19:7)**

Peter is saying that even Gentiles, such as Cornelius, who had faith were producing a life of *righteous* deeds even though they had not heard the gospel. Peter's introduction lets Cornelius know that the true *Word of God came through the children of Israel* and the originator of true peace was *Jesus Christ*, who was *Lord of all*; not only the Jews, but also the Gentiles. Thank God!

"That word, I say, ye know, which was published throughout all Judaea, and began from Galilee, after the baptism which John preached; How God anointed Jesus of Nazareth with the Holy Ghost and with power: who went about doing good, and healing all that were oppressed of the

devil; for God was with him." – Peter starts to deal with the life and ministry of Christ because Cornelius needed to know the beginning and the ending of the gospel. The Gentiles in the house of Cornelius had heard about this *Jesus of Nazareth who was from Galilee*, but Peter wanted them to know that He was the *anointed One*, the Messiah. The reason He was able to perform supernatural miracles and have power over *the devil* was because God was with Him. Jesus of Nazareth was a Man, but He was also God who had come to save His people.

THE APOSTOLIC WITNESS

Acts 10:39-41 - *And we are witnesses of all things which he did both in the land of the Jews, and in Jerusalem; whom they slew and hanged on a tree: Him God raised up the third day, and shewed him openly; Not to all the people, but unto witnesses chosen before God, even to us, who did eat and drink with him after he rose from the dead.*

Try to imagine Cornelius and his Gentile friends listening to Peter tell them that he was actually there and *witnessed* the ministry of Jesus from Galilee to Jerusalem. It's interesting that when Peter moves on to the death of Jesus in Jerusalem, he doesn't mention the Jews or the Romans; he just simply says, *"they slew and hanged on a tree."* It wasn't important to place the blame on anyone because God sent Jesus into the world to die for the sins of humanity, including the Gentiles, and Jesus freely gave Himself. Peter says that Jesus was *hanged on a ★tree*, not a cross.

(Archaeologists tell us that most likely Jesus was crucified on the center beam of an olive tree, being nailed to a crossbeam that was fastened onto the tree. His arms were tied by ropes while His hands and feet were nailed. He was probably on the side of a road for all to see, and the apostles were eyewitnesses.)

"Him God raised up the third day, and shewed him openly; Not to all the people, but unto witnesses chosen before God, even to us, who did eat and drink with him after he rose from the dead." - Peter then deals with the resurrection of Jesus, the event that forever changed the course of history. The greatest verse in the Holy Bible is *"He is not here; but is risen."* **(Luke 24:6)** The risen Christ was seen *openly*, but not to everyone, only to those *witnesses* who had been chosen by God, and Peter was one of them. Try to imagine the expressions on Peter's face as he was preaching, realizing how favored he had been to see the Lord resurrected and to be chosen to open the door to the Gentiles. What about the eyes of Cornelius and the faces of his guests? They were so privileged, as Gentiles, to hear the glorious gospel for the first time. Peter wanted them to know that after Jesus arose, He proved that He was alive in bodily form by *eating and drinking with them*. Just think about Jesus calling the fisherman Peter on the shore of Galilee, while knowing that within a few years he would be standing in the house of Cornelius in Caesarea.

PETER CONCLUDES HIS MESSAGE WITH THE COMMISSION

Acts 10:42-43 - *And he commanded us to preach unto the people, and to testify that it is he which was ordained of God to be the Judge of quick and dead.*

> *To him give all the prophets witness, that through his name whosoever believeth in him shall receive remission of sins.*

Peter tells Cornelius that the risen Jesus gave him and the apostles the great commission to *preach unto the people.* **(Matthew 28:16-20)** Because Peter was preaching to Gentiles, he wanted them to know that Jesus had been given the position of the *Judge of the living and dead.* Not only were the apostles witnesses, the prophets of old were also witnesses because Jesus was the Savior that they had written about who would come into the world. Although Jesus was a Jew in the flesh and He came to Israel, <u>whosoever</u> *believed in him would have forgiveness of his/her sins.* Jew or Gentile who believed in Jesus would be justified by his/her faith.

GENTILES RECEIVE THE HOLY SPIRIT BY FAITH

> **Acts 10:44-48 -** *While Peter yet spake these words, the Holy Ghost fell on all them which heard the word. And they of the circumcision which believed were astonished, as many as came with Peter, because that on the Gentiles also was poured out the gift of the Holy Ghost. For they heard them speak with tongues, and magnify God. Then answered Peter, Can any man forbid water, that these should not be baptized, which have received the Holy Ghost as well as we? And he commanded them to be baptized in the name of the Lord. Then prayed they him to tarry certain days.*

The Holy Spirit interrupted the scene when He knew that Cornelius and his friends truly believed the message that Peter was preaching. There was a secret transaction in their hearts! We must never forget what true faith in Christ does for an individual. It's not in raising one's hand, walking the aisle, or joining a local church. It's faith in the finished work of the Lord Jesus Christ as the Son of God!

The *circumcision* (Jews) that came with Peter were astonished that the Holy Spirit fell on the Gentiles without having to be circumcised to be completely converted to Judaism. This sounds so strange to us today, but the big wall that stood in the way of Gentiles who believed in the God of Israel being converted to the Jewish faith was the frightening ritual of circumcision.

"For they heard them speak with tongues (Greek *glossa*), **and magnify God."** – This verse has caused a lot of confusion in the body of Christ, particularly the last 100 years. Cornelius was a Latin-speaking Roman centurion, and after they were baptized in the Holy Spirit, they began to speak in other languages. The original word *glossa* means *"a language that had not been taught."* It may have been Hebrew, or Aramaic, to show Peter and the Jews that they were filled with the Spirit of God. The point is they were *magnifying God!* Wow!

"Then answered Peter, Can any man forbid water, that these should not be baptized, which have received the Holy Ghost as well as we? And he commanded them to be baptized in the name of the Lord. Then prayed they him to tarry certain days." – Jesus had commanded the apostles to *baptize* those who believed in Him. **(Matthew 28:19, Mark 16:16)** Because these Gentiles had experienced the same Holy Spirit as the believing Jews in **Acts 2**, there was no reason why they should not be water baptized. It was probably the Jews who came with Peter who actually performed the baptisms. We could say that this was *"the Pentecost of the Gentiles."* Water baptism was a Jewish way to be identified with Jesus and to be fully accepted within the Jewish community as followers of Jesus. Notice carefully that Cornelius and his friends were baptized in the Holy Spirit before they were baptized in water. Peter had also been commanded by the Lord to teach the people and make disciples, so he *tarried certain days* and taught the Gentiles more about the kingdom of God.

CHAPTER ELEVEN

THE CONTROVERSY IN JERUSALEM

Acts 11:1-3 - *And the apostles and brethren that were in Judaea heard that the Gentiles had also received the word of God. And when Peter was come up to Jerusalem, they that were of the circumcision contended with him, Saying, Thou wentest in to men uncircumcised, and didst eat with them.*

What had happened in Caesarea had quickly made its way to Jerusalem. There was a minority group of Jewish Christians who still believed that Gentiles should be circumcised to be fully accepted in the believing community. Their two other contentions were that Peter went into the house of a Gentile and *ate with them*. The Bible does not say if Peter ate non-kosher food, but the big issue here is that some of the circumcised Jews were more concerned with what Peter did than with what God was doing in spreading the glorious gospel of Christ to the Gentiles. Religion has a way of blinding people from what the Lord is really doing in the hearts of those who need Him.

Peter's Defense

Acts 11:4-15 - *But Peter rehearsed the matter from the beginning, and expounded it by order unto them, saying, I was in the city of Joppa praying: and in a trance I saw a vision, A certain vessel descend, as it had been a great sheet, let down from heaven by four corners; and it came even to me: Upon the which when I had fastened mine eyes, I considered, and saw fourfooted beasts of the earth, and wild beasts, and creeping things, and fowls of the air. And I heard a voice saying unto me, Arise, Peter; slay and eat. But I said, Not so, Lord: for nothing common or unclean hath at any time entered into my mouth. But the voice answered me again from heaven, What God hath cleansed, that call not thou common. And this was done three times: and all were drawn up again into heaven. And, behold, immediately there were three men already come unto the house where I was, sent from Caesarea unto me. And the Spirit bade me go with them, nothing doubting. Moreover these six brethren accompanied me, and we entered into the man's house: And he shewed us how he had seen an angel in his house, which stood and said unto him, Send men to Joppa, and call for Simon, whose surname is Peter; Who shall tell thee words, whereby thou and all thy house shall be saved. And as I began to speak, the Holy Ghost fell on them, as on us at the beginning.*

The importance of the vision that Peter had was that the Holy Spirit wanted Peter to repeat it after he had *rehearsed* it and had everything in perfect order. Without reiterating what we have already explained in the previous chapter, Peter wanted them to know that there was more to the vision than about food. It was the *Spirit* that compelled him to go to Caesarea, and it was an *angel* who told Cornelius to send for Peter. It was God supernaturally working it all out so the Gentiles *could be saved* and receive the *Holy Ghost*. God placed His approval on what had happened to the Gentiles in Caesarea. How could these circumcised Jews withhold their acceptance when God had already given His?

Remembering the Words of Jesus

Acts 11:16-18 - *Then remembered I the word of the Lord, how that he said, John indeed baptized with water; but ye shall be baptized with the Holy Ghost. Forasmuch then as God gave them the like gift as he did unto us, who believed on the Lord Jesus Christ; what was I, that I could withstand God? When they heard these things, they held their peace, and glorified God, saying, Then hath God also to the Gentiles granted repentance unto life.*

Peter tells them that when the Holy Spirit fell on Cornelius and his family, he remembered what Jesus had told them just before His ascension:

For John truly baptized with water; but ye shall be baptized with the Holy Ghost not many days hence. **(Acts 1:5)**

Activity is not enough to validate the work of God, it must also be in line with God's Word. What had happened in Caesarea passed both tests. Peter's defense can be summarized in these points:

* *Peter saw a vision telling him not to call others unclean*
* *The Holy Spirit directed Peter to go to Caesarea*
* *An angel was sent to Cornelius that Peter would give them the message of salvation*
* *The evidence was that the Holy Spirit fell on the Gentiles*
* *The same gift that had been given to the Jews in Acts 2*
* *The Holy Spirit was now available to the Gentiles who believed on the Lord Jesus Christ without the Law*
* *Peter could not withstand God*

The circumcised Jewish Christians in Jerusalem became silent and *glorified God*! If the Gentiles *repented* of their sins, they too would receive the gift of *eternal life*. Hallelujah!

THE CHURCH IN ANTIOCH

Acts 11:19-21 - *Now they which were scattered abroad upon the persecution that arose about Stephen travelled as far as Phenice, and Cyprus, and Antioch, preaching the word to none but unto the Jews only. And some of them were men of Cyprus and Cyrene, which, when they were come to Antioch, spake unto the Grecians, preaching the LORD Jesus. And the*

hand of the Lord was with them: and a great number believed, and turned unto the Lord.

The ministry of the early Jewish believers in Christ picks up here where **Acts 8:4** left off after the stoning of *Stephen*. This passage tells us how far the believers were scattered. They were *preaching the word to none but unto the Jews only* at this particular time in ★ *Phoenice* and areas that stretched along the northern coast of Israel; *Cyprus*, an island in the Mediterranean; and *Antioch*, a city in modern Syria.

★ *(About ten years earlier, the miracle of Jesus healing the daughter of the Syrophoenician woman in* **Mark 7:24-30** *was a prefigure that the gospel would go to the region of Phoenicia.)*

Simon Peter had opened the door to the Gentiles, and here certain men from *Cyprus and Cyrene* went into ★ *Antioch* and preached to the *Grecians*, or *Hellenized Gentiles*. They preached the *Lord Jesus*, or that Jesus was the Lord and Savior, not the Jewish Messiah. The Gentile mind would not have understood the Messianic title of Jesus. *The hand of the Lord was with them and a great number believed and turned to the Lord!* When God's hand is upon the preaching of His Word about Jesus, there is nothing that can stop the increase. Man can turn people to a preacher, to a church, to a social club, but only God's hand can cause people to turn to Christ for salvation. The first Gentile Christian church was founded in Antioch. As Jerusalem was the mother church of the early Jewish believers, Antioch was about 300 miles north of Jerusalem and became the mother church for the early Gentile believers in Christ. It even had a school of theology.

(Antioch was founded in 300BC by one of Alexander the Great's generals, Seleucus I Nicator. The Seleucid Dynasty fell to Rome in 64BC. The population was about 800,000 and was the third largest city in the Roman Empire, after Rome and Alexandria. While it was a very immoral city, it was a very beautiful place called, "The Queen of the East." The pagan gods of Artemis, Apollos, and Ashtaroth incorporated festivals that promoted ritual prostitution. Antioch was so corrupt that it impacted the lifestyles of Rome over 1,300 miles away. It would later become the city of the early church father, Ignatius, who was martyred around 108/140AD, and John Chrysostom who died in 407AD.)

The Ministry of Barnabas

Acts 11:22-24 - Then tidings of these things came unto the ears of the church which was in Jerusalem: and they sent forth Barnabas, that he should go as far as Antioch. Who, when he came, and had seen the grace of God, was glad, and exhorted them all, that with purpose of heart they would cleave unto the Lord. For he was a good man, and full of the Holy Ghost and of faith: and much people was added unto the Lord.

We are reminded of the generosity of *Barnabas* in **Acts 4:36-37** and his warm acceptance of Saul of Tarsus after he was converted in **Acts 9:26-28**. Because *Barnabas was a good man, and full of the Holy Ghost and of faith*, the church in Jerusalem decided to send him to Antioch to represent the apostles. When Barnabas *saw the grace of God* at work, he was *glad* and began to edify the believers to stay *close to the Lord* in a city that was filled with ungodliness. As mentioned in **Acts 4**, it's interesting that the name Barnabas means *"exhortation."* Because of his ministry there, *more people were added unto the Lord.*

BARNABAS AND SAUL WORK TOGETHER

Acts 11:25-26 - *Then departed Barnabas to Tarsus, for to seek Saul: And when he had found him, he brought him unto Antioch. And it came to pass, that a whole year they assembled themselves with the church, and taught much people. And the disciples were called Christians first in Antioch.*

Barnabas was sent to Tarsus to *seek for*, or to hunt everywhere until he found *Saul*. The same word is used when Joseph and Mary were seeking Jesus in the Temple in Jerusalem in **Luke 2:44-45**. When he found *Saul*, he brought him to Antioch to co-minister with him. Both of them spent a *whole year* teaching the Gentile believers there.

"And the disciples were called Christians first in Antioch." - The Jewish believers in Christ were called *"Nazarenes"* (**Acts 24:5**) and the title ★ *"Christian"* was given to the Gentile believers. In the Roman worldview, by adding the *"ian"* after the name of Christ meant that they were considered to be *soldiers of Christ*. A Roman soldier was identified this way by the name of the general he served under, such as a *Caesarian*. Today instead of being called a Baptist, a Methodist, a Pentecostal, or a Catholic, we should be called *"Jesus People"*

or *"Christians."* Notice the two other places the word is used in the New Testament:

> **Then Agrippa said unto Paul, Almost thou persuadest me to be a Christian. (Acts 26:28)**
>
> **Yet if any man suffer as a Christian, let him not be ashamed; but let him glorify God on this behalf. (I Peter 4:16)**

★ *(Over the course of history, the word "Christian" has become a disparaging term because of the many terrible things that have been committed by people who called themselves "Christians." The wars of the Crusaders killed many Jews; and the anti-Semitism theology of the Catholic Church ultimately resulted in the Holocaust of 6 million murdered Jews.)*

THE PROPHECY OF AGABUS

> **Acts 11:27-30 - And in these days came prophets from Jerusalem unto Antioch. And there stood up one of them named Agabus, and signified by the Spirit that there should be great dearth throughout all the world: which came to pass in the days of Claudius Caesar. Then the disciples, every man according to his ability, determined to send relief unto the brethren which dwelt in Judaea: Which also they did, and sent it to the elders by the hands of Barnabas and Saul.**

There were true prophets from Jerusalem who could predict an event that would come to pass in their lifetime. It is commonly believed that *Agabus*, was one of the 70 disciples in **Luke 10:1-24** and was in the Upper Room with the 120 when the Holy Spirit came. **(Acts 1:15)** The Holy Spirit was the Person who revealed to *Agabus* that there would be a ⋆ *great dearth*, or scarcity or famine, *throughout all the world*. The Greek wording here is where we get the English word, *"ecumenical,"* and implies that Luke was talking about the Roman Empire, not the entire globe. This famine happened during the reign of *Claudius Caesar* (41-54AD).

⋆ *(In the writing of "Antiquities," the historian Josephus records that many famines happened in Judea between the years 44-49AD. He wrote about the proselyte queen Helena of Adiabene, (present-day Iran) who turned to the Jewish faith and sent money and food to Jerusalem during these years. Queen Helena kept the Nazarite vow for 14 years, and some say even 21 years. She was buried in Jerusalem, and her sarcophagus was found in the Tomb of the Kings just north of Jerusalem in the 19th century.)*

"Then the disciples, every man according to his ability, determined to send relief unto the brethren which dwelt in Judaea:" - To prove that the disciples in Antioch were true Christians, they *determined* to give financial aid to the church in Jerusalem *according to every man's ability*. Some could give more and some gave less. This is the first time that we find that a Gentile church gave financial aid to the Jewish believers in Jerusalem. The money was not sent back to the apostles, but to *the elders* at the Jerusalem church, and was brought back by *Barnabas and Saul*.

CHAPTER TWELVE

THE MARTYRDOM OF JAMES

Acts 12:1-2 - *Now about that time Herod the king stretched forth his hands to vex certain of the church. And he killed James the brother of John with the sword.*

These two verses began the fourth persecution of the early church in Jerusalem. Who is this ★ *Herod the king*? It gets a little confusing, but it is important to try to untangle the Herodian web. This *Herod* was known as *Herod Agrippa I*, the grandson of *Herod the Great* in **Matthew 2:1,** who was king of Judea when Jesus was born. *Herod Agrippa I* was also the nephew of *Herod Antipas*, the tetrarch, one of the sons of *Herod the Great*, mentioned in **Matthew 14:1, Luke 3:1,** and **Luke 23:7-12**, and the nephew of *Herod Philip*, another son of *Herod the Great*, mentioned in **Luke 3:1**. *Herod the king* in **Acts 12:1** is the fourth ruler from the Herodian Dynasty mentioned in the New Testament thus far:

- ★ *Herod the Great of Matthew 2:1*
- ★ *Herod Antipas, a son of Herod the Great in Matthew 14:1, Luke 3:1, and Luke 23:7-12*

* *Herod Philip, a son of Herod the Great in Luke 3:1*
* *Herod Agrippa I, the grandson of Herod the Great*

* *(Herod Agrippa I who ruled Judea from 41-44AD was the son of Aristobulus IV, who was another son of Herod the Great and who was killed by his father along with his mother Mariamne, in 7BC for fear of losing his throne.)*

"And he killed James the brother of John with the sword." – By 44AD the early church has seen phenomenal success, and it was obvious that the message of the Lord Jesus Christ had already changed the known world. There were some of the early believers in Christ who thought that the 12 apostles enjoyed a unique divine protection. The killing of the apostle James proved that was not true. James was not the first martyr; Stephen was, but James was the first apostle to be martyred. Who was James? He was *not* James, the half-brother of Jesus who became one of the leaders of the early church and later wrote the book of James. The James who was killed by Herod Agrippa is not to be confused with *James the son of Alphaeus,* **(Mark 3:18)** or sometimes called *James the Less*, which may have meant *James the younger,* or smaller. The apostle *James* that Herod killed by the * sword was one of the three closest disciples to Jesus. Notice these intimate moments that James had with our Lord:

* *Mark 4:21 – James was called by Jesus in Galilee; the brother of John; both the sons of Zebedee*
* *Mark 5:37 – James was an eyewitness to the raising of Jairus' daughter*
* *Mark 9:2 – James was one of the three who was an eyewitness to the Transfiguration of Jesus*

* *Mark 14:33 – James was there at the Garden of Gethsemane when Jesus prayed*

* *(The killing of the sword probably means that James was beheaded. It is recorded in the writings of Eusebius, 260-340AD about a story from Clement of Alexandria, who said the soldier guarding James was so affected by his witness that he too became a Christian and was executed alongside James.)*

But there is another passage where Jesus pronounces a prophecy upon James that is directly connected to his martyrdom:

> **Matthew 20:20-23 – Then came to him the mother of Zebedees children with her sons, worshipping him, and desiring a certain thing of him. And he said unto her, What wilt thou? She saith unto him, Grant that these my two sons may sit, the one on thy right hand, and the other on the left, in thy kingdom. But Jesus answered and said, Ye know not what ye ask. Are ye able to drink of the cup that I shall drink of, and to be baptized with the baptism that I am baptized with? They say unto him, We are able. And he saith unto them, <u>Ye shall drink indeed of my cup, and be baptized with the baptism that I am baptized with:</u> but to sit on my right hand, and on my left, is not mine to give, but it shall be given to them for whom it is prepared of my Father.**

James fulfilled this prophecy by being the first apostle to be killed for the sake of the gospel. His brother lived to be an old man, but he suffered repeatedly. No one could kill John until the glorified Christ gave him the book of the Revelation on the isle of Patmos.

HEROD IMPRISONS PETER

Acts 12:3-4 - *And because he saw it pleased the Jews, he proceeded further to take Peter also. (Then were the days of unleavened bread.) And when he had apprehended him, he put him in prison, and delivered him to four quaternions of soldiers to keep him; intending after Easter to bring him forth to the people.*

Remember that Herod Agrippa, the grandson of Herod the Great, was of Edomite descent. This meant that he was always insecure about being ruler over the Jewish people:

Deuteronomy 17:15 - *Thou shalt in any wise set him king over thee, whom the Lord thy God shall choose: one from among thy brethren shalt thou set king over thee: thou mayest not set a stranger over thee, which is not thy brother.*

Herod Agrippa overcompensated by trying to appease the Jewish authorities. After killing James, he proceeded to arrest Peter and put him in prison.

"(Then were the days of unleavened bread.)" - This was the season of Passover and the seven days of the *Feast of Unleavened Bread*, in either 43 or 44AD. This important Jewish feast was also used as a protection for Simon Peter, because executions were not permitted during this religious feast.

*"delivered him to four quaternions of soldiers to keep him; intending after * Easter to bring him forth to the people."* - Because Peter was such an important figure in the spreading of the early church, 16 *soldiers* were appointed to watch, one set of four for each six-hour shift. We know that two of the soldiers were chained to Peter. Herod's intent was to execute Peter after the week of Passover.

* (The KJV translation of the Greek word "pascha" which should be translated "Passover" has caused a lot of debate over the centuries. The only explanation is the influences of the Catholic Church changing the Jewish holidays to so-called Christian holidays, and the 16th century worship of the German, pagan spring goddess, Ostara. The pagan festival celebrated that Ostara turned a bird into a rabbit, and the rabbit laid colored eggs. Sound familiar? But there is no doubt the KJV translators intended the word "Easter" here to have a Christian interpretation. The Greek word "pascha" is used 29 times in the Bible for "Passover" and why it is translated this one time in **Acts 12** *as "Easter" remains a mystery. Many Bible translations have made the correction.)*

THE CHURCH PRAYS FOR PETER

Acts 12:5 - *Peter therefore was kept in prison: but prayer was made without ceasing of the church unto God for him.*

Herod had his soldiers in charge of his prisons, but the early church had the power of prayer. When every gate is shut, the gate of heaven is always wide open. It wasn't only that the church was praying, it was praying *earnestly*. The Greek wording here is as if someone were stretching a muscle to its limits. It was the same idea when Jesus was praying in the Garden of Gethsemane. **(Luke 22:44)** How different our churches today would be if they prayed *earnestly unto God* and not just out of a routine!

GOD SENDS AN ANGEL

> **Acts 12:6-11** - *And when Herod would have brought him forth, the same night Peter was sleeping between two soldiers, bound with two chains: and the keepers before the door kept the prison. And, behold, the angel of the Lord came upon him, and a light shined in the prison: and he smote Peter on the side, and raised him up, saying, Arise up quickly. And his chains fell off from his hands. And the angel said unto him, Gird thyself, and bind on thy sandals. And so he did. And he saith unto him, Cast thy garment about thee, and follow me. And he went out, and followed him; and wist not that it was true which was done by the angel; but thought he saw a vision. When they were past the first and the second ward, they came unto the iron gate that leadeth unto the city; which opened to them of his own accord: and they went out, and passed on through one street; and forthwith the angel departed from him. And when Peter was come to himself, he said, Now I know of a surety, that the LORD hath sent his angel, and hath delivered me out of the hand of Herod, and from all the expectation of the people of the Jews.*

The last night of Passover had ended, and Peter was to be executed the next morning by Herod at the joy of the unbelieving Jewish authorities. It needs to be mentioned here that in spite of what Peter was facing, Peter was *asleep*. Peter was not too worried about Herod because he knew about the power of God. When the Lord God of heaven is with us, there are no soldiers, chains, guard posts, or iron-gate that can stop us. The iron-gate that led out of the city opened *of his own accord*, or the Greek *automate*, which means *automatically*. Here we see that * James the apostle was killed, and Peter the apostle was rescued.

* *(It is commonly taught that* **Hebrews 13:8**, *"Jesus Christ is the same yesterday, today, and forever," means that God always heals people today if they have enough faith. This is not true. God's character never changes, but the way He works does change. It was the appointed time for James to die, and Peter's time would come over 20 years later in Rome (64AD) when he would be killed by the Roman Emperor Nero, by being crucified upside down.)*

PETER PRESENTS HIMSELF TO THE CHURCH

Acts 12:12-17 - *And when he had considered the thing, he came to the house of Mary the mother of John, whose surname was Mark; where many were gathered together praying. And as Peter knocked at the door of the gate, a damsel came to hearken, named Rhoda. And when she knew Peter's voice, she opened not the gate for gladness, but ran in, and told how Peter stood before the gate. And they said unto her, Thou art mad. But she constantly affirmed* *that it was even so. Then said they, It is his angel. But Peter continued knocking: and when they had opened the door, and saw him, they were astonished. But he, beckoning unto them with the hand to hold their peace, declared unto them how the Lord had brought him out of the prison. And he said, Go shew these things unto James, and to the brethren. And he departed, and went into another place.*

"And when he had considered the thing, he came to the house of Mary the mother of John, whose surname was Mark;" – Peter came to a place where he knew other believers would be gathered. He wanted them to see firsthand that their prayers had been answered. He came to the house of *Mary*, the mother of *John Mark*, who was a prominent woman who had one of the house churches in her home. It was large enough to hold many believers. There were no church buildings in those days, so the early Jewish believers met in the ★ houses of devout followers of Christ, sometimes in the houses of one of the apostles or one of their relatives. There are several women in the New Testament named *Mary,* or the Hebrew *Miriam:*

★ *Mary, the mother of Jesus*
★ *Mary, of Bethany, the sister of Martha and Lazarus*
★ *Mary, Magdalene*
★ *Mary, the wife of Cleophas*
★ *Mary, the mother of James and John*
★ *Mary, the mother of John Mark*

★ *(In 1968, Virgilio Corbo and Stanislao Loffreda continued a work that had been started in 1905, excavating the ruins of*

Capernaum, the hometown of Jesus. They discovered underneath the ruins of an octagonal Byzantine Church, the simple dwelling of a fisherman from the 1st century AD. All of the archaeologists agreed that it was the house of Simon Peter where it was used as one of the early house churches in the Galilee.)

John, surnamed Mark, would later write the gospel of Mark under the eyewitness testimony of Peter. *John Mark* was a cousin to Barnabas **(Colossians 4:10),** and his name appears eight times in the New Testament. **(Acts 12:12, 25, 15:37, 39, Colossians 4:10, 2 Timothy 4:11, Philemon 24, and I Peter 5:13)** *John Mark* played a minor role in the book of Acts, but a major role in the history of the church by writing the gospel bearing his name. *John Mark* became a disciple of Simon Peter.

"And as Peter knocked at the door of the gate, a damsel came to hearken, named Rhoda." - Rhoda, or *"rose"* was a servant girl that lived in the house of Mary. Some scholars think that she is the same *damsel* that is mentioned in **John 18:17**. If this is true, it makes a very interesting connection to her hearing Peter's voice at the trial of Jesus and hearing Peter's voice at the door. When *Rhoda* told the group that Peter was at the gate, they thought she had seen *an angel*. It was a strong Jewish custom that a guardian angel had the same resemblance as the human he/she was assigned to watch over.

"But he, beckoning unto them with the hand to hold their peace, declared unto them how the Lord had brought him out of the prison. And he said, Go shew these things unto James, and to the brethren." - The whole group was *amazed* when they saw Peter! But Peter motioned with his hands for them to stay calm while he explained how the Lord rescued him from the prison of Herod. The word *declared*, or *diegesato*, means that Peter gave them *"the full story."* Peter told them to go tell *James*, the half-brother of Jesus, who was leading another house church and became the leader at the church in Jerusalem.

"And he departed, and went into another place." – Other than a brief mention in **Acts 15:7**, Peter is not mentioned again in the book of Acts. The narrative will start in **Acts 13** with Saul and Barnabas. Luke was not inspired to tell us where Peter went, but we know that he traveled to many places throughout the Roman world, such as Corinth, Antioch of Pisidia, Asia Minor, and Babylon.

THE EXECUTION OF THE SOLDIERS

Acts 12:18-19 - ***Now as soon as it was day, there was no small stir among the soldiers, what was become of Peter. And when Herod had sought for him, and found him not, he examined the keepers, and commanded that they should be put to death. And he went down from Judaea to Caesarea, and there abode.***

Herod was furious that Peter had escaped. It was the Roman custom that if a guard's prisoner escaped, the guard was given the penalty that was due to the prisoner. In this case it was death. We do not know if all 16 soldiers were put to death or just the soldiers who were chained to Peter. Most likely it was all 16 soldiers.

It was standard procedure for the ruler of Judea to leave Jerusalem after Passover and go back ★ *down to Caesarea*, the seaport town that was the political capital headquarters of Israel.

★ *(Leaving Jerusalem Herod would have traveled northwest about 75 miles to the coast of the Mediterranean Sea. He would have traveled over 2,400 feet downward geographically from the hills of Jerusalem to the coastal plain of Israel.)*

God Judges Herod Agrippa I

Acts 12:20-23 - ***And Herod was highly displeased with them of Tyre and Sidon: but they came with one accord to him, and, having made Blastus the king's chamberlain their friend, desired peace; because their country was nourished by the king's country. And upon a set day Herod, arrayed in royal apparel, sat upon his throne, and made an oration unto them. And the people gave a shout, saying, It is the voice of a god, and not of a man. And immediately the angel of the Lord smote him, because he gave not God the glory: and he was eaten of worms, and gave up the ghost.***

This is an interesting and unusual setting that the Holy Spirit inspired Luke to write. The cities of Phoenicia, *Tyre and Sidon,* were independent of Rome, but they relied on the grain and food supplies of the cities to come from the rich fields of Galilee that were controlled by Herod. Herod had cut off their supplies, and they tried to bribe a man named *Blastus*, his chamberlain who managed the household, to make peace.

"And upon a set day Herod, arrayed in royal apparel, sat upon his throne, and made an oration unto them. And the people gave a shout, saying, It is the voice of a god, and not of a man. And immediately the angel of the Lord smote him, because he gave not God the glory: and he was eaten of worms, and gave up the ghost." - God judged Herod because he enjoyed the praise of the people and wanted all of the glory to go to himself. It was such a display of evil debauchery and self-glory in his silver, glistening robe, that God had an *angel* to kill Herod. His flesh and intestines became so decayed and rotten that *worms* devoured his body. Herod Agrippa I died at the age of 54 in the seventh year of his reign. *(His death is recorded in detail by Flavius Josephus, Jewish Antiquities 19.343-350.)*

THE EARLY CHURCH GROWS

Acts 12:24-25 - *But the word of God grew and multiplied. And Barnabas and Saul returned from Jerusalem, when they had fulfilled their ministry, and took with them John, whose surname was Mark.*

Herod thought that he had the upper hand on the early church, but God showed that HE was in charge and orchestrated all of the events to spread the message of the risen Christ. Herod Agrippa I was judged and killed by God, and the early church grew. Notice the Bible says that the *word of God grew and multiplied*. The Word of God cannot be stopped by the evil deeds of men. The death of the apostle James and the escape of the apostle Peter impacted the church in a positive way.

Barnabas and Saul had completed distributing the gifts to the church in Jerusalem that were sent by the church in Antioch in **Acts 11:29-30**. They left Jerusalem to go back to Antioch and took *John Mark* with them.

CHAPTER THIRTEEN

THE APPOINTMENT OF BARNABAS AND SAUL

Acts 13:1-2 - *Now there were in the church that was at Antioch certain prophets and teachers; as Barnabas, and Simeon that was called Niger, and Lucius of Cyrene, and Manaen, which had been brought up with Herod the tetrarch, and Saul. As they ministered to the Lord, and fasted, the Holy Ghost said, Separate me Barnabas and Saul for the work whereunto I have called them.*

This chapter marks the final stage of the commission of Jesus in **Acts 1:8**. The order that our Lord gave them was to proclaim the gospel *in Jerusalem, and in all Judea and Samaria, and unto the uttermost part of the earth*. In the first 12 chapters of Acts, the gospel has been proclaimed in *Jerusalem, Judea, and Samaria*. Chapter 13 begins the final phase of proclaiming the gospel to the *uttermost parts of the earth*, which is also a fulfillment of **Isaiah 49:6**:

I will also give thee for a light to the Gentiles, that thou mayest be my salvation unto the end of the earth.

Antioch had become the base of Gentile evangelism. There were *prophets and teachers* who had been gifted to equip the saints in Antioch. They were a very unique and powerful group of men:

* *Barnabas - He was an apostle and a prophet*
* *Simeon called Niger - Niger is the Latin term for "black" and means that he was probably from Africa. Some believe he is the same Simon who carried the cross for Jesus, but there is no evidence.*
* *Lucius of Cyrene - He was probably one of the founders of the church at Antioch. (Acts 11:20)*
* *Manaen, or the Hebrew Menachem - He was the foster-brother of Herod Antipas and was brought up in the royal court. Interesting!*
* *Saul - He is not listed as an apostle here, but he would later become Paul and be one of the most important Christians who ever lived.*

"As they ministered to the Lord, and fasted," - These men were not merely holding a position to be seen of others, they were *ministering to the Lord*. The idea is akin to the priests ministering in the Tabernacle in the Old Testament, except here they were praying to God directly because the perfect Lamb of God had been given on the cross in Jerusalem. They were under the New Covenant now. Their sincerity was marked also by *fasting*. While fasting is not a commandment in the New Testament, it is an option for those who desire a closer walk with the Lord and to know more clearly His will for their lives.

"the Holy Ghost said, Separate me Barnabas and Saul for the work whereunto I have called them." - Because some of these men were prophets and because they were earnestly seeking God's will, God spoke to them through the Person of the *Holy Spirit*. There were no committee reports, no marketing surveys, or demographic analyses. The *Holy Spirit* is not a *force*, but the Third Person of the Triune Godhead. All of the men were divinely chosen for a certain purpose, but the *Holy Spirit* made it clear to them that *Barnabas and Saul* were especially gifted men and were *separated* to be missionaries. Salvation is to *whosoever will*, but God does *separate* certain people for specific purposes. God has a specific work for everyone to do, and we all need to seek the face of the Lord and find what is our real purpose in His kingdom. Most believers just coast along through life, living a nominal Christian life and never reach their full potential.

The Church at Antioch Sends Them Away

Acts 13:3 - *And when they had fasted and prayed, and laid their hands on them, they sent them away.*

The *laying on of hands* was a Jewish method of identification and appointment. This was not just a ritual or dry service, but an outward sign to the church that Barnabas and Saul had been consecrated for a special service. They were under the authority of the church at Antioch. They were an extension of the church. This is the first time mentioned in the Bible that a church *sent out* missionaries in an organized effort. This is the pattern of evangelists and missionaries today. It should be clear to the church just who the gifted ones are through *praying and fasting* and by *ministering unto the Lord*. Then they are to *send them out* with their full support.

The First Journey Begins

Acts 13:4-5 - *So they, being sent forth by the Holy Ghost, departed unto Seleucia; and from thence they sailed to Cyprus. And when they were at Salamis, they preached the word of God in the synagogues of the Jews: and they had also John to their minister.*

It is important to remember that Barnabas and Saul were not sent out by men, but they were sent *forth by the Holy Ghost*. If the Holy Spirit does not call or send out the preachers, the results will not be of eternal significance. From Antioch going west, there was a seaport about 16 miles away at *Seleucia*. It was from this seaport they sailed on to *Cyprus*, the home of Barnabas. **(Acts 4:36)** The island of Cyprus was about 130 miles southwest of Antioch. When they came to *Salamis*, the largest city on the island, they preached the word of God in the *synagogues of the Jews*. There was a large Jewish population on the island of Cyprus by New Testament times. In keeping with ★ God's orders, **(Romans 1:16)** they were to go to the Jews first then to the Gentiles.

★ *(One of the primary reasons why the modern-day churches are in spiritual trouble is because they do not follow this pattern. Gentile churches need to find ways to spread the gospel to the Jews and support*

Jewish Christian missions. *The Bible is a Jewish book and Jesus was a Jewish Messiah, and the world is indebted to Israel.* **(Romans 9:4-5)** *Gentile believers have been grafted into Israel and are not the natural branch.* **(Romans 11:17)** *The false doctrine of replacement theology (the Church replacing Israel) has grieved the Holy Spirit.)*

"and they had also John to their minister." - John Mark traveled with Barnabas and Saul on this journey and was an *attendant*. He was under their authority and served them and helped them in ministering to the people. As already mentioned, John Mark was the cousin to Barnabas. **(Colossians 4:10)**

Meeting the Roman Proconsul in Paphos

Acts 13:6-7 - *And when they had gone through the isle unto Paphos, they found a certain sorcerer, a false prophet, a Jew, whose name was Barjesus: Which was with the deputy of the country, Sergius Paulus, a prudent man; who called for Barnabas and Saul, and desired to hear the word of God.*

★ *Paphos* was on the western coast of Cyprus and was the capital of the Roman Senate, who had the control of the island instead of the Roman Emperor. Here we find a strange dichotomy: *a sorcerer who was a Jew, and a Gentile, Roman proconsul, who wanted to hear the word of God.*

★ *(Cyprus became a Roman senatorial province in 22BC. The city of Paphos was a very immoral city with a shrine to the cultic, sexual goddess, Aphrodite. In 1877, an inscription was found, "Under Paulus the proconsul" that dated to 53-54AD. The inscription also confirmed that he became a Christian, along with his entire family.)*

The Resistance of the Sorcerer

Acts 13:8-12 - *But Elymas the sorcerer (for so is his name by interpretation) withstood them, seeking to turn away the deputy from the faith. Then Saul, (who also is called Paul,) filled with the Holy Ghost, set his eyes on him. And said, O full of all subtilty and all mischief, thou child of the devil, thou enemy of all righteousness, wilt thou not cease to pervert the right ways of the Lord? And now, behold, the hand of the Lord is upon thee, and thou shalt be blind, not seeing the sun for a season. And immediately there fell on him a mist and a darkness; and he went about seeking some to lead him by the hand. Then the deputy, when he saw what was done, believed, being astonished at the doctrine of the Lord.*

The sorcerer's real name was *Elymas Bar-Yeshua*. He was an advisor to the proconsul and was the son of a man named *Yeshua*, which was a common name among the Jews in those days. This Jewish sorcerer, who was also an astrologer, was trying to turn the Roman official away from the faith that Saul was preaching. Barnabas and Saul found demonic opposition on their first missionary journey. Where the message of the Lord Jesus Christ is being proclaimed, we should always expect Satan to be in the shadows.

"Then Saul, (who also is called Paul,) filled with the Holy Ghost, set his eyes on him." - It has been commonly taught that after *Saul* was saved, his name was changed to *Paul*, but that is not true. Living in the Diaspora *(the dispersion of the Jews* *from their homeland)* as a Roman citizen, *Saul* had a Jewish name and a Roman name. His Jewish name was *Saul,* and his Roman name was *Paul.* Because Saul was now declared the apostle to the Gentiles, Luke now calls him *Paul.* And with only a few exceptions, *Paul* will now take the lead over Barnabas in the book of Acts. Imagine the scene here: *Paul* being filled with the discerning *Holy Ghost, (Old English term for the Holy Spirit)* and looking into the eyes of a demonic sorcerer!

"And said, O full of all subtilty and all mischief, thou child of the devil, thou enemy of all righteousness, wilt thou not cease to pervert the right ways of the Lord? And now, behold, the hand of the Lord is upon thee, and thou shalt be blind, not seeing the sun for a season. And immediately there fell on him a mist and a darkness; and he went about seeking some to lead him by the hand." - Notice the fivefold message that Paul brought forth to the sorcerer:

* *He was full of subtilty and a trickster*
* *He was full of mischief*
* *He was the son of the devil, while his name was Son-Yeshua*
* *He was the enemy of righteousness*
* *He was perverting the ways of the Lord*

It's interesting that Paul judged the sorcerer by pronouncing him blind. Paul had been blinded on the road to Damascus for his evil treatment of the church. And like Paul who had to be led by the hand after he was struck blind, this sorcerer would also have to be *led by the hand.* His blindness would be for only *a season,* and we never hear about *Elymas* again.

"Then the deputy, when he saw what was done, believed, being astonished at the doctrine of the Lord." - The result of seeing this judgment fall on the sorcerer and *the doctrine of the Lord* that Paul preached caused the Roman official to be converted to Christ. Wow! The point is that if the sorcerer chose to serve Satan, that was his personal mistake. To try and discourage *Sergius Paulus* from being converted to Jesus was too much for Paul to take.

From Paphos to Perga

Acts 13:13 - *Now when Paul and his company loosed from Paphos, they came to Perga in Pamphylia: and John departing from them returned to Jerusalem.*

Now the wording is changed from *Barnabas and Paul* to *Paul and his company*. From this point on, Paul's leadership will be evident. The distance from Paphos, Cyprus, to *Perga in Pamphilia*, was about 180 miles north-northwest to the southern part of Asia Minor, present day Turkey. The missionary journeys of Paul and Barnabas were not without problems. It was here at *Perga* that John Mark decided to go back to Jerusalem, and this was displeasing to Paul. **(Acts 15:37-39)** No one knows why, but here are a few thoughts:

* *Perhaps he was confused about Paul taking the leadership*
* *Perhaps the emphasis on Gentiles was too much of an adjustment*
* *Perhaps it was the dangerous Taurus mountains they were about to cross over*

* *Perhaps his confidence was weak because of Paul's poor health*
* *Perhaps John Mark was simply homesick*

PAUL PREACHES IN THE SYNAGOGUE AT PISIDIA

Acts 13:14-15 - But when they departed from Perga, they came to Antioch in Pisidia, and went into the synagogue on the sabbath day, and sat down. And after the reading of the law and the prophets the rulers of the synagogue sent unto them, saying, Ye men and brethren, if ye have any word of exhortation for the people, say on.

Paul and Barnabas traveled inland about 135 miles to *Pisidia*, which corresponds to the province of Antalya, Turkey, today. It was a difficult walk on foot, but the calling of God on their lives placed an unfailing fortitude in their sandals. They came to * *Antioch in Pisidia*, not to be confused with the Antioch in Syria.

* *(Antioch Pisidia was located on a military road called the Via Sebaste. It was founded between 312-280BC by Seleucus Nicator I. In 25BC Emperor Augustus made it a part of the province of Galatia, and was given the title Antiochia Caesarea. In 6BC it was made an important Roman colony where Roman soldiers could settle after 20 years of service to Rome. It had a large Jewish population by the time of Paul and Barnabas.)*

"and went into the synagogue on the sabbath day, and sat down" - Their purpose for going to the *synagogue* first was not only to worship, but to evangelize the Jews, keeping the principle of taking the gospel to the Jew first.

"And after the reading of the law and the prophets the rulers of the synagogue sent unto them, saying, Ye men and brethren, if ye have any word of exhortation for the people, say on." - Every Sabbath Day there was the reading from a section of the Law of Moses, *(Torah)* and then a section from the Prophets, *(Haftarah)* and then came the sermon. This was the custom of the Jewish synagogues in Jesus' time as well. Here is why the Old Testament was called in Hebrew, the *Tanach*, or *TNK*:

* ***T = Torah*** (Five books of Moses)
* ***N = Nevi'im*** (Prophets)
* ***K = Ketuvim*** (Psalms, Job, Poetry and Wisdom books)

It was also the custom for the rulers of the synagogue to give distinguished guests an opportunity to speak to the people. In other words, *"Do you men have any comments to make on the scriptures that have been read this day?"* Paul was more than happy to take advantage of the opportunity.

Paul's Message

Acts 13:16-23 - *Then Paul stood up, and beckoning with his hand said, Men of Israel, and ye that fear God, give audience. The God of this people of Israel chose our fathers, and exalted the people when they dwelt as strangers in the land of Egypt, and with an high arm brought he them out of it. And about the time of forty years suffered he their manners in the* *wilderness. And when he had destroyed seven nations in the land of Chanaan, he divided their land to them by lot. And after that he gave unto them judges about the space of four hundred and fifty years, until Samuel the prophet. And afterward they desired a king: and God gave unto them Saul the son of Cis, a man of the tribe of Benjamin, by the space of forty years. And when he had removed him, he raised up unto them David to be their king; to whom also he gave testimony, and said, I have found David the son of Jesse, a man after mine own heart, which shall fulfil all my will. Of this man's seed hath God according to his promise raised unto Israel a Saviour, Jesus:*

This begins the longest sermon ever recorded by the apostle Paul to a Jewish audience. There were probably some Gentiles in the synagogue as well who possibly had not been fully converted to Judaism. Paul begins by summarizing what took place in the book of Exodus and the wilderness wanderings, and finally the conquest into the Promised Land. Paul mentions that after *four hundred and fifty years* that *Samuel* was the *last* of the Judges and the *first* of the Prophets. After telling them about the 40 years of *king Saul, (after whom he was named)* Paul moved on to the *Davidic kingdom*. The reason God chose David was not because he was always so moral and good, but because he was *a man after God's own heart*. The point that Paul is making is that from Abraham to the rule of David, God had been preparing Israel for the coming of its Messiah, who He had promised would be the descendant of David. Paul combines the words *"Israel"* with *"Savior"* with *"Yeshua."* We can imagine the positive expressions on the people's faces in the synagogue until Paul talked about *Yeshua* being the *Savior*, and then their countenance changed. God's plan for history was all leading up to *Jesus* being the *Savior* of both the Jews *and* Gentiles. If we are *"in Jesus,"* we are in the flow of God's great plan of redemption.

Paul Preaches From John the Baptist to Jesus

> **Acts 13:24-29 -** *When John had first preached before his coming the baptism of repentance to all the people of Israel. And as John fulfilled his course, he said, Whom think ye that I am? I am not he. But, behold, there cometh one after me, whose shoes of his feet I am not worthy to loose. Men and brethren, children of the stock of Abraham, and whosoever among you feareth God, to you is the word of this salvation sent. For they that dwell at Jerusalem, and their rulers, because they knew him not, nor yet the voices of the prophets which are read every sabbath day, they have fulfilled them in condemning him. And though they found no cause of death in him, yet desired they Pilate that he should be slain. And when they had fulfilled all that was written of him, they took him down from the tree, and laid him in a sepulchre.*

John the Baptist was sent by God to preach the message of repentance with the sign of water baptism in preparation for the coming Messiah. As great as John was, he humbly admitted that he was not worthy *to loose the sandals of the Messiah.* There was no prophet after John. **(Matthew 11:13)**

Paul then told the Jewish listeners and the Gentile God-fearers that the *rulers in Jerusalem* did not know who their Messiah was when He came because they did not believe what was read every Sabbath Day in their synagogues that had been written by the prophets. They did not find any fault in Jesus, so they turned him over to the Roman procurator, Pontius Pilate, to be condemned to death. In their ignorance and unbelief, they were fulfilling what had been written by the prophets concerning the coming Messiah. Jesus was *slain on a tree,* **(Deut.21:22-23, Gal.3:13)** and then His body was taken down and placed in a *sepulchre.* Paul wanted them to know that Jesus was cursed on a tree so they could be blessed and forgiven. Notice that Paul didn't use the word *cross* because it was so offensive to the Jews.

PAUL PREACHES THE RESURRECTION OF JESUS

Acts 13:30-37 - ***But God raised him from the dead: And he was seen many days of them which came up with him from Galilee to Jerusalem, who are his witnesses unto the people. And we declare unto you glad tidings, how that the promise which was made unto the fathers, God hath fulfilled the same unto us their children, in that he hath raised up Jesus again; as it is also written in the second psalm, Thou art my Son, this day have I begotten thee. And as concerning that he raised him up from the dead, now no more to return to corruption, he said on this wise, I will***

> *give you the sure mercies of David. Wherefore he saith also in another psalm, Thou shalt not suffer thine Holy One to see corruption. For David, after he had served his own generation by the will of God, fell on sleep, and was laid unto his fathers, and saw corruption: But he, whom God raised again, saw no corruption.*

Paul is not focusing on philosophy or even theology, but he is just simply stating the historical fact that *God raised him from the dead.* Paul states that the risen Jesus was actually seen by the men and women who had followed Him from the Galilee. When David wrote the Psalms, he could not have been writing about his own resurrection because he died and his body did see corruption. David was writing about the resurrection of the Messiah. There are *three* important Old Testament prophecies mentioned here in Paul's sermon:

* *Psalm 2:7*
* *Isaiah 55:3*
* *Psalm 16:10*

PAUL'S MESSAGE OF FORGIVENESS

> **Acts 13:38-39** - *Be it known unto you therefore, men and brethren, that through this man is preached unto you the forgiveness of sins: And by him all that believe are justified from all things, from which ye could not be justified by the law of Moses.*

Paul concluded his message to the Jews at Antioch of Pisidia with the promise of *forgiveness*. Only by the very One who was killed in Jerusalem, who was buried and rose again, is the way they can find forgiveness and be *justified* in the eyes of a Holy God! By becoming a perfect sin sacrifice, Jesus the Messiah did what the *Law of Moses* could not do.

PAUL GIVES THEM A WARNING

Acts 13:40-41 - *Beware therefore, lest that come upon you, which is spoken of in the prophets; Behold, ye despisers, and wonder, and perish: for I work a work in your days, a work which ye shall in no wise believe, though a man declare it unto you.*

Paul is quoting from **Habakkuk 1:5**, where judgment was being pronounced upon Jerusalem through the invasion of the Babylonians. While God has sent His Son into the world and accomplished His great and mighty work, He will also judge those who *despise* His work. Judgment was about to fall on Jerusalem in 70AD, *(about 25 years later)* when the Romans would level the Temple to the ground. All of the individuals who rejected Jesus would *perish* as well. Paul was saying *because I am just a man declaring this truth unto you*, I have been called by the God of Israel to bring you this word, and it is God who will judge the world.

The Response to Paul's Message

> **Acts 13:42-43 - *And when the Jews were gone out of the synagogue, the Gentiles besought that these words might be preached to them the next sabbath. Now when the congregation was broken up, many of the Jews and religious proselytes followed Paul and Barnabas: who, speaking to them, persuaded them to continue in the grace of God.***

At this moment the positive response of the Gentiles seems to imply that at least some of them believed Paul's message. They wanted to hear his words again the next Sabbath Day because they were interested in his message. *Paul and Barnabas* encouraged some of the *Jews* and *Gentile proselytes* to *continue in the grace of God*. Just the words *"grace of God"* refers to the New Covenant that was brought in by the blood of Christ in contrast to the Old Dispensation based on the Law. It is God's *grace* that saves us, but we are to grow in His *grace*. The next Sabbath Day *Paul and Barnabas* would encounter opposition.

The Envy of the Unbelieving Jews

> **Acts 13:44-45 - *And the next sabbath day came almost the whole city together to hear the word of God. But when the Jews saw the multitudes, they were filled with envy, and spake against those things which were spoken by Paul, contradicting and blaspheming.***

On *the next Sabbath Day almost the whole city* of Pisidia was gathered together to hear Paul. Without the help of radio, TV, newspapers, or marketing, the power of God had drawn the multitude to hear Paul's message. When his message of grace attracted more people than the teachings of the Law, the unbelieving Jews were filled with *envy*. They spoke against Paul and told the people that he was *blaspheming*. They probably used abusive and degrading language against Jesus and Paul. Also, the unbelieving Jews wanted to keep a separation between themselves and the Gentiles. They could not accept the teachings of Paul that said that *all people* could be forgiven by trusting in the name of Jesus.

Paul and Barnabas Turn to the Gentiles

Acts 13:46-48 - *Then Paul and Barnabas waxed bold, and said, It was necessary that the word of God should first have been spoken to you: but seeing ye put it from you, and judge yourselves unworthy of everlasting life, lo, we turn to the Gentiles. For so hath the Lord commanded us, saying, I have set thee to be a light of the Gentiles, that thou shouldest be for salvation unto the ends of the earth. And when the Gentiles heard this, they were glad, and glorified the word of the Lord: and as many as were ordained to eternal life believed.*

We must not overlook the fact that Paul said that *it was necessary that the word of God should first have been spoken to the Jews*. God laid down that pattern in the Holy Bible, and it will never change. Because this group of Jews rejected the gospel, they were considered *unworthy to receive everlasting life*. Paul and Barnabas obeyed what God had told them to do, and now *they turn to the Gentiles*. Again, the first stage of the presenting the gospel is to the Jews and then to the Gentiles. **(Romans 1:16)** Paul repeated this pattern in every city where he was led to travel.

Paul is quoting from **Isaiah 49:6** about *a light going to the Gentiles*. The Gentiles in Pisidia had been taught that they were not as important as the Jews. When they heard this new message from Paul, *they were glad, and glorified the word of the Lord*. It broke Paul's heart for his fellow Jews to reject the gospel, but it did not keep him from spreading the gospel to the Gentiles.

"as many as were ordained to eternal life believed." - This is one of the phrases that Calvinists use to teach that some have been *ordained* for salvation, and some have not been *ordained* for salvation. The ones who were *ordained* were the ones who received the message of Christ. There are countless verses that uphold that God desired for all to be saved, and that Jesus died for the sins of the whole world. Here are just a few: **John 3:16-17, John 5:40, Mark 16:15, I Timothy 2:4, 2 Peter 3:9, I John 2:2**

PAUL AND BARNABAS EXPELLED FROM THE CITY

Acts 13:49-52 - *And the word of the Lord was published throughout all the region. But the Jews stirred up the devout and honourable women, and the chief men of the city, and raised persecution against*

Paul and Barnabas, and expelled them out of their coasts. But they shook off the dust of their feet against them, and came unto Iconium. And the disciples were filled with joy, and with the Holy Ghost.

The *word of the Lord* spread like wild fire because the city of Pisidia was strategically located on one of the main Roman roads. Whenever God is bringing about a revival, Satan is always stirring up trouble. The unbelieving Jews had strong connections in the city with *the devout and honorable women, and the chief men of the city*. We need to always remember that Satan has control of many of the powerful people in our world. These influential people *expelled Paul and Barnabas out of their coasts*. Paul and Barnabas knew what Jesus had said about *shaking the dust off of their feet*. **(Matthew 10:14, Mark 6:11, Luke 9:5)** This was a symbolic and yet physical measure of completely breaking fellowship. By literally taking their sandals and shaking the dust toward the unbelievers, this showed that they had heard the gospel and had rejected it. It was time to move to the next city of *Iconium*.

"And the disciples were filled with joy, and with the Holy Ghost." - The opposition in Pisidia did not prevent the believers there, nor Paul and Barnabas from being *filled with joy and with the Holy Ghost*. The *joy* of the disciples of Christ cannot be extinguished by the devil's crowd. The gospel going forth sends up a sweet aroma unto God, even if there are those who reject the message.

CHAPTER FOURTEEN

MANY BELIEVE IN JESUS AT ICONIUM

Acts 14:1 - *And it came to pass in Iconium, that they went both together into the synagogue of the Jews, and so spake, that a great multitude both of the Jews and also of the Greeks believed.*

Iconium was about 85 miles east of *Antioch, Pisidia. Iconium, Antioch, Lystra, and Derbe* were all in the southern part of the province of Galatia. After they had been expelled from Antioch, what an encouragement this must have been to see a *multitude of Jews and* ★ *Greeks* believe in Christ. It sounds redundant, but again they started their ministry in *Iconium* by going to the Jews first.

★ *(The Greeks in Iconium were mostly Phrygians, who migrated down from the north. The city was known for its weaving industry. This group were God-fearing Gentiles who believed in the God of Israel. After they heard Paul preach about Jesus being Israel's Messiah and Savior of the Jews <u>and</u> Gentiles, they believed the gospel and became Christians.)*

Opposition from Unbelieving Jews & Gentiles

Acts 14:2-7 - But the unbelieving Jews stirred up the Gentiles, and made their minds evil affected against the brethren. Long time therefore abode they speaking boldly in the Lord, which gave testimony unto the word of his grace, and granted signs and wonders to be done by their hands. But the multitude of the city was divided: and part held with the Jews, and part with the apostles. And when there was an assault made both of the Gentiles, and also of the Jews with their rulers, to use them despitefully, and to stone them, They were ware of it, and fled unto Lystra and Derbe, cities of Lycaonia, and unto the region that lieth round about: And there they preached the gospel.

Not only did some of them reject the gospel message of Paul, they ★ stirred up a group of the Gentiles causing them to reject the message. Unbelief sometimes attracts unbelief. What is so sad is that the Jews were called by God to be a light to the Gentiles, but here this group is taking them away from the light. This opposition, however, did not prevent Paul and Barnabas from preaching *boldly in the Lord* and spending a significant amount of time in Iconium. This period of time allowed Paul to help the believers there and to show them the contrast between the believers and unbelievers. In order to be good soldiers of the cross of Christ, we must realize that we are up against Satan, and he is the ruler of this present evil world and has countless people under his demonic control.

★ *(Paul mentioned these persecutions later in* **2 Timothy 3:11**, *and that God delivered him.)*

God gave Paul and Barnabas the grace to perform ★ *signs and wonders* to authenticate their message. These miracles were not done because of the Law of Moses, but on the basis of God's grace through faith. **(Galatians 3:5)** As a result, the entire city was *divided*; part of the city stood on the side of the unbelieving Jews, and part of them agreed with the believing Jews and *the apostles*.

★ *(The subject of signs and wonders has caused much debate and division in the body of Christ. The apostles could only perform miracles when God ordained it and only at certain times. In* **2 Corinthians 12:7-10**, *Paul could not heal himself. In* **2 Timothy 4:20**, *Paul left Trophimus sick in Miletus. Divine miracles still happen, but only at God's timing.)*

This division led to a conspiracy against the apostles, and they wanted to *stone them*. When they were forced, Paul and Barnabas left Iconium for ★ *Lystra and Derbe*, in the region of *Lycaonia*. The whole purpose of the apostles traveling from town to town was not for a sightseeing tour, they went to *preach the gospel*.

★ *(History records that Lystra and Derbe were indeed cities in the Roman province of Lycaonia, but only between the periods of 32-72AD. This is the time period when the book of Acts was written. This accuracy has persuaded many to believe the Bible is true. Why would anyone ever doubt it?)*

A Lame Man Healed in Lystra

Acts 14:8-10 - *And there sat a certain man at Lystra, impotent in his feet, being a cripple from his mother's womb, who never had walked: The same heard Paul speak: who stedfastly beholding him, and perceiving that he had faith to be healed, Said with a loud voice, Stand upright on thy feet. And he leaped and walked.*

The physician writer, Luke, makes mention that this man was *impotent in his feet, being a cripple from his mother's womb*. This poor man listened so intently, that Paul, with his divine apostolic gift, could tell by the expressions on the man's face that he believed the gospel. His faith resulted in his immediate healing. Paul wanted everyone to hear him, so he *Said with a loud voice, Stand upright on thy feet*. The man *leaped and walked*! The same thing happened when Peter healed the lame man in **Acts 3:8**.

Paul and Barnabas are Declared to be gods

Acts 14:11-13 - *And when the people saw what Paul had done, they lifted up their voices, saying in the speech of Lycaonia, The gods are come down to us in the likeness of men. And they called Barnabas, Jupiter; and Paul, Mercurius, because he was the chief speaker. Then the priest of Jupiter, which was before their city, brought oxen and garlands unto the gates, and would have done sacrifice with the people.*

In the pagan mythological worldview of that region, the people didn't know what to do but declare in their Lycaonian language that Paul and Barnabas were *gods*, who had come down to earth disguised as mortals. Because Paul was the chief speaker, they called him the Latin, *Mercury*, the Greek *Hermes*. Because Barnabas probably had a beard and was taller, they called him *Jupiter*, the Greek *Zeus*. In mythology, *Jupiter/Zeus* was the chief among the gods and the ruler of the world. According to archaeology findings, Zeus and Hermes were the two gods that were jointly worshipped by the people in Lystra.

"Then the priest of Jupiter, which was before their city, brought oxen and garlands unto the gates, and would have done sacrifice with the people." - These were the common sacrifices for the Roman gods, and they were about to * sacrifice them to Paul and Barnabas.

* (There was a strong legend in Lystra recorded by the Roman historian, Ovid. It claimed that Jupiter and Mercury were disguised as men and came down to a hill in that region. No one showed them hospitality but an elderly couple named Baucis and Philemon. The two gods destroyed the population before rewarding Baucis and Philemon by making them a priest and priestess of Jupiter. Because the people at Lystra had seen Paul perform the miracle of raising the lame man, they thought they had better reward them or they might be destroyed.)

PAUL APPEALS TO THE CROWD

Acts 14:14-18 - *Which when the apostles, Barnabas and Paul, heard of, they rent their clothes, and ran in among the people, crying out, And saying, Sirs, why* *do ye these things? We also are men of like passions with you, and preach unto you that ye should turn from these vanities unto the living God, which made heaven, and earth, and the sea, and all things that are therein: Who in times past suffered all nations to walk in their own ways. Nevertheless he left not himself without witness, in that he did good, and gave us rain from heaven, and fruitful seasons, filling our hearts with food and gladness. And with these sayings scarce restrained they the people, that they had not done sacrifice unto them.*

When the apostles *rent their clothes*, they were showing the people that they were human. It was also a Jewish symbol of blasphemy. Barnabas and Paul told the crowd to turn from their idolatry and believe in the *living God*! They had been worshipping the dead gods of paganism who were only man-made stone statues. They couldn't just add Jesus to their list of gods; He was the only true God! Praise God! Jupiter didn't create the world, Jesus did! Mercury did not provide them crops to eat, Jesus did! Poseidon didn't rule the sea, Jesus ruled the sea! Paul was telling them that the One I have been preaching to you about is the One who gives you rain from heaven, fruitful seasons, and fills your physical lives with food. He is the One who will fill your spiritual lives with salvation, joy, and peace by coming to die on the cross for your sins. Notice that Paul was not quoting from the Jewish Old Testament because he was speaking to pagan Gentiles who needed to hear in a language about ★ creation they could understand.

(It's very important to our faith to always connect Jesus with creation. **John 1:1-5, 10, 14, Colossians 1:15-19, I Timothy 3:16, Revelation 1:8***)*

"And with these sayings scarce restrained they the people, that they had not done sacrifice unto them." - Paul and Barnabas were not like the Roman leaders, such as Augustus, Tiberius, Agrippa, Antiochus, or Caligula; they would not receive worship of themselves.

THE STONING OF PAUL

Acts 14:19-20a - *And there came thither certain Jews from Antioch and Iconium, who persuaded the people, and having stoned Paul, drew him out of the city, supposing he had been dead. Howbeit, as the disciples stood round about him, he rose up, and came into the city:*

The Jewish adversaries of Paul were so filled with anger that they traveled about 100 miles to persecute him. This was an attempt to execute Paul and Barnabas. The stoning of Paul here is mentioned later in **2 Corinthians 11:25**, and may be one of the sources of the marks in his body that Paul referred to in **Galatians 6:17**. Even though Luke does not actually say, many scholars believe that Paul was actually killed here, or at least beaten unconscious, and this is where he saw the vision that he mentioned in **2 Corinthians 12:1-4**, where he was caught up into the * third heaven. The restoration of Paul's health here is a miracle indeed as he gained his strength to go back into the city.

* *(The first heaven is where the clouds are; the second heaven is where the stars are; and the third heaven is the abode of God.)*

PAUL AND BARNABAS WITNESS IN DERBE

Acts 14:20b-22 - …..and the next day he departed with Barnabas to Derbe. And when they had preached the gospel to that city, and had taught many, they returned again to Lystra, and to Iconium, and Antioch, Confirming the souls of the disciples, and exhorting them to continue in the faith, and that we must through much tribulation enter into the kingdom of God.

After Paul had been stoned, the next day he and Barnabas walked some 40 miles to *Derbe*. They preached the gospel freely in *Derbe* and then returned to the cities of *Lystra, Iconium,* and *Antioch of Pisidia*. There they made many *disciples* for Christ. Paul didn't preach an easy-believism gospel. He told the disciples on his journeys that they would go *through much tribulation* before they would physically *enter into God's kingdom*. The Christian faith is not for the faint hearted. It takes a strong faith to walk with the Lord year after year, trial after trial. The trials that we face today are nothing compared to what the early believers in Jesus endured.

PAUL AND BARNABAS RETURN TO ANTIOCH IN SYRIA

Acts 14:23-28 - And when they had ordained them elders in every church, and had prayed with fasting,

they commended them to the Lord, on whom they believed. And after they had passed throughout Pisidia, they came to Pamphylia. And when they had preached the word in Perga, they went down into Attalia: And thence sailed to Antioch, from whence they had been recommended to the grace of God for the work which they fulfilled. And when they were come, and had gathered the church together, they rehearsed all that God had done with them, and how he had opened the door of faith unto the Gentiles. And there they abode long time with the disciples.

Paul and Barnabas were committed to make new believers in Christ and also to establish churches where the Christians could grow and be established in the Lord. There were no church buildings; the small groups of believers met in homes. Most of the time they had to worship in private while being surrounded by the paganism of the Roman world. There were no paid salaries. They considered God's kingdom work much too sacred to turn it into a business. The church in our modern-day world has drifted far from what God started in the first century. The apostles knew that the churches needed leaders, so they *ordained elders in every church and after fasting they commended them to the Lord*. The original wording here means that Paul *deposited* them into the hands of the Lord. These churches did not belong to Paul or Barnabas, but to Jesus! The churches were not governed by a democracy, but by a theocracy where Christ ruled the churches. The *elders* were such devout men that God revealed to them about what decisions needed to be made concerning the churches. One of the weakest links in the churches today is the lack of godly, Holy Spirit-filled leadership.

On their way back to Antioch in Syria, they did not go back through the island of Cyprus, but traveled through the southwestern part of Asia Minor through the towns of *Pamphylia, Perga, and Attalia,* and then sailed back to *Antioch.* This concluded their first missionary journey, and Paul and Barnabas shared with their home congregation all *the mighty works that God had done and how the gospel had been opened to the Gentiles.* What a glorious reunion this must have been, and that is why the Bible says they stayed a *long time with the disciples in Antioch.* Though they had experienced great opposition, their first journey was a tremendous success. We can summarize this first missionary journey with these points:

- **God had opened the door for Paul and Barnabas**
- **The gospel had officially gone out to the Gentiles**
- **It was clear that salvation was by grace through faith**
- **The Gentiles did not enter the church by circumcision**
- **The pattern was clear that the gospel went to the Jew first**
- **The results would lead to the first Jerusalem council**

CHAPTER FIFTEEN

CERTAIN MEN FROM JUDEA

Acts 15:1 – *And certain men which came down from Judaea taught the brethren, and said, Except ye be circumcised after the manner of Moses, ye cannot be saved.*

The issue that led to the debate was *Gentile circumcision* and would be brought before the Jerusalem Council. This was a group of Jews who were *believers*, according to **verse 5**, and they were not sent by the church in Jerusalem, but came of their own accord. You could call them the *"circumcision denomination."* They were teaching that Gentiles in Antioch *could not be saved* by faith in Christ alone without submitting to the Jewish ritual of *circumcision after the manner of Moses*. Much like those today that believe in Jesus as the Son of God, they also believed no one could be saved without being water baptized. There have always been religious groups who teach that faith in the Christ and His finished work on the cross is not enough, and they lead people astray by teaching a salvation by works. However, Paul made mention of another group of Judaizers in **Galatians 2:4,** and called them *"false brethren:"*

And that because of false brethren unawares brought in, who came in privily to spy out our liberty which we have in Christ Jesus, that they might bring us into bondage.

PAUL AND BARNABAS GO TO JERUSALEM

Acts 15:2-4 - *When therefore Paul and Barnabas had no small dissension and disputation with them, they determined that Paul and Barnabas, and certain other of them, should go up to Jerusalem unto the apostles and elders about this question. And being brought on their way by the church, they passed through Phenice and Samaria, declaring the conversion of the Gentiles: and they caused great joy unto all the brethren. And when they were come to Jerusalem, they were received of the church, and of the apostles and elders, and they declared all things that God had done with them.*

Paul and Barnabas showed the heart of being *true* shepherds. They would not stand for this group of radical Pharisees *(even though they were believers in Christ)* trying to undermine the work that God had already started doing in the hearts of the Gentile believers. Satan is always using his children to break up unity in the church. The church at Antioch made the wise decision to send *Paul and Barnabas, and certain other of them,* (**Galatians**

2:1-5, & *Titus*) to Jerusalem and present this question to *the apostles and elders.*

"And being brought on their way by the church, they passed through Phenice and Samaria, declaring the conversion of the Gentiles: and they caused great joy unto all the brethren." - Paul and Barnabas accumulated support from the Gentile churches in *Phenice (Phoenicia) and Samaria*. While the Judaizers had caused disunity among the Gentile believers in Antioch, there was continual joy when Paul and Barnabas shared what God was doing on their journey up to Jerusalem. Notice that when they arrived in Jerusalem, they did not boast about what they were doing, but *they declared all things that God had done with them.*

The Issue is Re-Stated

Acts 15:5-6 - But there rose up certain of the sect of the Pharisees which believed, saying, That it was needful to circumcise them, and to command them to keep the law of Moses. And the apostles and elders came together for to consider of this matter.

This group of Pharisees did believe in Jesus as their Messiah, but were holding on to the Law of Moses. While it may sound foreign to us Gentiles today, one can understand how they were still confused and not yet grown to maturity in Christ. Again, this sub-group of Jews believed that Gentiles could be saved, but they could not be part of the congregation of Israel without the law of circumcision.

The Jerusalem Council Declaration by Peter

Acts 15:7-11 - *And when there had been much disputing, Peter rose up, and said unto them, Men and brethren, ye know how that a good while ago God made choice among us, that the Gentiles by my mouth should hear the word of the gospel, and believe. And God, which knoweth the hearts, bare them witness, giving them the Holy Ghost, even as he did unto us; And put no difference between us and them, purifying their hearts by faith. Now therefore why tempt ye God, to put a yoke upon the neck of the disciples, which neither our fathers nor we were able to bear? But we believe that through the grace of the LORD Jesus Christ we shall be saved, even as they.*

This was such a serious matter, that it required debate and questioning. The church today should have a time when people can ask questions about salvation. Is salvation by works? Is it by faith in Christ? Is it by a combination of both? After there had been much *disputing, the apostle Peter rose up,* and this would be his last address in the book of Acts.

"Men and brethren, ye know how that a good while ago God made choice among us, that the Gentiles by my mouth should hear the word of the gospel, and believe." – Peter is referring to **Acts 10** that occurred some eight to ten years before, when God sent him to preach to Cornelius in Caesarea. Peter was the one who had the keys of the kingdom and opened the door for the Gentiles to come in by faith.

"And God, which knoweth the hearts, bare them witness, giving them the Holy Ghost, even as he did unto us; And put no difference between us and them, purifying their hearts by faith." - Peter is recalling vocally what happened eight or ten years before when Cornelius and his family received the Holy Spirit in Caesarea without having to keep the Law of Moses. He was an eyewitness that there was *no difference* between the Jews and Gentiles when it came to salvation.

"Now therefore why tempt ye God, to put a yoke upon the neck of the disciples, which neither our fathers nor we were able to bear? But we believe that through the grace of the LORD Jesus Christ we shall be saved, even as they." - Peter is saying that for the Jews to challenge Gentile salvation by faith in Christ alone was to *tempt God*. God's eternal plan of salvation was not for the Jews only, and Jesus not only died for the sins of the lost sheep of the house of Israel, but for the whole world. (**I John 2:2**) Peter was saying, *"why force the Gentiles to do something that we or our forefathers were not even able to do?"* They were putting a *yoke (hardship)* upon the *necks of the Gentile disciples*. Notice that Peter here calls *Jesus* the *"Christ"* and the *"Lord,"* and that salvation is by grace through faith. Three points can summarize Peter's argument:

* *It was God's choice that the Gentiles hear the gospel*
* *The Holy Spirit gave witness that there was no distinction*
* *The Law was unbearable to the Jews, why inflict it on the Gentiles*
* *Jesus is not only the Christ, but He is the Lord of all*

Paul would later write about what really happened when Jesus died on the cross concerning the Law of Moses:

Blotting out the handwriting of ordinances that was against us, which was contrary to us, and took it out of the way, nailing it to his cross. **(Colossians 2:14)**

THE TESTIMONY OF PAUL AND BARNABAS

Acts 15:12 - *Then all the multitude kept silence, and gave audience to Barnabas and Paul, declaring what miracles and wonders God had wrought among the Gentiles by them.*

The fact that there was a moment of *silence* shows how effective Peter's speech was, and the Jews were willing to listen to the testimonies. *Paul and Barnabas* not only reiterated what Peter had said, but were also stating that God was using them to perform *miracles and wonders among the Gentiles* on their first missionary journey.

THE TESTIMONY OF JAMES

Acts 15:13-21 - *And after they had held their peace, James answered, saying, Men and brethren, hearken unto me: Simeon hath declared how God at the first did visit the Gentiles, to take out of them a people for his name. And to this agree the words of the prophets; as it is written, After this I will return, and will build again the tabernacle of David, which is fallen down; and I will build again the ruins thereof, and I will set it up: That the residue of men might seek after the Lord, and all the Gentiles, upon whom my* *name is called, saith the Lord, who doeth all these things. Known unto God are all his works from the beginning of the world. Wherefore my sentence is, that we trouble not them, which from among the Gentiles are turned to God: But that we write unto them, that they abstain from pollutions of idols, and from fornication, and from things strangled, and from blood. For Moses of old time hath in every city them that preach him, being read in the synagogues every sabbath day.*

"James answered, saying, Men and brethren, hearken unto me:" – This was the half-brother of Jesus and an apostle of the second category. He was the head of the church in Jerusalem and was responsible for giving a solution to the question of should the Gentiles be circumcised. When James uses the word *brethren*, he is referring to his fellow Jewish Christians.

"Simeon hath declared how God at the first did visit the Gentiles, to take out of them a people for his name." – James uses the Aramaic form of the name *Shimon*, which is *Symeon*. Peter would use this Aramaic name of himself in **2 Peter 1:1**. James was simply saying that God officially first used Simon Peter to evangelize the Gentiles. There was a remnant of the Jews who would embrace Jesus as their Messiah, and there would be a larger remnant of the Gentiles who would come to know Christ. Three important reasons why God is saving Gentiles today:

* *To bring glory to His name*
* *To provoke the Jews to jealousy* (**Romans 11:11-14**)

* *To support the Jewish Christians financially* (**Romans 15:25-27**)

"And to this agree the words of the prophets; as it is written, After this I will return, and will build again the tabernacle of David, which is fallen down; and I will build again the ruins thereof, and I will set it up:" - The situation in Jerusalem inspired James to quote from this passage:

In that day will I raise up the tabernacle of David that is fallen, and close up the breaches thereof; and I will raise up his ruins, and I will build it as in the days of old: That they may possess the remnant of Edom, (original Hebrew may be translated as seek the remnant of Adam) *and of all the heathen, which are called by my name, saith the* LORD *that doeth this.* (**Amos 9:11-12**)

James reminded his fellow Jewish brothers that the *prophets* predicted the salvation of the Gentiles. He could have used other prophetic writings, but he used the book of Amos as a point of similarity and prophecy. The tent of David had fallen, having no power, but Gentile salvation would be part of God's plan in restoring *the tabernacle of David*. God was using the partial blindness of Israel to give the Gentiles an opportunity to be saved, and then He will return and rebuild the house of David. (**Romans 11:25-26**)

It is also interesting that the passage from **Amos 9:11-12** is a Messianic passage, and one of the rabbinic titles of the Messiah is *Bar Naphli*, which means, *"son of the fallen one,"* because Jesus the Messiah will rebuild the house of David that had fallen.

"That the residue of men might seek after the Lord, and all the Gentiles, upon whom my name is called, saith the Lord, who doeth all these things. Known unto God are all his works from the beginning of the world." - The majority of the world is filled with Gentiles, and many will *seek after the Lord*. They will remain Gentile believers in Christ and will not have to be converted to Judaism in order to be saved. God had designed His plan of salvation for both Jews and Gentiles before the world was ever created.

"Wherefore my sentence is, that we trouble not them, which from among the Gentiles are turned to God: But that we write unto them, that they abstain from pollutions of idols, and from fornication, and from things strangled, and from blood. For Moses of old time hath in every city them that preach him, being read in the synagogues every sabbath day." - James made a decision that was so powerful that it represented the mutual decision of everyone present. James would pronounce the definitive *sentence* on the matter. James was telling the council *not to trouble the Gentiles* with the burden of circumcision. They should not make it difficult for the Gentiles to be saved. Peter, Paul, and Barnabas were correct, and the sect of the Pharisees was wrong. If the Gentiles turned to Jesus as the Son of God, they would be saved, period!

But James told the council to write that the Gentiles needed to obey the *Law of Love* and consider their Jewish brethren when it came to social interactions. While they were Gentile believers, they were not to deliberately go against the Law of Moses to antagonize or offend the Jews:

* ***Pollution from idols*** - (**Exodus 34:15**) Foods that had been sacrificed to idols, or even using the utensils that had been used.
* ***Fornication*** - Or unlawful close family marriages (**Lev.18:6-18**)
* ***Eating what meats had been strangled*** - Meat from which the blood had not been drained. (**Lev.17:13**)
* ***Drinking blood*** - This was a pagan practice that was forbidden by the Law (**Lev.17:10-14**)

"For Moses of old time hath in every city them that preach him, being read in the synagogues every sabbath day." - There were Jewish synagogues in almost every city throughout the Roman world that preached these prohibitions. Gentile Christians were saved without keeping the Law of Moses, but they were not to *offend* the Jewish Christians or the unbelieving Jews. Paul would later write to the church in Rome that Christians should not be a stumbling block to others. (**Romans 14:13**) This should be a biblical rule for all of us who profess the name of Jesus Christ, to live our lives each day that even the lost people around us would have nothing to say against us.

Sending Paul, Barnabas, Judas, and Silas

Acts 15:22 - *Then pleased it the apostles and elders with the whole church, to send chosen men of their own company to Antioch with Paul and Barnabas; namely, Judas surnamed Barsabas and Silas, chief men among the brethren:*

The certain men of **Acts 15:1** were shown they were wrong, and the Jerusalem council decided to send *Judas and Silas* back to Antioch with *Paul and Barnabas* to give witness of the report. Not much is known about *Judas or Barsabas*, but we know that *Silas*, also mentioned as *Silvanus*, became Paul's companion on his second missionary journey. **(Acts 15:40, 16:19, 25, 29, 17:4, 10, 14-15, 18:5)** *Silvanus* in mentioned in several of the Epistles; **2 Cor.1:19, I Thess.1:1, 2 Thess.1:1, and I Peter 5:12.**

A Letter is Written and Sent

Acts 15:23-27 - *And they wrote letters by them after this manner; The apostles and elders and brethren send greeting unto the brethren which are of the Gentiles in Antioch and Syria and Cilicia. Forasmuch as we have heard, that certain which went out from us have troubled you with words, subverting your souls, saying, Ye must be circumcised, and keep the law: to whom we gave no such commandment: It seemed good unto us, being assembled with one accord, to send chosen men unto you with our beloved Barnabas and Paul, Men that have hazarded their lives for the name of our Lord Jesus Christ. We have sent therefore Judas and Silas, who shall also tell you the same things by mouth.*

The authors were *the apostles and the elders and brethren* of the Jerusalem church. The recipients were the brethren of the *Gentile churches in Antioch, Syria, and Cilicia.* Coming from the

Jewish believers in Christ in Jerusalem, they are calling the Gentile believers in Christ *"brethren."* The Jewish Christian church in Jerusalem wanted the Gentile churches to know that the Gentile believers did not have to be circumcised in order to be saved, and they wanted them to hear it from the *mouths* of their *beloved Paul and Barnabas*, who had already suffered for the cause of the *Lord Jesus Christ*. Try to imagine the unrest and emotional feelings the Gentile believers must have had when the Judaizers came to them, *subverting* them with their words. Then how they would be relieved when they got direct words from Jerusalem that the apostles, the elders, and the church as a whole did not authorize or give commandment to the sect of Pharisees to trouble them. The Jewish believers in Jerusalem sending *Judas and Silas* along with *Paul and Barnabas* was in keeping with the Jewish Law of more than one witness:

> **One witness shall not rise up against a man for any iniquity, or for any sin, in any sin that he sinneth: at the mouth of two witnesses, or at the mouth of three witnesses, shall the matter be established. (Deut.19:15)**

THE HOLY SPIRIT WAS PLEASED

> **Acts 15:28-29 -** *For it seemed good to the Holy Ghost, and to us, to lay upon you no greater burden than these necessary things; That ye abstain from meats offered to idols, and from blood, and from things strangled, and from fornication: from which if ye keep yourselves, ye shall do well. Fare ye well.*

The decision of the Jerusalem church was not just a work of men, it was a work of the ⋆ *Holy Ghost, or Holy Spirit.* They were all in one accord and unity concerning the Gentiles. The emissaries read the letter, and it stated the four things the Gentiles were to refrain from that had been stated by James in **verse 20** as a basis for fellowship. These restrictions were not sent out to every Gentile church, but to those who were mixed congregations of both Jews and Gentiles. Two other important Epistles that parallel the Jerusalem Council are the books of **James,** written by James the leader of the Jerusalem church, and **Galatians**, written by Paul.

⋆*(Jesus promised to send the Holy Spirit to guide them into all truth in* **John 16:13.***)*

"Fare ye well" – This simple ending, *"errosthe"* to the letter shows that the Hebrew/Aramaic speaking Jews in Jerusalem sent the letter back to the Gentile church in Antioch in the Greek language.

The Joyful Reception in Antioch

> **Acts 15:30-35 -** *So when they were dismissed, they came to Antioch: and when they had gathered the multitude together, they delivered the epistle: Which when they had read, they rejoiced for the consolation. And Judas and Silas, being prophets also themselves, exhorted the brethren with many words, and confirmed them. And after they had tarried there a space, they were let go in peace from the brethren unto the apostles. Notwithstanding it pleased Silas to abide there still. Paul also and Barnabas continued*

in Antioch, teaching and preaching the word of the Lord, with many others also.

What rejoicing to know that you are truly saved by grace through faith apart from the Law of Moses! The center of Jewish evangelism in Jerusalem was at peace with the center of Gentile evangelism in Antioch. This was a major turning point in the growth of Christianity in the first century.

"And Judas and Silas, being prophets also themselves, exhorted the brethren with many words, and confirmed them." – One of the reasons why the Jerusalem church sent *Judas and Silas* along was because they were *prophets* themselves, and to *exhort and to confirm* the Gentile believers. They helped to settle the hearts of the Gentiles and let them know that they were complete in Christ alone. What a blessing they must have been to the Antioch church!

"And after they had tarried there a space, they were let go in peace from the brethren unto the apostles. Notwithstanding it pleased Silas to abide there still." – We do not know exactly how long they stayed in Antioch, but according to the original language, it was for a lengthy period. There seems to be a variation in the last part where *they* were let go in peace, and then *it pleased Silas to abide there still*. Some translations have the last part in the margin, while some have it in the primary text. Either way, apparently Silas went back to Antioch later to accompany Paul on his next missionary journey.

"Paul also and Barnabas continued in Antioch, teaching and preaching the word of the Lord, with many others also." – The ministry in Antioch had been interrupted by the Judaizers; but *Paul and Barnabas* were now able to ★ *continue teaching and* *preaching the Word of the Lord.* The Bible does not say who *the many others were*, but it was also during this time when the apostle Peter came to Antioch. **(Galatians 2:11)**

★ *(It needs to be mentioned that while the Gentile believers were free from the Law of Moses, the Jewish believers still had their liberty in Christ to keep certain facets of the Torah as long as it didn't contradict New Testament revelation. Those Jews who were residents of Israel still observed certain customs and servant, Jewish lifestyles.* **(Acts 21:20)** *Circumcision is still practiced by Jewish Christians today because of the Abrahamic Covenant,* **(Gen.12:1-3, 7, 13:14-17, 15:1-21, 17:1-2, 22:15-18)** *not only because of the Law of Moses. Gentile Christians are also free to observe certain laws in the Torah based upon their liberty and conscience. The matter of salvation must always be taught that the Lord Jesus Christ fulfilled the sacrificial law, and believers are complete in Him. Jewish customs and traditions brought into the Gentile church have caused much confusion today.)*

DIVISION BETWEEN PAUL AND BARNABAS

Acts 15:36-41 - *And some days after Paul said unto Barnabas, Let us go again and visit our brethren in every city where we have preached the word of the Lord, and see how they do. And Barnabas determined to take with them John, whose surname was Mark. But Paul thought not good to take him with them, who departed from them from Pamphylia, and went not with them to the work. And the contention was so sharp between them, that they departed asunder one from the other: and so Barnabas took Mark, and sailed unto Cyprus; And Paul chose Silas, and* *departed, being recommended by the brethren unto the grace of God. And he went through Syria and Cilicia, confirming the churches.*

After some time of ministering in Antioch, Paul wanted to go and visit the brethren in the cities where they preached on their first missionary journey. It was Paul's love and devotion to those churches that motivated him to go back and to see how they were doing spiritually.

"And Barnabas determined to take with them John, whose surname was Mark. But Paul thought not good to take him with them, who departed from them from Pamphylia, and went not with them to the work." - Because John Mark was Barnabas's cousin, (**Colossians 4:10**) he was determined to take John on their second missionary journey. Because of John Mark's abrupt departure on their first journey, (**Acts 13:13**) Paul thought it was unwise to take him along. We need to understand that while Paul and Barnabas were godly men and chosen by God, they were still human, and one of them here was not acting according to the Holy Spirit. No one is so super godly that they do not make the wrong decisions from time to time.

"And the contention was so sharp between them, that they departed asunder one from the other: and so Barnabas took Mark, and sailed unto Cyprus;" - In spite of the sharp disagreement between Paul and Barnabas, God still worked His divine plan by sending out *two* missionary teams. We do know that the schism was later healed because Barnabas is mentioned a few years later in **I Corinthians 9:6,** and fellowship was restored. (**Colossians 4:10**) Later on Paul valued the contributions

of John Mark (*Marcus*). (**Philemon 24, 2 Timothy 4:11**) Servants of Christ may disagree at times about many things, but at the end of the day we need to reconcile, forgive, and keep fellowship with each other. Barnabas went first back to his home country of *Cyprus* to disciple the brethren there.

"And Paul chose Silas, and departed, being recommended by the brethren unto the grace of God. And he went through Syria and Cilicia, confirming the churches." - Paul may have chosen Silas because he was a leading believer from Jerusalem (**Acts 15:22, 27**) and a Roman citizen (**Acts 16:37**) who would be a tremendous help to Paul. It is noteworthy here that the church at Antioch sent out *Paul and Silas*. This may imply that the church at Antioch sided with Paul in his disagreement with Barnabas, but we cannot be sure. Luke may have mentioned this because it was Silas (*Silvanus*) who wrote one of Simon Peter's letters (**I Peter 5:12**) and possibly Paul's letters to the Thessalonians. (**I Thess.1:1, 2 Thess.2:1**) Paul would go back to his hometown of Tarsus, which was in *Cilicia*, and disciple the brethren there first.

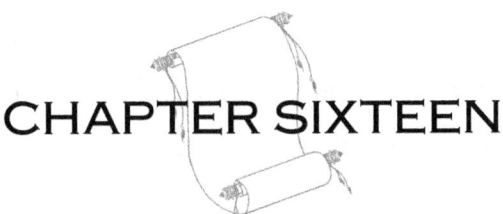

CHAPTER SIXTEEN

PAUL MEETS TIMOTHY IN LYSTRA

Acts 16:1-2 - *Then came he to Derbe and Lystra: and, behold, a certain disciple was there, named Timotheus, the son of a certain woman, which was a Jewess, and believed; but his father was a Greek: Which was well reported of by the brethren that were at Lystra and Iconium.*

About five years had passed since the time Paul had preached at Lystra. (**Acts 14:6**) According to I **Timothy 1:2**, ★ Timothy was converted to Jesus Christ under the ministry of Paul in Lystra. His name, *Timotheus,* means *"God honored,"* and is called a *certain disciple.* His name appears some 17 times in Paul's writings. We know that his mother was Jewish, (*Eunice*) and his grandmother was named *Lois*; both were women of faith. They trained *Timothy* in the Holy Scriptures from an early age. (**2 Timothy 1:5, 3:15**) They had a *good report among the brethren that were in Lystra and Iconium.* Normally a person's Jewishness is traced through his father, but Timothy's father was a Gentile, and Luke doesn't say if he was a believer.

* *(In Jewish writings in 97AD, Timothy was 80 years of age when he was dragged and stoned to death in Ephesus for trying to stop a procession honoring the pagan god, Diana. His remains were taken to Constantinople in the 4th century, transferred to the Termoli Cathedral in Italy in the 13th century, and later rediscovered in 1945.)*

PAUL CIRCUMCISES TIMOTHY

Acts 16:3 - Him would Paul have to go forth with him; and took and circumcised him because of the Jews which were in those quarters: for they knew all that his father was a Greek.

Paul was impressed enough with Timothy's faith and reputation that he wanted him to go with them. It's as if Timothy took the place of John Mark just as Silas took the place of Barnabas. It was well known that Timothy's father was Greek, and he had not been * *circumcised*. Paul knew this would be a hindrance going into the Jewish synagogues, so he *circumcised* Timothy.

* *(The circumcision of Timothy seems contrary to the Jerusalem council in* **Acts 15** *and contrary to Paul's teaching (***Gal.2:3-4, 5:2-11***), but this is Luke's larger portrayal of Paul as being someone the unbelieving, religious Jews would not have any legitimate reason to object. The circumcision of Timothy was also based on the Abrahamic Covenant for the Jewish people. Paul did not circumcise Titus because he was a Gentile.)*

Decrees of the Jerusalem Council Delivered

Acts 16:4-5 - *And as they went through the cities, they delivered them the decrees for to keep, that were ordained of the apostles and elders which were at Jerusalem. And so were the churches established in the faith, and increased in number daily.*

Paul, showing that he was loyal to the leadership of the *apostles and elders that were in Jerusalem, delivered the decrees* to the churches that he had started on his first missionary journey. Those decrees were again threefold:

* *Salvation was by faith, not by the law of circumcision*
* *Fornication was forbidden*
* *Blood and meats offered to idols were forbidden*

When the truth was preached about biblical salvation and how that fellowship with the Jews was not to be broken, then the churches were *established in the faith, and increased in number daily*. Biblical truth solidifies our faith and causes the Holy Spirit to move freely in our churches.

The Macedonian Call

Acts 16:6-10 - *Now when they had gone throughout Phrygia and the region of Galatia, and were forbidden of the Holy Ghost to preach the word in Asia, After they were come to Mysia, they assayed to go into Bithynia: but the Spirit suffered them not. And they passing by Mysia came down to Troas. And a vision appeared to Paul in the night; There stood a man* *of Macedonia, and prayed him, saying, Come over into Macedonia, and help us. And after he had seen the vision, immediately we endeavoured to go into Macedonia, assuredly gathering that the Lord had called us for to preach the gospel unto them.*

Here we can learn a tremendous lesson in preaching the gospel. The Holy Spirit *closes* doors as He *opens* doors. It was not time for Paul, Silas, and Timothy to minister in Asia Minor, present-day Turkey. The text does not tell us just how the Holy Spirit made it clear to them, but God's timing would bring Paul back into the region of Asia Minor in **Acts 19**.

"the Spirit suffered them not." - The original language of Acts is the *Spirit of Jesus*, and this is the only time the Holy Spirit is referred to in this way. In **Romans 8:9**, He is called the *Spirit of Christ*, and in **Philippians 1:19**, He is called the *Spirit of Jesus Christ*.

"And they passing by Mysia came down to Troas." - *Troas* was the primary seaport city on the Aegean Sea from Asia Minor to Macedonia. One could ٭ see Greece across the Aegean Sea from this city. Paul would return later to *Troas* in **Acts 20:6** and **2 Corinthians 2:12.**

٭ *(This author toured the journeys of Paul in 2010. While riding on a ship across the Aegean Sea one night as the moon glistened across the waves, the seriousness of the divine call on Paul's life was so real.)*

'**And a vision appeared to Paul in the night; There stood a man of Macedonia, and prayed him, saying, Come over into Macedonia, and help us."** - The vision that Paul had was from *a man of Macedonia*. This man was probably wearing the distinctive Macedonian attire. The call for Paul to *come over into Macedonia* is so important because this would be the launching of the gospel of the Lord Jesus Christ into Europe for the very first time.

"And after he had seen the vision, immediately we endeavoured to go into Macedonia, assuredly gathering that the Lord had called us for to preach the gospel unto them." - The pronouns *we* and *us* show that it was in Troas that *Luke*, the author of the book of Acts, joined Paul, Silas, and Timothy. It's a good thing to preach the gospel, it is a powerful thing when the Lord leads and calls someone to an exact place to preach the gospel. Paul had been called to go and preach the gospel into Macedonia. The world would never be the same!

THE STORY OF LYDIA IN PHILIPPI

Acts 16:11-14 - *Therefore loosing from Troas, we came with a straight course to Samothracia, and the next day to Neapolis; And from thence to Philippi, which is the chief city of that part of Macedonia, and a colony: and we were in that city abiding certain days. And on the sabbath we went out of the city by a river side, where prayer was wont to be made; and we sat down, and spake unto the women which resorted thither. And a certain woman named Lydia, a seller of purple, of the city of Thyatira, which worshipped God, heard us: whose heart the Lord opened, that she attended unto the things which were spoken of Paul.*

With the wind at their backs, the missionary team including Luke, sailed over 150 miles across the Aegean Sea from the continent of Asia to Europe. They first came to the island of *Samothracia*, midway between *Troas* and *Neapolis*. *Neapolis* was only about ten miles from the important European city of * *Philippi*. The capital city of that region was *Amphipolis*.

* *(Philippi was named after Philip II of Macedon in 356BC. The major Roman road called the Via Egnatia ran through the city. This famous road connected the east to the west Appian Way in Italy, all the way to Rome. Today one can see the ruins of a theatre, a Roman forum, a 5th century Byazantine Basilica, and chariot markings in the Roman road from Paul's time. This author had the wonderful experience of walking in Philippi and teaching the Bible in 2010.)*

"And on the sabbath we went out of the city by a river side, where prayer was wont to be made; and we sat down, and spake unto the women which resorted thither." - There was a small Jewish community in Philippi not large enough to have a * Jewish synagogue, so Paul went outside the gate to the *river* known as *Gangites*. Oftentimes Jewish prayer services were held near flowing water, and this time there were only *women* meeting for prayer.

* *(It took a "minyan" of at least ten Jewish men to start a Jewish synagogue. The reason this custom originated was because of Abraham asking God not to destroy Sodom if there were only ten righteous men.* **Genesis 18:32***)*

"And a certain woman named Lydia, a seller of purple, of the city of Thyatira, which worshipped God, heard us: whose heart the Lord opened, that she attended unto the things which were spoken of Paul." - A prominent woman named

Lydia became the first European convert to the Lord Jesus Christ. She sold expensive purple fabric that was used to make Roman togas. She was originally from *Thyatira*, but migrated to Philippi for business reasons. It's interesting that later a church would be formed in *Thyatira*. (**Revelation 2:18-29**) Five things about *Lydia* are worthy to mention:

* *Lydia was a woman of wealth*
* *Lydia worshipped God*
* *Lydia heard the new, strange preachers*
* *Lydia's heart was opened*
* *Lydia listened carefully to the apostle Paul*

THE BAPTISM OF LYDIA

Acts 16:15 - *And when she was baptized, and her household, she besought us, saying, If ye have judged me to be faithful to the Lord, come into my house, and abide there. And she constrained us.*

Not only was *Lydia* identified with Christ by immersion in water in the *Gangites River*, but also her household. She was so changed by the preaching of Paul and his missionary team that she persuaded them to start a church in her home. (**Acts 16:40**) Lydia was faithful to the Lord, and this was one of the primary reasons why Paul received the Macedonia call in **verse 9**. This church would start small but would reach out and convert countless souls to our precious Lord.

A Demon-Possessed Girl Follows Paul

Acts 16:16-17 - *And it came to pass, as we went to prayer, a certain damsel possessed with a spirit of divination met us, which brought her masters much gain by soothsaying: The same followed Paul and us, and cried, saying, These men are the servants of the most high God, which shew unto us the way of salvation.*

The prayer meeting at *Philippi* started to grow, and *a certain damsel possessed with a spirit of divination,* (*pneuma Pythona,* or a *"spirit of Python,"*) was there who was a source of money as a wizard, fortune-teller, *for her masters.* **(Lev.19:31, 20:6, 27)** The * *python snake* was associated with the pagan god, *Apollo,* who had a shrine not far from Philippi. The spirit of Satan was living in this girl, and Satan wanted to be at this prayer meeting. We shouldn't be surprised!

* *(It's important to realize the existence of the pagan, demonic world in which the apostles carried the gospel. This girl had been a victim of the evil influence of the Greco-Roman world. Most of the supposed powers of these mythological gods were borrowed and twisted from the Holy Bible and still influence the modern world today. For example, Apollo was said to have defeated the giant serpent, "Python," in the 6th century BC in Delphi, Greece. This serpent was believed to have been guarding the center of the earth. It was believed that this giant serpent was created from the rot and slime of the flood in Noah's time. Apollo's son in mythology was Asclepius, who was the healing god of the Roman world. One of the cultic practices was to have snakes crawling all over the floor in the Asclepeion Temples. There were over*

300 such temples in Greece alone. The rod of Ascelpius was a snake-entwined staff that is still the symbol of modern medicine today. The idea of snakes being involved with healing is borrowed from the brazen serpent during the time of Moses in **Numbers 21:5-9.** This author visited the well-preserved ruins of one of the Asclepeion Temples in Pergamum, Turkey, in 2010.)

"The same followed Paul and us, and cried, saying, These men are the servants of the most high God, which shew unto us the way of salvation." - Not only did the demon-possessed girl know who Jesus was, she knew who His servants were. This should be a troubling reminder to all followers of Christ; even the devil believes, and he also knows *the way of salvation.* Satan is a religious being and has been damning the souls of men for centuries with his evil devices. (**James 2:19, Matthew 7:21-23, 2 Cor.11:14-15**)

Paul Casts the Demon Out

Acts 16:18 - *And this did she many days. But Paul, being grieved, turned and said to the spirit, I command thee in the name of Jesus Christ to come out of her. And he came out the same hour.*

This demon-possessed girl followed Paul *for many days.* Paul did not need or want the advertising from the devil. Neither did Jesus! (**Matthew 8:28-34, Mark 3:11-12**) There are four important truths from Paul's casting out the demon here:

* *Paul was grieved*
* *Paul spoke to the demon, not the girl*

* *Paul knew to use only the name of Jesus Christ*
* *Paul's command caused the demon to leave immediately*

PAUL AND SILAS BEATEN AND IMPRISONED

Acts 16:19-24 - *And when her masters saw that the hope of their gains was gone, they caught Paul and Silas, and drew them into the marketplace unto the rulers, And brought them to the magistrates, saying, These men, being Jews, do exceedingly trouble our city, And teach customs, which are not lawful for us to receive, neither to observe, being Romans. And the multitude rose up together against them: and the magistrates rent off their clothes, and commanded to beat them. And when they had laid many stripes upon them, they cast them into prison, charging the jailor to keep them safely: Who, having received such a charge, thrust them into the inner prison, and made their feet fast in the stocks.*

Sometimes we overlook the real reason why Paul and Silas were put into prison. It was because the girl who had been demon-possessed had stopped making money for her masters. *The masters saw that the hope of their gains was gone.*

"These men, being Jews, do exceedingly trouble our city, And teach customs, which are not lawful for us to receive, neither to observe, being Romans." - For some reason the masters left Timothy and Luke alone and laid hold on *Paul and Silas*. It may have been because they looked the most Jewish, and the anti-Semitic sentiment was very obvious. They brought them to the *marketplace* that was the public Roman forum. Here *the rulers and magistrates* who were accompanied by *lictors*, or *serjeants*, were the ones who used the beating rods. **(Acts 16:35)** There was the issue of the masters losing money, and the crowd's issue was nationalism and religion. Judaism was a legal religion under the Roman Empire, but it could not attempt to convert Romans citizens.

"And the multitude rose up together against them: and the magistrates rent off their clothes, and commanded to beat them." - Beating Roman citizens was illegal, but because of the mob situation, Paul and Silas did not have a chance to make their Roman citizenship known. Paul mentioned this violent treatment in **I Thess.2:2**.

"And when they had laid many stripes upon them, they cast them into * prison, charging the * jailor to keep them safely: Who, having received such a charge, thrust them into the inner prison, and made their feet fast in the stocks." - This was the first of three times that Paul was beaten with rods. **(2 Corinthians 11:25)** The *charge* that was given to *the jailor* involved the death penalty if Paul and Silas escaped. While their backs were bloody and sore from being beaten, they were cast into the *inner prison*, which was akin to a dungeon with no light and very little air to breathe. The stocks were made of wood, possibly a long timber with two holes for the wrists, two for the ankles, and one for the neck. Paul and Silas were being tortured for doing God's work in Philippi. They were truly taking up their crosses and following Jesus!

(There are ruins today in Philippi of the small, simple dungeon where Paul and Silas were kept. The jailor's name is believed to have been Stephanus of Achai mentioned in **I Corinthians 1:16, 16:15, 17.**)

Paul and Silas Rejoice

Acts 16:25 - *And at midnight Paul and Silas prayed, and sang praises unto God: and the prisoners heard them.*

This verse shows that Paul experienced what he would later write about:

***Rejoice in the Lord always: and again I say, Rejoice.* (Philippians 4:4)**

The prison walls and the other prisoners had never heard such a sound before. God's grace was there to help Paul and Silas praise God in the midst of horrific circumstances. They were rejoicing that God had counted them worthy enough to suffer for His name.

A Great Earthquake

Acts 16:26 - *And suddenly there was a great earthquake, so that the foundations of the prison were shaken: and immediately all the doors were opened, and every one's bands were loosed.*

The results of the *great earthquake* were fourfold:

★ *The earthquake was supernatural*

- *The foundations of the prison were shaken*
- *All of the vestibule doors were opened and in the inner prison*
- *Everyone's bands were loosed*

THE JAILOR'S RESPONSE

Acts 16:27-29 - *And the keeper of the prison awaking out of his sleep, and seeing the prison doors open, he drew out his sword, and would have killed himself, supposing that the prisoners had been fled. But Paul cried with a loud voice, saying, Do thyself no harm: for we are all here. Then he called for a light, and sprang in, and came trembling, and fell down before Paul and Silas,*

The supernatural earthquake caused the jailor to awake from his natural sleep. When he saw that the *doors were open*, he *supposed that the prisoners had escaped*. Instead of allowing the Romans to kill him for not doing his job, the jailor thought it was best to *draw out his sword and kill himself.*

"But Paul cried with a loud voice, saying, Do thyself no harm: for we are all here. Then he called for a light, and sprang in, and came trembling, and fell down before Paul and Silas," - When Paul saw that a life was about to commit suicide, his love for the jailor caused him to *cry out with a loud voice*. There must have been torches there in the dungeon because there were no windows in the inner prison. The earthquake and the compassion of Paul touched the jailor so much that he came running into the inner prison and was *trembling as he fell down*

before Paul and Silas. We see God working even through the sufferings of Paul and Silas to bring others to faith in Christ. Paul saved the jailor's physical life, which would later lead to his spiritual salvation.

The Conversion of the Philippian Jailor

> **Acts 16:30-34** - *And brought them out, and said, Sirs, what must I do to be saved? And they said, Believe on the Lord Jesus Christ, and thou shalt be saved, and thy house. And they spake unto him the word of the Lord, and to all that were in his house. And he took them the same hour of the night, and washed their stripes; and was baptized, he and all his, straightway. And when he had brought them into his house, he set meat before them, and rejoiced, believing in God with all his house.*

The jailor wanted the joy that Paul and Silas had. What a beautiful thing it is when the lives of the followers of Christ draw others to Him. Preaching the gospel is one way that God chose, but He also wants us to live the Christian life in such a way that we point others to Christ. This jailor knew that Paul and Silas *indeed* had the message of spiritual salvation.

"Sirs, what must I do to be saved?" - What an excitement it brings to this author's heart when someone asks this question. This is the most important question that anyone could ever ask. This jailor was asking this all-important question out of a heart of conviction. Possibly at that moment the jailor thought there was something that he was supposed to *do* morally, or to *do* religiously, or some sacrifice that he could give.

"Believe on the Lord Jesus Christ, and thou shalt be saved, and thy house." - Paul and Silas gave the jailor the most important answer! It's not in doing, or praying; it's in *believing on the Lord Jesus Christ*. Here we have the essence of the gospel. Salvation is by grace through faith alone. This has been a stumbling block to countless people over the centuries. It sounds too simple! It sounds too good to be true! Just *believe and be saved*?

> *For by grace are ye saved through faith; and that not of yourselves: it is the gift of God: Not of works, lest any man should boast.* **(Ephesians 2:8-9)**

Paul and Silas didn't mention repentance to the jailor because he was already in the attitude of repentance. Every individual has to be handled differently. Some religious fundamentalists have caused a false sense of security to many people by believing that the same memorized wording should be given to each person. We must meet each person where he/she is and discern how they need to be approached with the gospel. Jesus talked to the Samaritan woman about water. (**John 4**) Jesus talked to the religious Nicodemus about being born again, and that being born a Jew was not enough. (**John 3**)

Here Paul did not give the jailor a *lecture on theology. He did not talk about the sacraments of the church or joining a church. He pointed him to faith in the *Lord Jesus Christ!* Hallelujah!

⭐ *(One old chaplain of the British Army, Bishop John Taylor Smith, used a test for candidates for the chaplaincy. If they could not tell a dying soldier how to be saved in three minutes, they were not qualified. The mountain preacher, Vance Havner, once said, "A person can stay close to Jesus if he/she stays away from institutionalized theologians.")*

"....and thy house. And they spake unto him the word of the Lord, and to all that were in his house" - Paul came to the house of the jailor and had the freedom to speak *the word of the Lord* to everyone there. The power of *the word of the Lord* brought the entire house to salvation. The jailor's household was not automatically saved because he was saved, they had to choose Christ for themselves. At this time in the Roman world the father of a family was called the *paterfamilias*, the head of the house. His position was so authoritative that his decision to believe in Christ would free his family to also believe, and they did.

"And he took them the same hour of the night, and washed their stripes; and was baptized, he and all his, straightway. And when he had brought them into his house, he set meat before them, and rejoiced, believing in God with all his house." - Notice the results of the jailor's salvation:

⭐ *The jailor washed their stripes*
⭐ *The jailor and his house were water baptized*
⭐ *The jailor brought Paul and Silas to his house*
⭐ *The jailor showed hospitality and gave them food*

* *The jailor and his house were rejoicing*
* *The jailor's house became a place of fellowship*

THE MAGISTRATES SET PAUL & SILAS FREE

Acts 16:35-39 - And when it was day, the magistrates sent the serjeants, saying, Let those men go. And the keeper of the prison told this saying to Paul, The magistrates have sent to let you go: now therefore depart, and go in peace. But Paul said unto them, They have beaten us openly uncondemned, being Romans, and have cast us into prison; and now do they thrust us out privily? nay verily; but let them come themselves and fetch us out. And the serjeants told these words unto the magistrates: and they feared, when they heard that they were Romans. And they came and besought them, and brought them out, and desired them to depart out of the city.

Paul wasn't going to let the *magistrates* get away with breaking Roman law. Notice the reasons why Paul wasn't leaving Philippi just by the second-hand words of the *serjeants* that had previously treated them as criminals:

* *They had been beaten and openly uncondemned*
* *Paul & Silas were Roman citizens*
* *They had been cast into prison*
* *The magistrates wanted to free them privily (secretly)*

The *magistrates* had violated two Romans laws: *Lex Valeria*, which passed in 509BC, and the *Leges Porciae*, issued between 248-195BC. These laws exempted true Roman citizens from shameful punishment, especially beating in public. The Roman citizen had the right to appeal to the local Roman authorities. Paul knew the Roman law, and he wanted the *magistrates* to come themselves and set them free. Notice that when they heard that Paul and Silas were Roman citizens, they were afraid. They were afraid for their own lives, and they brought Paul and Silas out of the city to personally set them free.

Acts 16:40 – *And they went out of the prison, and entered into the house of Lydia: and when they had seen the brethren, they comforted them, and departed.* **–** What a beautiful picture we find here! A church had been planted in Philippi; the very first church in * Europe. *Lydia's house* became the headquarters of the church, *the brethren*. Sometimes we forget that when we read the powerful book of Philippians, written about ten years later, that Paul was writing back to those precious believers in Philippi. The church consisted of Lydia, the slave girl, the jailor and his household, and others who were converted under Paul's preaching. Lydia was a woman of business whose heart had been tenderly opened when she heard the preaching of Paul. The slave girl had to be set free from the grip of the devil. The jailor had to be confronted with an earthquake. It was a strange group, but a wonderful group that Christ had changed. Praise God!

⋆ *(This was the first church in Europe, thus explaining the Macedonian call of Paul in* **Acts 16:6-10**. *The gospel of Christ had been planted in a new continent along a major Roman trade route, the Via Egnatia, where it would quickly spread. The pagan Roman Empire could not and would not stop Christianity from changing the course of history. It's interesting that the pronoun "they" in* **vs.40** *and the pronoun "us" in* **Acts 20:5-6** *imply that Luke most likely stayed behind to help care for the congregation in Philippi.)*

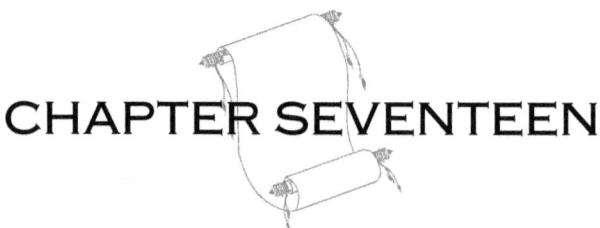

CHAPTER SEVENTEEN

PAUL PREACHES IN THESSALONICA

Acts 17:1-4 - *Now when they had passed through Amphipolis and Apollonia, they came to Thessalonica, where was a synagogue of the Jews: And Paul, as his manner was, went in unto them, and three sabbath days reasoned with them out of the scriptures, Opening and alleging, that Christ must needs have suffered, and risen again from the dead; and that this Jesus, whom I preach unto you, is Christ. And some of them believed, and consorted with Paul and Silas; and of the devout Greeks a great multitude, and of the chief women not a few.*

Leaving Philippi, Paul, Silas, and Timothy took the famous *Egnatian Way* and passed through *Amphipolis and Apollonia*. Because there was no Jewish synagogue in those towns, they traveled about 100 miles from Philippi to the ★ free city of *Thessalonica*, where Paul found a synagogue. He would follow the pattern that God commanded him to do, preach to the Jew first then to the Greek. (**Romans 1:16**)

The custom was to preach in the Jewish synagogue first before preaching on the streets. Jesus followed that custom. (**Luke 4:16**)

* *(Thessalonica was founded by the king of Macedonia, Cassander, in 315BC. He named the city after his wife, who was also the step-sister of Alexander the Great. Thessalonica became part of the Roman Empire in 168BC, and became a free city in 42BC, where it would be self-governed and print its own coins, etc. It was a very important city and had a population of about 200,000.)*

".......and three sabbath days reasoned with them out of the scriptures, Opening and alleging, that Christ must needs have suffered, and risen again from the dead; and that this Jesus, whom I preach unto you, is Christ." - Paul ministered longer than three weeks, but he deliberately went into the Jewish synagogue for *three Sabbaths*. He used the style of *reasoning* with the Jews by asking questions and interchanging ideas. The key is that Paul *reasoned out of the scriptures, as* Jesus did in **Luke 24:44-46**. It's one thing for a group to talk about worldly matters and religious opinions and quite another to be talking about the *Holy Scriptures*. The goal was to lead the Jews to believe that the One who *suffered and died, and rose again* was none other than *Jesus the Christ, or Israel's Messiah*. Paul came *not* into the synagogue to discuss their Jewish traditions or to follow their calendar reading of the Hebrew *Tanakh*, which is an acronym for the *Torah*, (5 books of Moses) the *Nevi' im*, (the Prophets) and the *Ketuvim*, (the Psalms and historical books) which make up what we call today the Old Testament. He set before them the scriptures in such a way that showed them how to connect the truths together. We do not know what specific scriptures that Paul used, but he explained to them that Jesus of Nazareth was the One the prophets wrote about.

The Jews had no understanding of *two comings* of the Messiah, or a *suffering* Messiah, so Paul probably took the passages in the Old Testament such as **Isaiah 53** and **Psalm 22** to show them the mission of the Messiah at His first coming. Because the cross was a stumbling block to the Jews, Paul took the scriptures that spoke about His suffering.

"And some of them believed, and consorted with Paul and Silas; and of the devout Greeks a great multitude, and of the chief women not a few." - Some of the Jews believed in Jesus and were identified with Paul and Silas. Two of them were *Aristarchus and Secundus*. (**Acts 20:4**) The majority of the people who believed were *Gentiles*, called *God-fearers*. They had believed in the God of Israel, but now they could become followers of Christ without having to be circumcised. There were many of the *honorable Jewish women* in Thessalonica who became followers of Christ. We are reminded of some of the women who followed Jesus:

> *And it came to pass afterward, that he went throughout every city and village, preaching and shewing the glad tidings of the kingdom of God: and the twelve were with him, And certain women, which had been healed of evil spirits and infirmities, Mary called Magdalene, out of whom went seven devils, And Joanna the wife of Chuza Herod's steward, and Susanna, and many others, which ministered unto him of their substance.* **(Luke 8:1-3)**

JEWISH OPPOSITION IN THESSALONICA

Acts 17:5-9 - *But the Jews which believed not, moved with envy, took unto them certain lewd fellows of the baser sort, and gathered a company, and set all the city on an uproar, and assaulted the house of Jason, and sought to bring them out to the people. And when they found them not, they drew Jason and certain brethren unto the rulers of the city, crying, These that have turned the world upside down are come hither also; Whom Jason hath received: and these all do contrary to the decrees of Caesar, saying that there is another king, one Jesus. And they troubled the people and the rulers of the city, when they heard these things. And when they had taken security of Jason, and of the other, they let them go.*

Not only were there Jews who did not believe the message of Paul, they were *moved with envy* and hatred. It's amazing how religious people can become filled with envy when they see others coming to Christ. This group of Jews incited a mob of rabble-rousers that were common in the Greek and Roman cities. One could offer them money, and they would cause a riot in a city over just about anything.

"*.....and assaulted the house of Jason, and sought to bring them out to the people. And when they found them not, they drew Jason and certain brethren unto the rulers of the city*" - Evidently the *house of Jason* was where Paul and Silas were staying, alike Lydia's house in Philippi. When the rioters could not find Paul and Silas, *they drew Jason and other believers unto the magistrates of the city.*

"…..crying, These that have turned the world upside down are come hither also; Whom Jason hath received: and these all do contrary to the decrees of Caesar, saying that there is another ★ king, one Jesus." – The evil men of the marketplace gave an unintended compliment to the effectiveness of God's work through Paul and Silas. The message of the Lord Jesus Christ had already *turned the world upside down*. The charges were that *Jason* and others had received the message of Paul and Silas, and they were claiming that Caesar was not king; *Jesus was the true king*. This of course went against *the decrees of Caesar*.

★ *(Jesus was King when He was born. He was King during His ministry. He was King on the cross. He will return as King of Kings and Lord of Lords.* **Matt.2:2, John 1:49, Luke 23:38, Revelation 19:16**)

"And they troubled the people and the rulers of the city, when they heard these things. And when they had taken security of Jason, and of the other, they let them go." – The reason why the *rulers of the city were troubled* is because if they could not keep peace in the cities, then Caesar would dispatch a legion of soldiers to that city to restore order. While Caesar was to be worshipped as king, Rome was really more concerned about keeping down riots than the personal faith of the individuals. The word here for *security* is *hikanon*, and it means *"bond."* *Jason and other believers* had to put up a *security deposit* to guarantee against any future riots. This may very well be one of the reasons why Paul wrote after a short while that Satan hindered him from returning to Thessalonica. **(I Thess.2: 17-18)**

While Jason and the believers were *let go*, the believing Jews that remained in Thessalonica continued to suffer persecution from the unbelieving Jews. **(2 Thess.1: 6-7)**

GOD'S KINGDOM ADVANCED IN BEREA

Acts 17:10-12 - *And the brethren immediately sent away Paul and Silas by night unto Berea: who coming thither went into the synagogue of the Jews. These were more noble than those in Thessalonica, in that they received the word with all readiness of mind, and searched the scriptures daily, whether those things were so. Therefore many of them believed; also of honourable women which were Greeks, and of men, not a few.*

The *brethren* had to pay a deposit for Paul and Silas to leave Thessalonica. Paul wanted to leave to keep from causing more trouble, but the church in Thessalonica had been established. Berea was about 60 miles southwest of Thessalonica. It was a much smaller city, but there were enough Jews who lived there to have a synagogue. The Jews in Berea were *more noble* than the Jews in Thessalonica, as they were more open-minded with a generous spirit. The reason was because they were Jews who *searched the scriptures daily.* When people are careful students of the scriptures, the Holy Spirit gives them the faith and mind they need to be open to receive truth. Although the Bereans were hearing the famous Apostle Paul, they searched the scriptures to see if what he was saying was true. Everyone needs to take a lesson from the Bereans. Just because we like a certain preacher or grow up in a certain church doesn't mean we are given biblical, sound truth. We need to be people who carefully search and examine the Holy Bible daily! The Holy Bible is not just a book of poetry and nice thoughts, it is truth that we live by. It is the eternal Word of God!

"Therefore many of them believed; also of honourable women which were Greeks, and of men, not a few." - This time *many* of the Jews believed the gospel was true. One of them we know was *Sopater* of Berea. (**Acts 20:4**) Notice here that many of the Gentiles, *honorable men and women* were saved. God's kingdom was advanced with many Jews and Gentiles, male and female, coming to know Christ as their Savior. Hallelujah! Berea was a small town with many people who embraced Jesus!

Paul Was Forced to Leave Berea

Acts 17:13-14 - But when the Jews of Thessalonica had knowledge that the word of God was preached of Paul at Berea, they came thither also, and stirred up the people. And then immediately the brethren sent away Paul to go as it were to the sea: but Silas and Timotheus abode there still.

The opposition came from the unbelieving Jews in Thessalonica. They were willing to travel some 60 miles to stir up trouble when they heard that *Paul was preaching the word of God in Berea*. Again there was a sense of urgency, so the believers in Berea took Paul *to the sea* to escape to Athens, while *Silas and Timotheus* were left behind to help edify the new converts. In spite of the opposition from the unbelieving Jews, a church had been established in Berea, and the work of the kingdom of God continued.

Paul Sails to Athens, Greece

Acts 17:15-16 – ***And they that conducted Paul brought him unto Athens: and receiving a commandment unto Silas and Timotheus for to come to him with all speed, they departed. Now while Paul waited for them at Athens, his spirit was stirred in him, when he saw the city wholly given to idolatry.***

Some of the brethren from Berea escorted Paul to Athens. It would have taken a considerable amount of time for Paul to travel over 200 miles south to Athens. Paul gave them a commandment to tell *Silas and Timotheus* to come be with him as soon as possible. *While Paul was waiting for them in Athens, he was troubled deeply when he saw that the entire city was given over to* ⋆ *idolatry.* Paul's spirit was strongly moved to have seen the acceptance of the gospel of Christ by the Bereans and then to see the paganism in Athens. He was about to experience something totally different from what he had ever seen before. Athens was one of the most beautiful cities in the world, and the average tourist would have been impressed. Paul was depressed when he saw the spiritual condition of the city. Many times beautiful places attract people who are very worldly-minded.

(We must remember that it was not the Jews, but the Gentiles who were given over to the idolatry in Athens. The Jews learned their lesson about idolatry after the Babylonian captivity. While many of the Jews did not believe in Jesus, they were not bowing down to the pagan gods and goddesses of Rome.)

Paul Preaches in the Synagogue & Marketplace

Acts 17:17 - *Therefore disputed he in the synagogue with the Jews, and with the devout persons, and in the market daily with them that met with him.*

Paul could not wait on Silas and Timotheus to arrive, so he started preaching in the Jewish synagogue. In contrast to Berea, Paul didn't have much success with the Jews in Athens. It's interesting that Paul was not able to start a church there. When one is preaching the gospel of Christ, he/she must always remember what our Lord told His disciples:

And whosoever shall not receive you, nor hear your words, when ye depart out of that house or city, shake off the dust of your feet. **(Matthew 10:14)**

Paul started in the synagogue then moved out into the marketplace. Try to imagine the Jewish Paul being surrounded by a new culture, the beauty of Athens with the best sculptors and architects the world had ever seen. There were temples to pagan gods, colonnaded streets, and the intellectual capital of the Greco-Roman world.

The Epicureans and the Stoicks

Acts 17:18-21 - Then certain philosophers of the Epicureans, and of the Stoicks, encountered him. And some said, What will this babbler say? other some, He seemeth to be a setter forth of strange gods: because he preached unto them Jesus, and the resurrection. And they took him, and brought him unto Areopagus, saying, May we know what this new doctrine, whereof thou speakest, is? For thou bringest certain strange things to our ears: we would know therefore what these things mean. (For all the Athenians and strangers which were there spent their time in nothing else, but either to tell, or to hear some new thing.)

The *Epicureans* followed the teachings of Epicurus, a Greek philosopher who lived between the years of 341-270BC. When Epicurus could not find the true reason for life through human reasoning, he turned to pleasure being the real reason for living. He said the goal of life should not be knowledge, but pleasure. The Epicureans did not believe in an afterlife, so there was nothing to fear or nothing to look forward to. They believed that life should be lived to the fullest by pursuing pleasure. Their philosophy degenerated into sensualism.

The *Stoicks* were philosophers that went to the other extreme, that life had no real direction or destiny. They were followers of *Zeno* (334-262BC) and *Chrysippus* (279-206BC). Their belief was all about human reasoning, and they believed in removing one's self from emotions. Man had the power within himself to be self-sufficient, which was attractive to many of the Romans. The *Stoicks* believed that man should just be happy within himself, and being brave when facing death was a human virtue. Their belief in life having no real meaning was one reason why so many of the Roman Emperors committed suicide.

"And some said, What will this babbler say? other some, He seemeth to be a setter forth of strange gods: because he preached unto them Jesus, and the resurrection" – The intellectual world of Athens called Paul a *babbler*, or a *seed picker*. They saw Paul as someone who gained knowledge from hearing different thinkers and then passing it on to others. Because Paul was *preaching Jesus and His resurrection*, they thought he was presenting some new foreign god to them. Notice that though Paul was in a strange place with a different kind of an audience, his message stayed the same.

"And they took him, and brought him unto Areopagus, saying, May we know what this new doctrine, whereof thou speakest, is? For thou bringest certain strange things to our ears: we would know therefore what these things mean. (For all the Athenians and strangers which were there spent their time in nothing else, but either to tell, or to hear some new thing.)" – They took Paul to * *Areopagus*, which means *"the Hill of Ares"* or *"Mars Hill."* This was an outcropped hill about 490 feet above sea level, northwest of the Acropolis of Athens. The sarcastic invitation was given to Paul because the Athenians were always anxious to hear *some new thing*. They were reading the apostle Paul as someone today would read the newspaper to find out what was the latest, worldly news.

(In Roman times, the Areopagus also refers to an important tribunal that was composed of city leaders responsible for supervising religion, culture, and education in Athens. This council was in charge of giving traveling lecturers a hearing. It was here where the apostle Paul would give his first sermon to a pagan, Gentile audience that had no understanding of the Hebrew Scriptures. This is why Paul did not quote scripture, but relied on the subject of the nature of God versus idolatry.)

PAUL'S INTRODUCTION AT MARS HILL

Acts 17:22-23 - *Then Paul stood in the midst of Mars' hill, and said, Ye men of Athens, I perceive that in all things ye are too superstitious. For as I passed by, and beheld your devotions, I found an altar with this inscription, TO THE UNKNOWN GOD. Whom therefore ye ignorantly worship, him declare I unto you.*

When Paul said *"I perceive that in all things ye are too superstitious,"* he was referring to the reverence the people of Athens gave to their pagan deities. They were religious in a bad sense, and he was not giving them a compliment.

"For as I passed by, and beheld your devotions, I found an altar with this inscription, TO THE UNKNOWN GOD. Whom therefore ye ignorantly worship, him declare I unto you." - Paul could easily see that in their pantheistic mind, the Greeks had an UNKNOWN GOD who covered any god that they may have missed or neglected so the city would be protected. Paul wanted to reveal the identity of the UNKNOWN GOD. This

is the only time in the New Testament that a pagan *altar* is mentioned. Paul was going to place his emphasis on *ignorance*, not on worship. He was not going to introduce to them a new religion, but the existence of the one true God of old.

Paul Tells The Athenians Who God Is

> **Acts 17:24-28 -** *God that made the world and all things therein, seeing that he is Lord of heaven and earth, dwelleth not in temples made with hands; Neither is worshipped with men's hands, as though he needed any thing, seeing he giveth to all life, and breath, and all things; And hath made of one blood all nations of men for to dwell on all the face of the earth, and hath determined the times before appointed, and the bounds of their habitation; That they should seek the Lord, if haply they might feel after him, and find him, though he be not far from every one of us: For in him we live, and move, and have our being; as certain also of your own poets have said, For we are also his offspring.*

Very different from what the philosophers taught, the one true God is the Creator of everything and the very source of life; *the Lord of heaven and earth*. He does not *dwell in temples made with hands*. This was in total contradiction to their belief that there was a god for this and a god for that. *God does not need anything for His happiness, He gives life and breath to all things.* This was a real arrow shot to the hearts of the *Epicureans and Stoicks*.

"And hath made of one blood all nations of men for to dwell on all the face of the earth, and hath determined the times before appointed, and the bounds of their habitation;" - The Greeks believed that their origin came from their own soil of Attica, the beautiful peninsula that jotted out into the Aegean Sea. With their myriads of gods and goddesses, they believed Greece was special in its origin and creation. Paul tells them that God Almighty created the human race and has determined the boundaries of the nations. The Greeks were no more important than any other people. God is in control of human history.

"That they should seek the Lord, if haply they might feel after him, and find him, though he be not far from every one of us" - God desires that mankind should *seek after Him*. In the Greeks groping in the darkness to find God, they had turned away from Him and invented their own gods. In spite of all the pagan temples around them, the one true God could be found and *is not far from any of us.*

"For in him we live, and move, and have our being; as certain also of your own poets have said, For we are also his offspring." - This is the proof of God's nearness. There is life; *we live*. There is movement; *we move*. There is being; *we have existence*. It's interesting that Paul mentioned their own ★ *poets* to build a bridge to his pagan audience.

★ *(Paul was referring to poets, such as Aratus of Soli, (315-240BC) Clemanthes, the son of Phanius of Assos, (263-232BC) and Epimenides of Crete (around 600 BC). Epimenides wrote these words about Zeus: (They fashioned a tomb for thee, O holy and high one, The Cretans, always liars, evil beasts, idle bellies! But thou art not dead: though livest and abidest for ever, For in thee we live and move and have our being.) Paul quoted this same poet in* **Titus 1:12**. *Paul did not quote these poets because they were prophets, but because they spoke some truth even though they were pagans.)*

PAUL DEALS WITH THEIR RESPONSIBILITY TO GOD

Acts 17:29-31 - *Forasmuch then as we are the offspring of God, we ought not to think that the Godhead is like unto gold, or silver, or stone, graven by art and man's device. And the times of this ignorance God winked at; but now commandeth all men every where to repent: Because he hath appointed a day, in the which he will judge the world in righteousness by that man whom he hath ordained; whereof he hath given assurance unto all men, in that he hath raised him from the dead.*

Paul took another aim at the philosophers by telling them that since we are all God's *offspring*, that they must reject the wrong idea that He can be represented *with gold, or silver, or stone, graven by art and man's device.* They were worshipping the gods of their own minds. In reality, they were worshipping demons, and Satan had taken them away from their Creator.

"And the times of this ignorance God winked at; but now commandeth all men every where to repent:" - Before the coming of the Lord Jesus Christ into the world, God overlooked the Gentile *ignorance*. God never overlooked it with the Jews, but dealt with them with divine judgment. Because Christ has come, now *God commands all men everywhere to repent,*

not only to change their minds, but to also change the way they live. What faith and courage God gave Paul to speak to these pagans in Athens while being surrounded by intellectual philosophers. Notice how Paul structures his message to this pagan audience:

* *Knowing the one true God as Creator*
* *Knowing that they are His offspring*
* *Their responsibility to seek Him*
* *They will be judged if they do not repent*

"Because he hath appointed a day, in the which he will judge the world in righteousness" - Paul is referring to the Great White Throne judgment, when all of the unsaved will be judged by the standard of *righteousness*.

"by that man whom he hath ordained; whereof he hath given assurance unto all men, in that he hath raised him from the dead." - For the first time in his message Paul references Jesus when he says that all will be judged by the righteousness of Christ Jesus. The *resurrection of Jesus* is the assurance that this judgment will take place. Everyone who has not been declared righteous through embracing Jesus as the Son of God will face the divine judgment, Jews or Gentiles. Just believing in God was not enough. They had to believe in the Man named Jesus who died in Jerusalem and was buried, and that *God raised him from the dead*.

THE RESULTS OF PAUL'S MESSAGE

Acts 17:32-34 - *And when they heard of the resurrection of the dead, some mocked: and others*

> *said, We will hear thee again of this matter. So Paul departed from among them. Howbeit certain men clave unto him, and believed: among the which was Dionysius the Areopagite, and a woman named Damaris, and others with them.*

Some mocked and some said we will hear thee again of this matter. The Greeks had no concept of the resurrection of the body. Believing that the body was evil, how could someone be raised from the dead? Basically, the *Epicureans* and the *Stoicks* refused Paul's message.

"*So Paul departed from among them. Howbeit certain men clave unto him, and believed: among the which was Dionysius the Areopagite, and a woman named Damaris, and others with them.*" - There is no mention that Paul ever returned to Athens. However, his ministry was not in vain; there were *some* who believed in Jesus, ★ *Dionysius the Areopagite, and a woman named Damaris, and others*. These were probably aristocrats from the council of *Areopagus*.

★ *(According to the historian Eusebius (260-340AD), Dionysius became the bishop of the church in Athens and died as a martyr. Even though the Bible does not say that Paul ever started a church there, history does record that a church was later started. This author had the privilege to visit Athens in the year 2010, and today 90 percent of Greece is Christian. Greek Orthodox is the primary religion in Greece. Interesting!)*

We are reminded of what Paul wrote in **I Corinthians: 1:21**:

For after that in the wisdom of God the world by wisdom knew not God, it pleased God by the foolishness of preaching to save them that believe.

The great human wisdom of the Greeks could not bring them to Christ, yet the foolishness of preaching did save those who believed. A great lesson can be learned from Paul's message on Mars Hill. The gospel cannot be properly preached without the *Doctrine of God, Creation, the Cross, the Resurrection, and the Judgment to come.* They all must be connected.

CHAPTER EIGHTEEN

Paul's Arrival at Corinth

Acts 18:1-4 - *After these things Paul departed from Athens, and came to Corinth; And found a certain Jew named Aquila, born in Pontus, lately come from Italy, with his wife Priscilla; (because that Claudius had commanded all Jews to depart from Rome:) and came unto them. And because he was of the same craft, he abode with them, and wrought: for by their occupation they were tentmakers. And he reasoned in the synagogue every sabbath, and persuaded the Jews and the Greeks.*

Paul travels some 50 miles west of Athens to the important city of ★ Corinth, having a population of about 500,000.

★ *(The city of Corinth was just across the narrow land bridge that connected the Peloponnese and the mainland of Greece. On the east was the Aegean Sea and on the west was the Ionian Sea. Corinth was known as the center of the worship of the sexual goddess, Aphrodite. On top of the Acrocorinth, a hill 1,800 feet high, the temple stood overlooking the city. One thousand cultic prostitutes worked in the* temple, so Corinth was famous for its immorality. It was also known for dishonesty, drunkenness, and promiscuous lifestyles. Corinth was also a commercial city and was noted for being important for trade. While Paul would have many issues to deal with, planting a church in Corinth would touch lives all over the Roman Empire.)

"And found a certain Jew named Aquila, born in ★ Pontus, lately come from Italy, with his wife Priscilla; (because that ★ Claudius had commanded all Jews to depart from Rome:) and came unto them." - One of the bright spots in Paul's visit to Corinth was meeting *Aquila and his wife, Priscilla*. Her name is mentioned in several places in the New Testament. **(Rom.16:3, I Cor.16:19, 2 Tim.4:19, Acts 18:18, 26)**

★ *(Pontus was much farther east on the southern coast of the Black Sea, the extreme northern part of Asia Minor, present-day Turkey. There were people from Pontus who came to the Feast of Pentecost in* **Acts 2:9.***)*

★ *(The Roman Emperor Claudius expelled the Jews from Rome in 49AD because of a riot that broke out in the Jewish community over Chrestus, or Christ. Though the Romans did not understand what it was all about, Claudius just signed an edict for all Jews to leave. Interestingly enough there was already a church in Rome, and Aquila and Priscilla were already believers. Possibly the church was founded after some of the Jews and Greeks, who believed on the Day of Pentecost, returned to Rome.)*

"And because he was of the same craft, he abode with them, and wrought: for by their occupation they were tentmakers. And he reasoned in the synagogue every sabbath, and persuaded the Jews and the Greeks." - Possibly Paul met them because they were ★ *tentmakers* as well. The Greek word for tentmakers, *skenopoioi*, means "leather workers." They did more than just build tents. Aquila and Priscilla found such common ground with Paul, that he stayed in their home.

★ *(In Jewish thinking, someone who brought forth the scriptures was not supposed to receive payment for his teaching. Paul practiced a trade.)*

As was always his pattern, Paul began to preach Christ in the synagogue in Corinth. He was able to persuade the Jews and the Greeks. Among some of the ones who believed in Jesus were the house of *Crispus,* the house of *Gaius,* and the house of *Stephanas.* (I Cor.1:14, 16)

SILAS AND TIMOTHEUS ARRIVE FROM MACEDONIA

Acts 18:5 - *And when Silas and Timotheus were come from Macedonia, Paul was pressed in the spirit, and testified to the Jews that Jesus was Christ.*

We know from **2 Cor.1:19** that when *Silas and Timotheus* arrived from *Macedonia,* they brought financial gifts to help Paul, and they gave him great encouragement to keep preaching. The first emphasis was for Paul to preach to the *Jews that Jesus was Christ.* Try to imagine the Jewish apostle Paul in a very ungodly city with the boldness to stand in the synagogue, with the unction of the Holy Spirit, and tell the Jews that Jesus of Nazareth was the long-awaited Messiah of Israel. Wow!

Opposition From the Jews

Acts 18:6 - *And when they opposed themselves, and blasphemed, he shook his raiment, and said unto them, Your blood be upon your own heads; I am clean; from henceforth I will go unto the Gentiles.*

The fact that this group of Jews *blasphemed* meant that they rejected the preaching that Jesus was the Son of God. It was the proclamation of the deity of Christ that caused them to *blaspheme*. Paul *shook off his clothes and told them that their blood would be upon their own heads*. This was a solemn disclaimer of responsibility on their behalf. When Paul said that *he would go unto the Gentiles*, this was not a turning point for the church age, or some dispensational change, it was a turning point in Corinth.

The Positive Results of Paul's Ministry

Acts 18:7-8 - *And he departed thence, and entered into a certain man's house, named Justus, one that worshipped God, whose house joined hard to the synagogue. And Crispus, the chief ruler of the synagogue, believed on the Lord with all his house; and many of the Corinthians hearing believed, and were baptized.*

Here we find a Gentile named *Justus*, who *lived close to the synagogue*, who became a believer in Jesus. He had been a God-fearer, (*worshipped God*) but now he was a true follower of Christ. And we see a Jewish ruler, *Crispus*, who came to believe in Jesus and *all his house*. There were *many more of the Corinthians*, probably Gentiles, *who believed and were baptized*. We know that Paul did baptize *Crispus*, (**I Cor.1:14**) but Paul only baptized a few. Most likely Silas and Timotheus did most of the baptizing. (**I Cor.14-17**) Paul described the kind of people the Corinthians were in **I Corinthians 1:26**:

> *For ye see your calling, brethren, how that not many wise men after the flesh, not many mighty, not many noble, are called.*

GOD GIVES PAUL ENCOURAGEMENT

> **Acts 18:9-11 - *Then spake the Lord to Paul in the night by a vision, Be not afraid, but speak, and hold not thy peace: For I am with thee, and no man shall set on thee to hurt thee: for I have much people in this city. And he continued there a year and six months, teaching the word of God among them.***

God gives Paul four revelations, **Acts 9:4, 16:9, 18:9-10,** and **22:17-18**. The reason for this revelation came to Paul *in the night* because evidently he was afraid. We do not know all of the circumstances and personalities that Paul was encountering. God knew exactly what Paul's fear was, and He knew when to come to him. Jesus told His disciples in the midst of a storm, *"Be not afraid."* (**Matthew 14:27**) We all face fears during our journey here on earth, and we need to be reminded of this truth:

> *For God hath not given us the spirit of fear; but of power, and of love, and of a sound mind.* **(2 Timothy 1:7)**

"For I am with thee, and no man shall set on thee to hurt thee: for I have much people in this city. And he continued there a year and six months, teaching the word of God among them." – The presence of Jesus, the sympathy of Jesus, and the cooperation of Jesus would help Paul to continue his work in Corinth. He did not tell Paul that he would not be attacked, but that no harm would come to him. God knew there would be many others who would be saved, and this revelation gave Paul the encouragement to stay in Corinth for *a year and six months, teaching the word of God among them.* This was the longest time that Paul ever stayed in one city. It helps us to remember that this was a major seaport town that was filled with immorality and cultic prostitutes. We are reminded of a biblical truth that Jesus said:

> *Verily I say unto you, That the publicans and the harlots go into the kingdom of God before you.* **(Matthew 21:31b)**

Great sinners realize their need to be saved, while the religious are trusting in their own self-righteousness. Paul was in a very sinful city, but God was about to save many from their sins and enable Paul to start a church there. When we understand all of the history of Corinth, it helps us understand the writings of both letters that Paul wrote to the Corinthians.

Paul Before Gallio

Acts 18:12-17 - *And when * Gallio was the deputy of Achaia, the Jews made insurrection with one accord against Paul, and brought him to the judgment seat, Saying, This fellow persuadeth men to worship God contrary to the law. And when Paul was now about to open his mouth, Gallio said unto the Jews, If it were a matter of wrong or wicked lewdness, O ye Jews, reason would that I should bear with you: But if it be a question of words and names, and of your law, look ye to it; for I will be no judge of such matters. And he drave them from the judgment seat. Then all the Greeks took Sosthenes, the chief ruler of the synagogue, and beat him before the judgment seat. And Gallio cared for none of those things.*

* (Gallio, being the proconsul of Achaia, is well documented outside of the scriptures. He served for only two years, 51-52AD. He was known to be a pleasant man and kind to everyone. It is written about Gallio in the Delphi Inscription. (nine fragments that were found in Delphi, Greece, that had been written by Emperor Claudius, "my friend and proconsul".))

When *Gallio* was *deputy of Achaia*, the unbelieving Jews made a rush against Paul and brought him into the *agora*, or the *public marketplace.*

"Saying, This fellow persuadeth men to worship God contrary to the law." - Their argument was that Paul was teaching men contrary to the Law of Moses. Judaism was allowed in the Roman Empire as a unified religion, but these Judaizers were claiming that Paul was preaching a different religion from Judaism. Was he? It may have seemed to be different to the unbelieving Jews, but in reality Paul was teaching the *completeness* of Judaism. Jesus, being Israel's Messiah, was what the Hebrew Scriptures were referring to. Paul was teaching that a person could be saved through faith in Christ, not in trying to obey the commandments of the Torah. It was the same religion, but with Jesus as the fulfillment.

"And when Paul was now about to open his mouth, Gallio said unto the Jews, If it were a matter of wrong or wicked lewdness, O ye Jews, reason would that I should bear with you: But if it be a question of words and names, and of your law, look ye to it; for I will be no judge of such matters. And he drave them from the judgment seat." - At the moment when Paul was trying to defend himself, *Gallio* interrupted. *Gallio* knew that Paul had committed no crime, and he also knew that any matters concerning the Jews would have to be dealt with themselves. What Paul was doing had nothing to do with the Roman law. *Gallio* wanted the Jews to see the difference between religious and civil matters. ★ *Gallio* thought Paul's message using the name, *Yeshua,* was just a part of Judaism.

★ *(This decision by Gallio was God using a pagan to free Paul to preach the gospel all over the territory. God orchestrates the events in human history to accomplish His divine mission.)*

"Then all the Greeks took Sosthenes, the chief ruler of the synagogue, and beat him before the judgment seat. And Gallio cared for none of those things." - The former ruler of the synagogue was *Crispus,* (**vs.8**) but when he became a believer in Jesus, he had to give up his position in the synagogue. It was Gentile, anti-Semitic bystanders who attacked and beat ★ *Sosthenes*. The original wording says, "Not one of these things was a care to Gallio--not the issue of the new Jewish faith in Jesus, not the issue of Judaism, and not the issue of Jews being beaten."

★ *(It seems that Sosthenes later became a believer in Jesus as well: "Paul called to be an apostle of Jesus Christ through the will of God, and Sosthenes our brother.")* **(I Cor.1:1)**

Paul Departs Corinth

Acts 18:18 - ***And Paul after this tarried there yet a good while, and then took his leave of the brethren, and sailed thence into Syria, and with him Priscilla and Aquila; having shorn his head in Cenchrea: for he had a vow.***

While Paul ministered for a *good while* in Corinth, he felt in his spirit that it was time to depart. He traveled a few miles east of Corinth to the seaport town of *Cenchrea* on the Aegean coast. This is where Paul *shaved his head,* which has caused much debate over the centuries. This author would like to give three possible reasons why Paul *shaved his head*:

- ★ *The revelation from God in vs. 9-10 moved Paul to consecrate himself*
- ★ *Paul wanted to protect himself from the sinfulness of Corinth*
- ★ *Paul had taken the Nazarite vow* **(Numbers 6:1-21)**

Shaving one's head was the *completeness* of the temporary Nazarite vow:

And the Nazarite shall shave the head of his separation at the door of the tabernacle of the congregation, and shall take the hair of the head of his separation, and put it in the fire which is under the sacrifice of the peace offerings. **(Numbers 6:18)**

Paul would have sailed across the Aegean Sea to Asia Minor with *Aquila and Priscilla* stopping in Ephesus. His ultimate destination would be *Syria*. While the Bible does not say, it is very likely that he offered up his hair as a * sacrifice in the Temple in Jerusalem.

* (Paul saw no contradiction between believing in Jesus as the Messiah and keeping some of the Jewish customs. He never tried to impose those things on Gentile believers, but he was a Jew preaching a Jewish Messiah, and certain Jewish laws were still important to Paul.)

PAUL IN EPHESUS

Acts 18:19-21 - *And he came to Ephesus, and left them there: but he himself entered into the synagogue, and reasoned with the Jews. When they desired him to tarry longer time with them, he consented not; But bade them farewell, saying, I must by all means keep this feast that cometh in Jerusalem: but I will return again unto you, if God will. And he sailed from Ephesus.*

Paul had received the Macedonian call to leave Asia Minor in **Acts 16:6-11**. *Now* the Holy Spirit is giving Paul the liberty to preach in the important seaport city of * *Ephesus*.

(At the time of Paul, Ephesus was the greatest commercial city in Asia Minor. Being a major seaport city, it was considered "the gateway to Asia." It could boast about the streets being made of white marble, bathhouses with beautiful mosaic walls and floors, and a theatre that would seat 25,000. The visitors could see the huge theatre as they walked up the beautiful Arcadian Street. Ephesus was also a very corrupt city with the temple to Diana, (or the Greek Artemis) the multi-breasted goddess of fertility. The temple was one of the seven wonders of the ancient world. The temple had 127 columns, four to six feet in diameter, and 60 feet high, twice the size of the Parthenon in Greece. Ephesus was the fourth largest city next to Rome, Alexandria of Egypt, and Antioch of Syria. Ephesus had a population of about 250,000.)

"....and left them there: but he himself entered into the synagogue, and reasoned with the Jews. When they desired him to tarry longer time with them, he consented not" - The good news is that God did a great work in the lives of many people in Ephesus, and Paul wanted to leave Aquila and Priscilla there to comfort the saints and to edify them. Once again, Paul would go into the Jewish *synagogue and reason with the Jews.* They desired for Paul to stay but when doing God's work, there is a time to stay and there is a time to leave. Paul's heart was set on going to Jerusalem and Antioch.

"But bade them farewell, saying, I must by all means keep this feast that cometh in Jerusalem: but I will return again unto you, if God will. And he sailed from Ephesus." - Paul had his mind on keeping the feast in Jerusalem. *(either the Feast of Passover or Pentecost)* It was probably at this feast Paul would offer up his hair as a sacrifice in Jerusalem. Notice that Paul says, *"but I will return again unto you, if God will."* The phrase *if God will* is a Jewish saying that meant that God was in control. (**James 4:15**)

PAUL'S RETURN TO ANTIOCH

Acts 18:22-23 - ***And when he had landed at Caesarea, and gone up, and saluted the church, he went down to Antioch. And after he had spent some time there, he departed, and went over all the country of Galatia and Phrygia in order, strengthening all the disciples.***

Paul first landed at the seaport town of *Caesarea*, on the west coast of Israel. He traveled some 40 more miles east, and *went up* to Jerusalem and *saluted the church* there. We must remember that Jerusalem is almost 2,500 feet above sea level, and *Caesarea* lies on the coastal plain almost at sea level. Paul probably reported to the church at Jerusalem all of the wonderful things that God had done on his missionary journey and the churches that had been established. This shows that Paul still held the *first church at Jerusalem* in high regard. Finally, Paul went down to his home congregation in *Antioch* for his last visit there. Paul had fond memories of the Holy Spirit working in *Antioch* from the first time he worked there with Barnabas. (**Acts 13**)

***"And after he had spent some time there, he departed, and went over all the country of Galatia and Phrygia in order, strengthening all the disciples."* -** Paul then traveled northward some 1,500 miles into Asia Minor to the regions of *Galatia* *and Phrygia*. His purpose was to *strengthen the disciples there* who had been converted on his previous journey to places such as *Tarsus, Derbe, Lystra, and Iconium*. Paul had been given a heart that was filled with compassion to win others to Christ and also to see them become true disciples of Jesus. Paul would tell us today to grow in our faith and make the end of our lives stronger than the beginning.

APOLLOS IN EPHESUS

> **Acts 18:24-28 -** *And a certain Jew named Apollos, born at Alexandria, an eloquent man, and mighty in the scriptures, came to Ephesus. This man was instructed in the way of the Lord; and being fervent in the spirit, he spake and taught diligently the things of the Lord, knowing only the baptism of John. And he began to speak boldly in the synagogue: whom when Aquila and Priscilla had heard, they took him unto them, and expounded unto him the way of God more perfectly. And when he was disposed to pass into Achaia, the brethren wrote, exhorting the disciples to receive him: who, when he was come, helped them much which had believed through grace: For he mightily convinced the Jews, and that publicly, shewing by the scriptures that Jesus was Christ.*

A *certain Jew* named *Apollos* came from *Alexandria, Egypt*, and by many measures was a remarkable man:

* *He was an eloquent man*
* *He was mighty in the scriptures*

- *He was instructed in the way of the Lord*
- *He was fervent in the spirit*
- *He spoke and taught diligently the things of the Lord*

"knowing only the baptism of John. And he began to speak boldly in the synagogue:" - As great of a man as *Apollos* was, his understanding was limited to the *baptism of John the Baptist*. (**Isaiah 40:3-5, Luke 3:1-20**) In other words, his knowledge was *incomplete,* and he could only speak with the limited knowledge he had. He knew about Jesus, and that John came baptizing as the means of preparing the way for the Messiah to come. He did not know about the death, burial, and the resurrection of Jesus. Isn't it timely that Paul left Aquila and Priscilla behind in Ephesus, and they heard *Apollos speak boldly in the Jewish synagogue.*

"whom when Aquila and Priscilla had heard, they took him unto them, and expounded unto him the way of God more perfectly" - What a divinely appointed blessing! Aquila and Priscilla saw that God had his hand on *Apollos* and that he would be valuable in God's kingdom. They taught *Apollos* the rest of the story. *Apollos* knew about Jesus, but now he would know about His finished work on the cross.

"And when he was disposed to pass into Achaia, the brethren wrote, exhorting the disciples to receive him: who, when he was come, helped them much which had believed through grace: For he mightily convinced the Jews, and that publicly, shewing by the scriptures that Jesus was Christ." - *Apollos* traveled across the Aegean Sea to the southern part of Greece to *Achaia*. He went with a letter of commendation. With his complete understanding about Jesus now, *Apollos*

could edify and build up the saints wherever he went. Notice that he *mightily convinced the Jews,* and he did it by *showing from the scriptures that Jesus was the Messiah. Hallelujah!* We know that
★ *Apollos* had a powerful ministry in Corinth. (**I Cor.1:12**)

   ★ *(There are some Hebrew scholars who believe that the mighty Apollos wrote the Book of Hebrews. However, the Latin historian Tertullian, (155-220AD) wrote that it was written by Barnabas. What causes some to believe this is that the Book of Hebrews is not Pauline in its style.)*

CHAPTER NINETEEN

PAUL COMES BACK TO EPHESUS

Acts 19:1-7 - *And it came to pass, that, while Apollos was at Corinth, Paul having passed through the upper coasts came to Ephesus: and finding certain disciples, He said unto them, Have ye received the Holy Ghost since ye believed? And they said unto him, We have not so much as heard whether there be any Holy Ghost. And he said unto them, Unto what then were ye baptized? And they said, Unto John's baptism. Then said Paul, John verily baptized with the baptism of repentance, saying unto the people, that they should believe on him which should come after him, that is, on Christ Jesus. When they heard this, they were baptized in the name of the Lord Jesus. And when Paul had laid his hands upon them, the Holy Ghost came on them; and they spake with tongues, and prophesied. And all the men were about twelve.*

Paul returns to Ephesus as he promised in **Acts 18:21**.

Apollos was still at Corinth, Greece, across the Aegean Sea. This is the last mention of *Apollos* in the book of Acts, but other references to him are found in **I Cor.1:12, 3:5-6, 22, 4:6, 16:12,** and **Titus 3:13.**

"and finding certain disciples, He said unto them, Have ye received the Holy Ghost since ye believed?" - Paul recognized that there was something missing in the lives of these disciples. This is an unusual situation, and Paul didn't make it a habit to ask people this question. The original wording is more clear: *Did ye receive the Holy Spirit <u>when ye believed?</u>* This one verse had caused tremendous controversy over the years and has been the basis for many who teach that someone can be saved and then later receive the Holy Spirit. Receiving the Holy Spirit is simultaneous with salvation. We would be wise to pay close attention to this passage of scripture.

"And they said unto him, We have not so much as heard whether there be any Holy Ghost. And he said unto them, Unto what then were ye baptized? And they said, Unto John's baptism." - This was a small group of men who were disciples of John the Baptist, and they had left the land of Israel before Jesus the Lamb of God came on the scene. The same situation with *Apollos* was in **Acts 18:25**. John baptized with water, but it would be the Messiah who would give the Holy Spirit baptism. (**Matt.3:11, Mark 1:8, Luke 3:16**) If these disciples had *not yet heard about the Holy Ghost, then what kind of baptism did they receive?* They were baptized of John in water and had never received Jesus as their Savior and experienced believer's baptism. This is the last mention of John the Baptist in the New Testament.

"Then said Paul, John verily baptized with the baptism of repentance, saying unto the people, that they should believe on him which should come after him, that is, on Christ Jesus. When they heard this, they were baptized in the name of the Lord Jesus." - These men had a heart ready to receive the message from Paul. Once Paul told them that they were to believe on the One who would come <u>after</u> John, *then they were baptized in the* * *name of the Lord Jesus.*

* *(There has also been much division over the recipe for saying certain names when one receives believer's baptism. Some say it should be in the name of the Father, the Son, and the Holy Spirit.* **(Matt.28:19)** *Some say it should be in Jesus' name,* **(Acts 2:38)** *and some say it should be in the name of the Lord Jesus.* **(Acts 19:5)** *This author has baptized people who desired a variety of these names to be spoken over them. The early church baptized in the name of the Father, the Son, and the Holy Spirit because all three were necessary for salvation to the world. However, the point is we are baptized in the authority of Jesus! In Jewish thought, to say "in the name of" meant "in the authority of someone." If we would only think about it deeper, what name do the Germans say when they are water baptized? What name would the Spanish say when they are water baptized, etc.? It's sad that so much division has been caused through ignorance of not understanding the Hebrew thought behind the text.)*

"And when Paul had laid his hands upon them, the Holy Ghost came on them; and they spake with tongues, and prophesied. And all the men were about twelve." - While Paul was not there at the baptism of John and did not walk with Jesus during His earthly ministry, he was still given the authority to lay hands on these people and they would receive the Holy

Spirit. This is not a universal doctrinal practice. It was given to the apostles, and Paul was an apostle, even though he was in the second category of apostles. To validate that these men had received the Holy Spirit, they began to speak in other *tongues,* or *languages.* Since it was a tri-lingual world, the gift of *languages* was needed to communicate the gospel. These were *languages* they had never been taught before. Also, they were given the gift of *prophecy,* or the gift of *preaching* the Old Testament. The Holy Spirit had given them the discernment of rightly dividing the Word of Truth to tell others that Jesus of Nazareth was the One the prophets wrote about who would come into the world. Notice *that all of the men were about twelve.* Again, these men did not have complete understanding of the gospel as the other believers in Ephesus. This was an isolated situation and must be understood as part of the *history* of the book of Acts, not as doctrine or theology.

PAUL IN THE SCHOOL OF TYRANNUS

Acts 19:8-10 - *And he went into the synagogue, and spake boldly for the space of three months, disputing and persuading the things concerning the kingdom of God. But when divers were hardened, and believed not, but spake evil of <u>that way</u> before the multitude, he departed from them, and separated the disciples, disputing daily in the school of one Tyrannus. And this continued by the space of two years; so that all they which dwelt in Asia heard the word of the Lord Jesus, both Jews and Greeks.*

As always, there were some Jews in the synagogue who rejected the message of Paul. The Jews were known to be stiff-necked and stubborn people. (**Exo.33:5, Acts 7:51**) This is a very interesting passage because here we find the term, *"that Way"* or *"the Way"* again. This connects us to **Acts 9:2**, where Paul had been persecuting the *"people of the Way,"* which means *"people of the Way of the Nazarene,"* and now he is one of the people of *the Way* and is *being persecuted himself* by some of the unbelieving Jews.

Paul leaves the synagogue and begins to teach *the word of the Lord Jesus* in *the school of one* * *Tyrannus*. This was such a powerful ministry that Paul stayed here two years, and many *Jews and Greeks, which dwelt in Asia, heard the word*. It is believed that the official church of Ephesus was really started at this time, and many of the churches in places such as *Colossae, Smyrna, Pergamum, Thyatira, Sardis, Philadelphia,* and *Laodicea* may have been started as a result of Paul's preaching here.

* *(Little is known about Tyrannus. He had a Greek name and may have been a rhetorician, but he could have been a Hellenized Jew who was a believer, or maybe a businessman who wanted Paul's work to continue. All we know is that he opened his school or lecture hall for Paul to preach the Word. It is recorded in the history of Ephesus that the people rested from their work between 11:00 am and 4:00 pm from the heat of the day. They worked at night and the wee hours of the morning. It is believed that Paul used those afternoon hours each day for two years to preach to the people. Evidently there were countless people who became followers of Christ during this time; "all they that dwelt in Asia heard the word of the Lord Jesus".)*

Unusual Miracles by God Through Paul

Acts 19:11-12 - *And God wrought special miracles by the hands of Paul: So that from his body were brought unto the sick handkerchiefs or aprons, and the diseases departed from them, and the evil spirits went out of them.*

These were not ordinary miracles, and they were performed by *the power of God through the hands of Paul.* This once again showed Paul's apostolic authority. As previously stated, the miracles in the book of Acts were performed by the apostles, and not by believers in general. Even Paul did not always have this supernatural power. **(2 Cor.12:8-10, Phil.2:25-27, I Tim.5:23, 2 Tim.4:20)** The * *handkerchiefs* were sweatbands that Paul wore around his head, and the *aprons* were the front coverings worn by artisans and workmen, such as Paul when he made tents. Notice also that *evil spirits* went out of the people. This distinguishes sickness from demonic possession.

* (As mentioned in the beginning of this commentary, the Book of Acts is a transitional book, and many false teachers and charismatic preachers have taken verses out of context to mislead people. Today some offer handkerchiefs, oils, and holy water to raise money for their so-called ministries. These type ministries prey upon the simple and the ignorant. We all need to know God's Word in its historical context to refrain from falling victim to these religious charlatans.)

SEVEN SONS OF SCEVA

Acts 19:13-17 - *Then certain of the vagabond Jews, exorcists, took upon them to call over them which had evil spirits the name of the LORD Jesus, saying, We adjure you by Jesus whom Paul preacheth. And there were seven sons of one Sceva, a Jew, and chief of the priests, which did so. And the evil spirit answered and said, Jesus I know, and Paul I know; but who are ye? And the man in whom the evil spirit was leaped on them, and overcame them, and prevailed against them, so that they fled out of that house naked and wounded. And this was known to all the Jews and Greeks also dwelling at Ephesus; and fear fell on them all, and the name of the Lord Jesus was magnified.*

This bizarre passage introduces us to some strolling Jews, or traveling fortune-tellers. These Jews were living in disobedience to the Law of Moses because they were practicing sorcery. This was a perversion of Judaism, and they were doing their spells *in the* * *name of the Lord Jesus.* They thought they could repeat the formula that Paul was using. They did not know Jesus as their Lord and Savior. They were itinerant Jewish exorcists.

* *(This author was visiting someone in a hospital years ago, and the family was all praying out loud using the name of "Jesus" as a magical formula to heal their sick loved one. After the loved one passed away, their faith was weakened and their minds were confused even until this day.)*

"And there were seven sons of one Sceva, a Jew, and chief of the priests, which did so." - Although *Sceva* was a Latin name, he was a Jewish priest who was living far from Jerusalem, in Ephesus. He would not have been allowed to practice such sorcery in Jerusalem. His *seven sons* were attempting to cast out an evil spirit from a man by using the vain superstitions they had learned from their father and by using the *Jesus* name that Paul was preaching about.

"And the evil spirit answered and said, Jesus I know, and Paul I know; but who are ye?" - Twice the demon said *"I know."* This is a very intriguing passage because when the demon said *"Jesus I know,"* the word for *know,* is *ginosko,* and it means *"to know by experience."* When the demon said *"Paul I know,"* the word for *know,* is *epistamai,* and it means *"to know about."* The evil spirit knew Jesus *by experience* and knew *about Paul.* The evil spirit *did not know who* * the sons of Sceva were. Wow!

* *(The sons of Sceva had no right to use the name of Jesus because they did not have a personal relationship with Him. There are many people who attend churches who will perish in hell because they have no real relationship with Jesus. They only know the Jesus their pastor preaches about, or their spouse believes in, instead of the Jesus of their own salvation.)*

"And the man in whom the evil spirit was leaped on them, and overcame them, and prevailed against them, so that they fled out of that house naked and wounded. And this was known to all the Jews and Greeks also dwelling at Ephesus; and fear fell on them all, and the name of the Lord Jesus was magnified." - The literal wording means that *the evil spirit leaped on them like* *a panther.* The evil spirit mastered all of the *seven sons of Sceva. They fled out of the house naked and wounded.* The good news is that *all of the Jews and Greeks in Ephesus were filled with fear, and the name of the Lord Jesus was magnified.* It was a great victory over demonism in Ephesus. The people learned that demons were real, and Jesus was real.

THE VICTORIES IN EPHESUS

> **Acts 19:18-20 -** *And many that believed came, and confessed, and shewed their deeds. Many of them also which used curious arts brought their books together, and burned them before all men: and they counted the price of them, and found it fifty thousand pieces of silver. So mightily grew the word of God and prevailed.*

Ephesus had been a stronghold of Satan. Sorcery and satanic practices were plentiful in the city. Even some of the Christians were still caught up in occult practices. When many of them saw the reality of demonic power, they confessed their sins and even revealed what they had been doing. They *brought their books,* scrolls, magic charms, incantations, and *burned them before all men.* Fifty thousand pieces of silver would equal millions of dollars in today's money. When the Bible says that *the word of God grew mightily and prevailed,* it means that that the Word of God kept increasing and increasing. This unusual passage of the imitating *sons of Sceva* needs a recap so we will not forget the results:

* *Reality of demons*
* *Demons know who Jesus is*
* *Jesus was glorified*
* *Confession of the saints*
* *Destruction of occult books*
* *God's Word grew mightily*

Paul's Future Plans

Acts 19:21-22 - *After these things were ended, Paul purposed in the spirit, when he had passed through Macedonia and Achaia, to go to Jerusalem, saying, After I have been there, I must also see Rome. So he sent into Macedonia two of them that ministered unto him, Timotheus and Erastus; but he himself stayed in Asia for a season.*

Paul was being led by the Holy Spirit to travel through *Macedonia* and *Achaia*, to *Jerusalem*, and then to *Rome*. One of the primary reasons was to collect and to deliver a collection of funds from other churches to help out the church in Jerusalem. (**Romans 15:25-31, I Cor.16:1-4**) Paul had a passion to visit the Christians in Rome who were already serving there. (**Romans 1:8-15**)

"So he sent into Macedonia two of them that ministered unto him, Timotheus and Erastus; but he himself stayed in Asia for a season." - We already know about *Timotheus*, but the other disciple, *Erastus*, we know very little about. He is mentioned in **Romans 16:23** and **2 Timothy 4:20**. They were truly assistants to the apostle Paul and helped him to

maximize his ministry. Their willingness to go ahead into *Macedonia* gave Paul the extra time he needed in Asia. Paul had to deal with many adversaries in Ephesus. **(I Cor.16:8-9)**

Demetrius and the Goddess Diana

Acts 19:23-28 - *And the same time there arose no small stir about that way. For a certain man named Demetrius, a silversmith, which made silver shrines for Diana, brought no small gain unto the craftsmen; Whom he called together with the workmen of like occupation, and said, Sirs, ye know that by this craft we have our wealth. Moreover ye see and hear, that not alone at Ephesus, but almost throughout all Asia, this Paul hath persuaded and turned away much people, saying that they be no gods, which are made with hands: So that not only this our craft is in danger to be set at nought; but also that the temple of the great goddess Diana should be despised, and her magnificence should be destroyed, whom all Asia and the world worshippeth. And when they heard these sayings, they were full of wrath, and cried out, saying, Great is Diana of the Ephesians.*

Notice again that a tremendous riot broke out about the preaching of *that way*, or *the Way*. We have already mentioned that the gigantic temple to the goddess Diana was one of the seven wonders of the ancient world. *Demetrius, a silversmith,* and others were *making silver shrines,* trinkets and idols *for Diana,* and their wealth was being affected because of the preaching of Paul. This may be what Paul was talking about when he *fought with the beasts at Ephesus.* (**I Cor.15:32**) This shows the powerful change that was going on in the Roman world through the preaching of the gospel. When people came to believe in Christ as the Lord, they stopped worshipping the false deities. Christianity was affecting the economy of the pagans. The world doesn't need Congress of Parliaments to change the world. The power of the gospel changes the hearts of the people; thus, changing the course of the world.

"Whom he called together with the workmen of like occupation, and said, Sirs, ye know that by this craft we have our wealth. Moreover ye see and hear, that not alone at Ephesus, but almost throughout all Asia, this Paul hath persuaded and turned away much people, saying that they be no gods, which are made with hands: So that not only this our craft is in danger to be set at nought; but also that the temple of the great goddess Diana should be despised, and her magnificence should be destroyed, whom all Asia and the world worshippeth." - *Demetrius* was making small figurines of the multi-breasted Diana that were placed in niches in the homes or worn around their necks as amulets. After more than two years of Paul preaching in Ephesus, many had come to faith in Jesus. While Paul was totally against paganism, he wasn't on an anti-everything campaign. He was on a pro-Jesus campaign. *Demetrius* called a meeting with his fellow workers and made a speech. He mentioned two ways that Paul's preaching was a threat to them:

* ***Their craft was in danger of losing business***
* ***The temple of Diana could be exposed***

"And when they heard these sayings, they were full of wrath, and cried out, saying, Great is Diana of the Ephesians." – The crowd was filled with rage and began shouting, *"Great is Diana of the Ephesians."* The original wording means that they kept on shouting. Inscriptions have been found with these very words to confirm the account.

The Riot Gains More Momentum

Acts 19:29-34 - *And the whole city was filled with confusion: and having caught Gaius and Aristarchus, men of Macedonia, Paul's companions in travel, they rushed with one accord into the theatre. And when Paul would have entered in unto the people, the disciples suffered him not. And certain of the chief of Asia, which were his friends, sent unto him, desiring him that he would not adventure himself into the theatre. Some therefore cried one thing, and some another: for the assembly was confused: and the more part knew not wherefore they were come together. And they drew Alexander out of the multitude, the Jews putting him forward. And Alexander beckoned with the hand, and would have made his defence unto the people. But when they knew that he was a Jew, all with one voice about the space of two hours cried out, Great is Diana of the Ephesians.*

The second reaction was that *the whole city was filled with confusion and they rushed into the theatre.* This was the largest *theatre* of its kind in the Roman world. The original wording describes it as a flood of people pouring together, with yelling and screaming. On their way they seized *Gaius and Aristarchus.* **(Acts 20:4, I Cor.1:14, Acts 27:2, Colossians 4:10, Philemon 24)**

"And when Paul would have entered in unto the people, the disciples suffered him not. And certain of the chief of Asia, which were his friends, sent unto him, desiring him that he would not adventure himself into the theatre." - Paul was not afraid of the howling mob, and he also knew that it could possibly mean death. Two groups of people dissuaded Paul from entering into the theatre:

* *Some of the disciples who had been converted under Paul's ministry*
* *Some of the officials and officers who had respect for Paul*

"Some therefore cried one thing, and some another: for the assembly was confused: and the more part knew not wherefore they were come together" - Most of the people who had gathered in the theatre did not even know why they were there. It was a mob situation, not an orderly *assembly.*

"And they drew Alexander out of the multitude, the Jews putting him forward. And Alexander beckoned with the hand, and would have made his defence unto the people. But when they knew that he was a Jew, all with one voice about the space of two hours cried out, Great is Diana of the Ephesians." - *Alexander* wanted to make sure that the mob knew that the unbelieving Jews did not approve of Paul either. He didn't want the mob to turn on the other unbelieving Jews since they didn't practice idolatry. He accomplished nothing before the

angry crowd. This is probably the same *Alexander that caused Paul much evil* in **2 Timothy 4:14**.

When the crowd discovered that Alexander was a Jew, they shouted for two hours, *"Great is Diana of the Ephesians."* The context has anti-Semitic overtones. The acoustics in the theatre were so astounding that the echoes we still hear today as the world chants how great is their worldly idols, while the Christians shout *"Great is our Lord Jesus Christ!"* All idols will fall and crumble, but Christ will stand forever!

THE TOWN CLERK INTERVENES

Acts 19:35-41 - *And when the townclerk had appeased the people, he said, Ye men of Ephesus, what man is there that knoweth not how that the city of the Ephesians is a worshipper of the great goddess Diana, and of the image which fell down from Jupiter? Seeing then that these things cannot be spoken against, ye ought to be quiet, and to do nothing rashly. For ye have brought hither these men, which are neither robbers of churches, nor yet blasphemers of your goddess. Wherefore if Demetrius, and the craftsmen which are with him, have a matter against any man, the law is open, and there are deputies: let them implead one another. But if ye inquire any thing concerning other matters, it shall be determined in a lawful assembly. For we are in danger to be called in question for this day's uproar, there being no cause whereby we may give an account of this concourse.*

And when he had thus spoken, he dismissed the assembly.

The *town clerk* was what we would call a mayor of the town. His authority and respect were able to quiet the multitude. He had resided over many assemblies in that same theatre before. The *town clerk* confirmed that *the city of Ephesus worshipped the goddess Diana. He* told them not to do anything *rashly* because *Gaius, Aristarchus,* or Paul *had not stolen anything from their own churches or blasphemed the pagan goddess.* There were some Jews who robbed the treasures that were in pagan temples in parts of the Roman world. (**Romans 2:22**)

"Wherefore if Demetrius, and the craftsmen which are with him, have a matter against any man, the law is open, and there are deputies: let them implead one another. But if ye inquire any thing concerning other matters, it shall be determined in a lawful assembly." - The *clerk* told the mob that if *Demetrius* and his other *craftsman* had anything against any man, they should bring it before the proconsuls in an orderly fashion.

"For we are in danger to be called in question for this day's uproar, there being no cause whereby we may give an account of this concourse. And when he had thus spoken, he dismissed the * assembly." - Here is a very overlooked background to riots in the Roman world. Ephesus was one of the most beautiful cities in the Aegean Sea, and if they did not stop the riot, then they would have to give an account to Rome about the reason for their commotion. While the Romans were pagans, they prided themselves in keeping peace in their provinces. Once again God used a pagan official to protect Paul and preserve his work. The clerk dismissing the assembly gave the riot some official order.

★ (Interestingly enough, the Greek word here for "assembly" in these verses is "ekklesia," which is the Greek for "church." Of course it was used here as a non-religious word to describe a gathering of the people.)

CHAPTER TWENTY

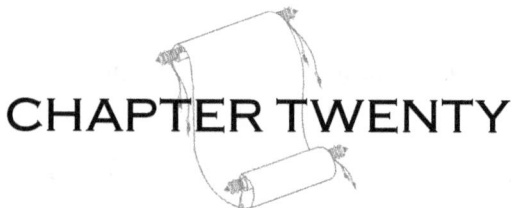

PAUL IN MACEDONIA AND GREECE

Acts 20:1-4 - *And after the uproar was ceased, Paul called unto him the disciples, and embraced them, and departed for to go into Macedonia. And when he had gone over those parts, and had given them much exhortation, he came into Greece, And there abode three months. And when the Jews laid wait for him, as he was about to sail into Syria, he purposed to return through Macedonia. And there accompanied him into Asia Sopater of Berea; and of the Thessalonians, Aristarchus and Secundus; and Gaius of Derbe, and Timotheus; and of Asia, Tychicus and Trophimus.*

After the citywide confusion in Ephesus had ended, it was time for Paul to *go into Macedonia.* Before Paul departed Ephesus, he embraced the disciples with a warm-hearted farewell.

"And when he had gone over those parts, and had given them much exhortation, he came into Greece" - Paul was not

evangelizing, but discipling the saints in Macedonia. *And when he had gone over those parts* covers a wide area. According to **Romans 15:19**, Paul traveled as far west as *Illyricum*. This corresponds to modern-day *Albania*. This is on the eastern coast of the Adriatic Sea, with the mainland of Italy westward across the water. Not every detail and every specific location of Paul's journeys are mentioned. Like the life and ministry of Jesus, we are not given a complete, chronological biography, but the most important events. (**John 20:30**) After Paul traveled as far as *Illyricum*, he then went south to Greece.

"And there abode three months. And when the Jews laid wait for him, as he was about to sail into Syria, he purposed to return through Macedonia." - It is believed that Paul spent the winter months of around 57 AD in Greece. It was during this time that he wrote the Epistle to the Romans and possibly to the Galatians. Paul had intended to sail from Corinth across the Aegean Sea back to *Syria*, or Israel, but after a Jewish plot to assassinate him, he had to change his plans. He decided to go back north up through Macedonia.

★ *(This plot may have happened while Paul was either getting ready to sail, or on a ship in the port of Corinth. Many of the Jews were preparing for the Passover in Jerusalem at this time. Paul ended up having to celebrate Passover in Phillipi.)*

"And there accompanied him into Asia Sopater of Berea; and of the Thessalonians, Aristarchus and Secundus; and Gaius of Derbe, and Timotheus; and of Asia, Tychicus and Trophimus." - This verse tells us that Paul had some representatives of various churches to accompany him. It's not surprising to see *Sopater* from the church of *Berea* and *Aristarchus* and *Secundus from Thessalonica* represented, but there were also *Gaius from Derbe,* and *Timothy from Lystra,* from the province of Galatia. *Tychicus* and *Trophimus* were from the province of Asia. As we will find in the following verses, *Luke,* the author of the Book of Acts, also was in the group.

PAUL AT TROAS

Acts 20:5-12 - These going before tarried for us at Troas. *And we sailed away from Philippi after the days of unleavened bread, and came unto them to Troas five days; where we abode seven days. And upon the first day of the week, when the disciples came together to break bread, Paul preached unto them, ready to depart on the morrow; and continued his speech until midnight. And there were many lights in the upper chamber, where they were gathered together. And there sat in a window a certain young man named Eutychus, being fallen into a deep sleep: and as Paul was long preaching, he sunk down with sleep, and fell down from the third loft, and was taken up dead. And Paul went down, and fell on him, and embracing him said, Trouble not yourselves; for his life is in him. When he therefore was come up again, and had broken bread, and eaten, and talked a long while, even till break of day, so he departed. And they brought the young man alive, and were not a little comforted.*

Luke adds the pronoun _we_ to **vs. 6** reminding us that Paul had left him in Philippi in **Acts 16:40**, and now he sails away with Paul for _five days_ back east to _Troas_, which was on the northwest corner of Asia Minor. Luke would stay with Paul from this point on through the rest of his journeys through the Book of Acts and all the way to Rome. Notice it was after they had kept the Jewish feast of _Unleavened Bread_, which included _Passover_, and they stayed in _Troas_ for _seven days_.

"And upon the first day of the week, when the disciples came together to break bread," - This is the very first example in the Bible where Christians made it a practice to gather together on _the * first day of the week_, the day our Lord Jesus Christ arose.

*(This subject has brought about much debate and division in the body of Christ over the centuries. Certain denominations still believe that what we call Saturday, or the seventh day of the week, is the day when Christians should gather to worship. Their reasoning comes from the fact that God rested on the seventh day of creation in **Genesis 2:2**, and God commanded Moses and the children of Israel to keep the Sabbath Day in **Exodus 20:8**. This verse, along with **Luke 24:1** and **I Corinthians 16:2**, shows us that the day of Christ's resurrection supersedes the Sabbath Day. Paul would later make it clear that the Sabbath Day was a shadow of things to come: "Let no man therefore judge you in meat, or in drink, or in respect of an holyday, or of the new moon, or of the Sabbath days: Which are a shadow of things to come; but the body is of Christ." **Colossians 2:16-17**)*

"Paul preached unto them, ready to depart on the morrow; and continued his speech until midnight." - Paul knew that he would never see many of these fellow believers again on this side of heaven, so he gave them a long sermon that lasted until midnight. The *next day he would depart,* but God had used Paul to establish the Christian faith in the hearts of many believers. God had prepared the geographical locations, the protection, the exact places, and the people to help Paul in his journeys. Rome and the world would never be the same!

"And there were many lights in the upper chamber, where they were gathered together. And there sat in a window a certain young man named Eutychus, being fallen into a deep sleep: and as Paul was long preaching, he sunk down with sleep, and fell down from the third loft, and was taken up dead." – The meeting took place in an *upper chamber* where there were many oil lamps and wicks burning. The name *Eutychus* means *"fortunate,"* and he was blessed and fortunate to have had the apostle Paul in his presence. Luke details to us that this *young man* had *fallen into a deep sleep,* and *he sunk down with sleep,* and *fell down from the third loft.* Because of the late hour, the heat and the fumes from the oil lamps and the length of Paul's message got the best of him. Luke, the doctor, tells us that the young man was *taken up dead.*

"And Paul went down, and fell on him, and embracing him said, Trouble not yourselves; for his life is in him." – Paul went down to the ground floor and threw himself on the dead body of *Eutychus.* This was a similar action that Elijah did in **I Kings 17:21** and Elisha did in **2 Kings 4:32-37**. It brought life back into the young man, *Eutychus.* This miracle is recorded because *Eutychus* was really dead, and God brought him back to life through Paul.

"When he therefore was come up again, and had broken bread, and eaten, and talked a long while, even till break of day, so he departed. And they brought the young man alive, and were not a little comforted." - This miracle of raising *Eutychus* from the dead and then showing him eating bread and talking afterwards reminds this author of the miracle of Jesus raising Lazarus. In **John 12:1-2**, Lazarus is sitting at the table with Jesus fellowshipping and eating bread.

Paul continued preaching until the sun came up. Try to imagine the tearful and joyful conversations the church had with the once dead and now alive *Eutychus*!

From Troas to Miletus

Acts 20:13-16 - *And we went before to ship, and sailed unto Assos, there intending to take in Paul: for so had he appointed, minding himself to go afoot. And when he met with us at Assos, we took him in, and came to Mitylene. And we sailed thence, and came the next day over against Chios; and the next day we arrived at Samos, and tarried at Trogyllium; and the next day we came to Miletus. For Paul had determined to sail by Ephesus, because he would not spend the time in Asia: for he hasted, if it were possible for him, to be at Jerusalem the day of Pentecost.*

This section of scripture deals with Paul and his companions, along with Luke, meandering their travels down the western coast of Asia Minor. On the first leg they sailed without Paul about 20 miles to *Assos*. Paul decided to walk the good paved road that connected the two cities.

"And when he met with us at Assos, we took him in, and came to Mitylene." - They were joined together again with Paul at *Assos*, and traveled about 30 miles to *Mitylene*. *Mitylene* was the capital of *Lesbos*, an island off the coast of Asia Minor.

"And we sailed thence, and came the next day over against Chios; and the next day we arrived at Samos, and tarried at Trogyllium; and the next day we came to Miletus. For Paul had determined to sail by Ephesus, because he would not spend the time in Asia: for he hasted, if it were possible for him, to be at Jerusalem the day of Pentecost." - Paul and his companions had a three-leg sailing journey in the Aegean Sea, and each leg took about one day to reach: from the island town of *Mitylene* to *Chios*; from the island town of *Chios* to the island town of *Samos*; then tarried at the mainland city of *Trogyllium* before arriving at ★ *Miletus*. *Miletus* is about 30 miles south of *Ephesus* where Paul was trying to bypass because of the bad riots he experienced before. Another reason why Paul did not want to spend time in the big city of *Ephesus* was because he desired to attend the *Feast of Pentecost in Jerusalem*, which was held during our month of May.

★ *(This author had the privilege to visit Miletus in 2010 and saw the inscription they found in the theatre there: "Place of the Jews, who are also called, God-fearing." Many of the Jews who lived in Miletus had become secularized and were attending this pagan theatre.)*

PAUL SUMMONS THE EPHESIAN ELDERS

Acts 20:17 - *And from Miletus he sent to Ephesus, and called the elders of the church.*

While Paul did not want to waste time in Ephesus, he was concerned about the church there. Paul sent for *the ★ elders of the church* to make the 30-mile walk to meet him in Ephesus.

★ *(The word "elders" is presbyterous, where we get the English word "Presbyterian." In the New Testament the word "elder" is sometimes called "bishop," or "pastor." Although they were appointed to be overseers of the churches that Paul started, the <u>apostle Paul</u> had authority over them.)*

PAUL REMINDS THE ELDERS OF THE PAST

Acts 20:18-21 - *And when they were come to him, he said unto them, Ye know, from the first day that I came into Asia, after what manner I have been with you at all seasons, Serving the Lord with all humility of mind, and with many tears, and temptations, which befell me by the lying in wait of the Jews: And how I kept back nothing that was profitable unto you, but have shewed you, and have taught you publicly, and from house to house, Testifying both to the Jews, and also to the Greeks, repentance toward God, and faith toward our Lord Jesus Christ.*

Notice that Paul did not set himself up before the elders as a celebrity to be worshipped. He always referred to his work as *serving the Lord with all humility of mind*. Although he was an apostle, he knew very well his own past and his experience on the Damascus Road never left his thoughts. Paul wanted to exemplify humility to help the elders be humble servants at the church of Ephesus. The elders knew quite well how Paul had lived among them, which would have started about four years earlier. Notice how Paul spoke of his service:

* *In humility of mind*
* *With many tears*
* *With trials and temptations from the Jews*

"And how I kept back nothing that was profitable unto you, but have shewed you, and have taught you publicly, and from house to house," – Paul taught them everything he knew from the Holy Scriptures. He did it privately and *publicly from*
* *house to house*. In Ephesus there were several small churches in the *houses* of the believers.

* *(When this author visited Ephesus, our tour guide showed us a secret code carved in a marble slab, from the first century, to let others believers know they were fellow Christians, and perhaps discuss where they would meet together. This protected the Christians from the Romans and the unbelieving Jews. The Greek letters, I-X-O-Y-E, were encoded in what looked like a chariot wheel's spokes. The letters in Greek meant JESUS-CHRIST-GOD-SON-SAVIOR.)*

"Testifying both to the Jews, and also to the Greeks, repentance toward God, and faith toward our Lord Jesus Christ." – Paul reminded them of his evangelistic efforts and desired for them to always remember to preach the gospel to the lost. The two-fold message of *repentance toward God and faith toward our Lord Jesus Christ* was meant to go forth not only to the *Greeks* living in Ephesus, but also to the *Jews*. In our

western world we have heard the names *Lord-Jesus-Christ* so many times that we forget what a powerful message that was in Paul's day. *Jesus of Nazareth* was the long-awaited *Messiah of Israel*, and He is *Lord* of all!

PAUL SPEAKS ABOUT THE FUTURE

Acts 20:22-27 - *And now, behold, I go bound in the spirit unto Jerusalem, not knowing the things that shall befall me there: Save that the Holy Ghost witnesseth in every city, saying that bonds and afflictions abide me. But none of these things move me, neither count I my life dear unto myself, so that I might finish my course with joy, and the ministry, which I have received of the Lord Jesus, to testify the gospel of the grace of God. And now, behold, I know that ye all, among whom I have gone preaching the kingdom of God, shall see my face no more. Wherefore I take you to record this day, that I am pure from the blood of all men. For I have not shunned to declare unto you all the counsel of God.*

Paul changes the subject from the past by saying *"And now, behold,"* to the future and his pending journey to *Jerusalem*. Paul had a sense of purpose in obeying the spirit that had compelled him to go to Jerusalem, not knowing what would happen to him. Paul's life was being controlled by the Spirit!

"Save that the Holy Ghost witnesseth in every city, saying that bonds and afflictions abide me." - Every place where Paul traveled, the Holy Spirit revealed to him that trouble would

await him. No doubt Paul had many revelations confirming that God's calling on his life involved suffering.

"But none of these things move me, neither count I my life dear unto myself, so that I might finish my course with joy, and the ministry, which I have received of the Lord Jesus, to testify the gospel of the grace of God." - Paul wasn't concerned about trying to live a long, prosperous life; his goal was to fulfill his calling. Paul's passion should be our passion, *to finish our course with joy.* The calling he received *from the Lord Jesus was to testify the gospel of the grace of God,* included going to Jerusalem. Paul knew that death was in his shadow, but he also knew that the gospel he was preaching was worth dying for.

"And now, behold, I know that ye all, among whom I have gone preaching the kingdom of God, shall see my face no more. Wherefore I take you to record this day, that I am pure from the blood of all men. For I have not shunned to declare unto you all the counsel of God." - What Paul would face in Jerusalem was unknown, and he didn't think that the elders in Ephesus would ★ *ever see his face* again. Paul's heart and conscious were clear because he had taught them the whole *counsel of God.* He could say that *he was pure from the blood of all men.*

★ *(As we search the Epistles of Paul, it does seem as though he did get to visit Ephesus again several years later, just prior to his death.* **(Philippians 2:24, Philemon 22, I Timothy 3:14, 4:13)** *Paul also returned to Troas and Miletus.* **(2 Timothy 4:13, 4:20)** *It helps to keep in mind that Paul would live several more years before being killed in Rome by Nero.)*

Paul Warns the Ephesian Elders

Acts 20:28-31 - *Take heed therefore unto yourselves, and to all the flock, over the which the Holy Ghost hath made you overseers, to feed the church of God, which he hath purchased with his own blood. For I know this, that after my departing shall grievous wolves enter in among you, not sparing the flock. Also of your own selves shall men arise, speaking perverse things, to draw away disciples after them. Therefore watch, and remember, that by the space of three years I ceased not to warn every one night and day with tears.*

Paul is pointing out the various responsibilities of the elders to the church at Ephesus. They were to *pay attention to their own minds and lives* because they had a very high standard to fulfill. A godly leader flows from a *godly life*, not just holding a position or having knowledge. The original word here for *"overseers"* is *episkopous*, and this is where we get the English word *"Episcopalian."* The word in this context means *"bishop."*

"to feed the church of God" - This means that the elders were *to shepherd*, or *to tend* to the flock. They were to be faithful pastors of their house-church congregations. The words *elder, bishop,* and *pastor,* are talking about the same person because:

* *Elders rule the flock*
* *Bishops oversee the flock*
* *Shepherds feed the flock*

"which he hath purchased with his own blood." - The church of born-again believers does not belong to a denomination, a board of deacons, or to the ones who give the most money. It was *purchased by the blood of Christ*! The number one problem in western world Christianity is that the local churches do not understand that the true church belongs to Jesus. The reason why Jesus shed His blood for the church was so he could reserve and preserve the church for Himself. These elders at Ephesus had a tremendous responsibility to take care of Christ's church.

"For I know this, that after my departing shall grievous wolves enter in among you, not sparing the flock." - One reason why the elders at Ephesus needed to take heed was that they would be attacked from the outside. The word for *"wolves"* in this verse is *lykoi*, and is the word that John wrote translating what Jesus had said:

> *But he that is an hireling, and not the shepherd, whose own the sheep are not, seeth the wolf coming, and leaveth the sheep, and fleeth: and the wolf catcheth them, and scattereth the sheep.* **(John 10:12)**

"Also of your own selves shall men arise, speaking perverse things, to draw away disciples after them." - Another reason why the elders needed to take heed was because they would be attacked from the inside by false teachers. From within the congregation would rise up false teachers who would pervert and twist the truth. This is why Paul taught them the whole counsel of God *for three years and ceased not to warn every one night and day with tears*. Satan has always been attacking God's people because this is the best way he can undermine the work of God's kingdom. While we do not understand why the battle rages, it shows us the reality of eternal things. The church is not a perfect place with perfect people, but is the most important organization in the world because the church is carrying the gospel. The gospel changes lives, and Satan is always trying to mix the truth with the false to either damn the souls of humans or to viciously divide and confuse the believers.

Paul Commends the Church to God

> **Acts 20:32-35 -** *And now, brethren, I commend you to God, and to the word of his grace, which is able to build you up, and to give you an inheritance among all them which are sanctified. I have coveted no man's silver, or gold, or apparel. Yea, ye yourselves know, that these hands have ministered unto my necessities, and to them that were with me. I have shewed you all things, how that so labouring ye ought to support the weak, and to remember the words of the Lord Jesus, how he said, It is more blessed to give than to receive.*

Paul is depositing the Ephesian elders into the hands of God. Only God and His Word can build the church. Programs cannot do it, entertainment cannot do it, marketing cannot do it, but only *God's word of grace* can build the church. Paul is reminding them that being a leader of a church is not supposed to turn into a financial business. While he was with them, he *coveted no man's silver, or gold, or apparel.*

"Yea, ye yourselves know, that these hands have ministered unto my necessities, and to them that were with me. I have

shewed you all things, how that so labouring ye ought to support the weak," - Paul wasn't afraid of hard work. A pastor of a church should lead by example by not being lazy or taking advantage of the people's generosity. It was a sad day when the church of God became a place for paid salaries to pastors, song leaders, organists, youth leaders, and janitors. Paul was letting the elders know that they were to be supporting the *weak* people in the church and to be careful not to offend them. They were to be more concerned about what they could give the flock than concerned about what their flock could give to them.

"and to remember the words of the Lord Jesus, how he said, It is more blessed to give than to receive." - This quote from Jesus is not recorded in the four gospels, but it summarizes the beatitudes that Jesus gave and was handed down orally to Paul. Not every miracle and teaching that Jesus gave is recorded. (**John 21:25**)

PAUL'S TEARFUL GOOD-BYE

Acts 20:36-37 - *And when he had thus spoken, he kneeled down, and prayed with them all. And they all wept sore, and fell on Paul's neck, and kissed him, Sorrowing most of all for the words which he spake, that they should see his face no more. And they accompanied him unto the ship.*

Paul ★ *kneeled down and probably led the prayer with them all.* Paul loved them, and they sincerely loved him. At this point *they wept and kept on weeping and kissed Paul.* They *sorrowed over all the words that Paul had spoken* because they knew that he was a chosen apostle of the Lord, and his words pierced their hearts. They also expected not to see Paul again until eternity. The elders of Ephesus *walked with Paul out to the ship.* What a heartbreaking moment for them that must have been! We are reminded of the condition of the church of Ephesus some 30-40 years later when Jesus sent them a letter in **Revelation 2:1-7.**

★ *(The words, "kneeled down" come from a Hebrew idiom, "kara," that is only recorded six times in the New Testament.* **(Mark 15:19, Luke 22:41, Acts 7:60, Acts 9:40, Acts 20:36, Acts 21:5)** *The fact that Jesus the Son of God kneeled down shows how powerful the meaning of this Hebrew word really is.)*

CHAPTER TWENTY-ONE

> PAUL ON HIS WAY TO JERUSALEM

Acts 21:1-2 - *And it came to pass, that after we were gotten from them, and had launched, we came with a straight course unto Coos, and the day following unto Rhodes, and from thence unto Patara: And finding a ship sailing over unto Phenicia, we went aboard, and set forth.*

The term *after we were gotten from them* means they had to *tear themselves away* from the Ephesian elders. After Paul and his companions launched, their first stop was ★ *Coos*, or *Cos*, a Greek island about 40 miles south of Miletus. The next day they arrive at ★ *Rhodes*, known as *"the island of the Roses."* Sailing east of *Rhodes*, they came to the seaport town of *Patara* in the province of Lycia. They found another ship, probably a larger one, because they would now have to sail across the northern part of the sometimes turbulent Mediterranean Sea. They were now on their way to *Phoenicia* in the province of Syria.

* *(Cos was the home of Hippocrates, the "father of medicine," born around 460BC. Even in Paul's day there was a large medical school there. Cos also had a large Jewish population.)*

* *(The city of Rhodes was famous for the Colossus of Rhodes, a statue of the Greek sun god Helios. It stood about 108 feet tall above the harbor and was considered one of the seven wonders of the ancient world. It was built in 280BC and was destroyed by the large earthquake in 226BC.)*

PAUL IS WARNED ABOUT GOING TO JERUSALEM

Acts 21:3-4 - Now when we had discovered Cyprus, we left it on the left hand, and sailed into Syria, and landed at Tyre: for there the ship was to unlade her burden. And finding disciples, we tarried there seven days: who said to Paul through the Spirit, that he should not go up to Jerusalem.

Once again Luke included the pronoun *we*, showing that he was aboard the ship with Paul. They bypassed *Cyprus* and sailed until they reached Syria, which included the land of Israel. The point of entry into Syria was *Tyre*, where the ship was to *unload her burden. Tyre* became part of the Roman Empire after the annexation of Phoenicia to Rome by Pompey the Great in 65BC. They *searched until they found some disciples* of Christ who were probably there as a result of the scattering of the believers from the stoning of Stephen in **Acts 7:54-60**. They stayed with them seven days while the ship was being unloaded.

These *disciples* who lived in *Tyre* tried to persuade Paul *not to go up to Jerusalem*. These disciples knew *through the Spirit* that Paul would suffer, but what they didn't know was that God had already revealed to Paul that he must go to Jerusalem. Paul was not being rebellious; he knew God's will for his life.

Paul Leaving Tyre for Jerusalem

Acts 21:5-6 - *And when we had accomplished those days, we departed and went our way; and they all brought us on our way, with wives and children, till we were out of the city: and we kneeled down on the shore, and prayed. And when we had taken our leave one of another, we took ship; and they returned home again.*

What a touching scene this is! This is the first time that *children* are mentioned in connection with the first church. These men with their wives and children escorted Paul and his companions all the way out of the city. When it was time to say farewell, Paul and his brethren *knelt down and prayed on the shore*. It was the custom to walk with the visiting travelers to the outskirts of the city, but it was not the custom to *kneel and pray*. Paul and his party took ship, and the other believers returned home.

This author finds a strong connection between Paul finding believers in Jesus in *Tyre* and the words of warning to the surrounding cities of Galilee from the mouth of Jesus some 30 years before:

Then began he to upbraid the cities wherein most of his mighty works were done, because they repented not: Woe unto thee, Chorazin! woe unto thee, Bethsaida! for if the mighty works, which were done in you, had been done in <u>Tyre and Sidon</u>, they would have repented long ago in sackcloth and ashes. But I say unto you, It shall be more tolerable for <u>Tyre and Sidon</u> at the day of judgment, than for you. **(Matthew 11:20-22)**

ARRIVAL IN PTOLEMAIS

Acts 21:7 - *And when we had finished our course from Tyre, we came to Ptolemais, and saluted the brethren, and abode with them one day.*

★ *Ptolemais* was located along the coastal plain of northern Israel, about twenty-five miles south of Tyre. There was a church there, and Paul stayed with them one day.

★ *(In Old Testament times the city was named Acco,* **Judges 1:31***, but in 285BC it was renamed Ptolemais after a Greek who ruled in Egypt. He named it in honor of himself and his father. When the Crusaders (1095-1291AD) captured Israel, they changed the name to Acre in honor of Joan of Arc. This is the name of the city in Israel today, and it has a population of almost 50,000.)*

PAUL ARRIVES AT CAESAREA

Acts 21:8-9 - *And the next day we that were of Paul's company departed, and came unto Caesarea:*

and we entered into the house of Philip the evangelist, which was one of the seven; and abode with him. And the same man had four daughters, virgins, which did prophesy.

The third leg of their journey brought them from *Ptolemias* to the seaport town of ★ *Caesarea*. They entered into the house of *Philip the evangelist*, not to be confused with Philip the apostle. This is the same Philip who brought the Ethiopian eunuch to faith in Christ in **Acts 8:27-39**. Many years later he is still there. What a wonderful title to be remembered in the sacred pages of the Holy Bible, *Philip the evangelist*! To be an *evangelist* was not a very common title, and the first time it is used. He was remembered for evangelizing the lost wherever he went. He was also *one of the seven*, meaning he was one of the first seven deacons of the church of Jerusalem. (**Acts 6:5**)

★ *(In the 4th century BC, this place was known as Strato's Tower. In 63BC it was taken over by Rome. In 22BC, Herod the Great began to rebuild the city and made it a beautiful and enormous seaport city to honor Caesar Augustus. He finished it around 10-12BC. Herod even built an aqueduct that brought in fresh water from the Carmel springs miles away. It was a major harbor and became the capital of the Roman province of Judea. Roman procurators, such as Pontius Pilate, lived there.)*

"And the same man had four daughters, virgins, which did prophesy." – Most likely these daughters were *virgins* for the sake of the ministry of Christ. They also *prophesied*, which shows that that spiritual gifts were available to women, as well as to men. These ★ *daughters* had the gift of teaching the deeper truths of the sacred scriptures as God had revealed to them. While the scriptures warn against women * usurping authority over a man in the church, (**I Corinthians 14:33-35**) they could use their gifts in many other situations, such as in their home.

* (Historians like Eusebius and Papias wrote that their names were Hermione, Eutychis, Irais, and Chariline. People came from long distances to hear their prophecies. They are said to have been buried in Heiropolis, Asia Minor, while others say they were buried in Caesarea.)

* (Much confusion and debate have risen up over the last 100 years about women being ministers. The Holy Bible makes it clear that women can be preachers of the gospel and are no less spiritual than men. We find the first person to see the resurrected Jesus was Mary Magdalene, and the other women from Galilee were there. (**Luke 24:10**) *Women are found in the Upper Room waiting for the coming of the Holy Spirit in* **Acts 1:14**. *While women have played a vital role in the spread of Christianity in the world, it is not clearly stated in the Bible that a woman should be a bishop or pastor of a local church. It seems that God desired for a man to hold the position of being a shepherd of the flock.* **I Timothy 2:11-14**)

AGABUS WARNS PAUL

Acts 22:10-13 - *And as we tarried there many days, there came down from Judaea a certain prophet, named Agabus. And when he was come unto us, he took Paul's girdle, and bound his own hands and feet, and said, Thus saith the Holy Ghost, So shall the Jews at Jerusalem bind the man that owneth this girdle, and shall deliver him into the hands of the Gentiles. And when we heard these things, both we,* *and they of that place, besought him not to go up to Jerusalem. Then Paul answered, What mean ye to weep and to break mine heart? for I am ready not to be bound only, but also to die at Jerusalem for the name of the Lord Jesus.*

Here we find a prophet named *Agabus, from* * *Judea*, that we studied about in **Acts 11:27-28**.

* *(Since Caesarea was part of Judea, how could Agabus come down from Judea to Caesarea? During Roman times, Caesarea was a part of Judea, but it was not a part of Old Testament Judah. This is something that only Jews would know. This implies that Luke was a Jew, not a Gentile, as some scholars say. This author made mention of this in an earlier work, "Luke, the Lord's Gospel.")*

"And when he was come unto us, he took Paul's girdle, and bound his own hands and feet, and said, Thus saith the Holy Ghost, So shall the Jews at Jerusalem bind the man that owneth this girdle, and shall deliver him into the hands of the Gentiles." - *Agabus* was performing a symbolic act. *Agabus* is warning Paul in a very real way what he had received from the *Holy Spirit*, not to go to Jerusalem. Notice that Agabus was prophesying that Paul would be *delivered into the hands of the Gentiles* (Romans). Paul confirmed this prophecy to be true in **Acts 28:17**. This is similar to what Jesus said would happen to him, when the Jews would turn Him over to the Gentiles in **Matthew 20:19.**

The prophecy of *Agabus* did not catch Paul by surprise. It only confirmed what God had already revealed to him. This was a prophecy of what would actually happen to Paul, not a command for Paul not to go to Jerusalem. Paul's going to Jerusalem would give him the opportunity to witness the gospel to mobs, kings, unbelieving Jews, the Sanhedrin, and to the Romans.

"And when we heard these things, both we, and they of that place, besought him not to go up to Jerusalem. Then Paul answered, What mean ye to weep and to break mine heart? for I am ready not to be bound only, but also to die at Jerusalem for the name of the Lord Jesus." - Even Luke was among the believers who tried to persuade Paul not to go up to Jerusalem. This was their emotional reaction to the vivid picture that *Agabus* had just painted for them, much like Peter when he didn't understand Jesus having to suffer in Jerusalem. (**Matthew 16:22**) They did not understand the calling that God had placed upon Paul's life. Sometimes godly people have good intentions, but they do not understand what the will of the Lord is for other people. Paul was willing to suffer anything for *the name of the Lord Jesus Christ*!

Paul at Jerusalem

Acts 21:14-17 - *And when he would not be persuaded, we ceased, saying, The will of the Lord be done. And after those days we took up our carriages, and went up to Jerusalem. There went with us also certain of the disciples of Caesarea, and brought with them one Mnason of Cyprus, an old disciple, with whom we should lodge. And when we were come to Jerusalem, the brethren received us gladly.*

It was indeed God's will for Paul to go up to Jerusalem. After many days *they took up their carriages, or baggage*, and walked over 50 miles ascending to Jerusalem.

"There went with us also certain of the disciples of Caesarea, and brought with them one Mnason of Cyprus, an old disciple, with whom we should lodge." - *Mnason* was from the island of Cyprus and had moved to Caesarea. He was probably one of the very first disciples of Jesus who was converted on the *Day of Pentecost* in **Acts 2**. *Mnason* may have had a home halfway between Caesarea and Jerusalem, or a house in Jerusalem. They received a warm welcome from their fellow believers in Jesus when they arrived in Jerusalem.

Paul Reports the Good Work of God

Acts 21:18-19 - *And the day following Paul went in with us unto James; and all the elders were present. And when he had saluted them, he declared particularly what things God had wrought among the Gentiles by his ministry.*

This moment marks the transition of Paul's third missionary journey and the beginning of the final stage of the book of Acts. Paul met with *James,* the half brother of Jesus, who was the leader of the Jerusalem church and *all of the elders.* The pronoun *us* is alluding to Luke again being with Paul. The other apostles were probably out of Jerusalem at this time. This would be the last time that Luke is recorded being with Paul until **Acts 27:1**.

> *"And when he had saluted them, he declared particularly what things God had wrought among the Gentiles by his ministry."* - Notice that Paul gives his respects to the elders of the Jerusalem church. In the original Greek, Paul went into every detail about his three journeys and the great miracles that God had done among the Gentiles. Here is the Jewish Paul giving details to the Jewish leaders in Jerusalem about what the God of Israel was doing among the Gentiles in the Roman world.

PAUL LEARNS OF HIS BAD REPUTATION

> **Acts 21:20-22** - *And when they heard it, they glorified the Lord, and said unto him, Thou seest, brother, how many thousands of Jews there are which believe; and they are all zealous of the law: And they are informed of thee, that thou teachest all the Jews which are among the Gentiles to forsake Moses, saying that they ought not to circumcise their children, neither to walk after the customs. What is it therefore? the multitude must needs come together: for they will hear that thou art come.*

Paul received a bittersweet welcome from the elders. They *glorified the Lord* in what he was doing among the Gentiles. The Jewish leaders in Jerusalem referred to Paul as *brother*.

"how many thousands of Jews there are which believe; and they are all zealous of the law:" - The Jewish leaders told Paul that *myriads,* or *tens of thousands* of the Jews had come to believe

in Jesus as their Messiah, but they were *zealous of the law*. Why? There are two possible reasons:

* *A Jewish believer is still free to keep the law if he/she desires. It's a voluntary decision.*
* *These Jews were immature, and they may have felt they were obligated to keep the law.*

"And they are informed of thee, that thou teachest all the Jews which are among the Gentiles to forsake Moses, saying that they ought not to circumcise their children, neither to walk after the customs." – They had heard some false rumors about Paul, most likely being spread by the Judaizers who had given him trouble along his journeys. The church leaders did not believe these rumors, but many of the congregants did believe them. Three things Paul was being accused of:

* *Jewish believers outside the land of Israel were to forsake the Law of Moses*
* *Jewish believers did not have to circumcise their male children*
* *Jewish believers did not have to keep the Jewish customs*

"What is it therefore? the multitude must needs come together: for they will hear that thou art come." – James and the elders knew that Paul was already too well known to conceal his visit in Jerusalem. They had a plan.

The Leaders Make a Recommendation

Acts 21:23-25 - *Do therefore this that we say to thee: We have four men which have a vow on them; Them take, and purify thyself with them, and be at* *charges with them, that they may shave their heads: and all may know that those things, whereof they were informed concerning thee, are nothing; but that thou thyself also walkest orderly, and keepest the law. As touching the Gentiles which believe, we have written and concluded that they observe no such thing, save only that they keep themselves from things offered to idols, and from blood, and from strangled, and from fornication.*

They recommended that Paul join himself to four other Jewish Christians who had taken the *Nazarite vow* that Paul had already taken in **Acts 18:18. (Numbers 6:1-21)**

"Them take, and purify thyself with them, and be at charges with them, that they may shave their heads" - Not only did they suggest that Paul join in the purification rites, but also to pay the peace offering for himself and the other four men. This would not only complete the vow, but also prove that these rumors about Paul were false. He was not trying to nullify the Law of Moses, and Paul was showing respect to the Jewish traditions. Paul wanted to show other Jews that trying to keep the Law would not give them salvation.

"As touching the Gentiles which believe, we have written and concluded that they observe no such thing, save only that they keep themselves from things offered to idols, and from blood, and from strangled, and from fornication." - The Jewish elders were confirming the decree of the Jerusalem Council in **Acts 15:22-29.** We can summarize two things that James was trying to say:

* *Gentiles were free from keeping the Law of Moses*
* *Jewish believers were also free to keep the Law of Moses*
   (Not as a means of salvation)

PAUL JOINS AND SPONSORS THE JEWISH RITE

Acts 21:26 - *Then Paul took the men, and the next day purifying himself with them entered into the temple, to signify the accomplishment of the days of purification, until that an offering should be offered for every one of them.*

Some scholars have written that Paul was being very hypocritical about keeping this vow. Paul was in the business of unifying the Jews and Gentiles. Paying for these offerings he considered as a memorial, not a means of salvation. It's always best when in doubt, allow the scriptures to speak:

And unto the Jews I became as a Jew, that I might gain the Jews; to them that are under the law, as under the law, that I might gain them that are under the law. **(I Corinthians 9:20)**

JEWS FROM ASIA STIR UP TEMPLE RIOT

Acts 21:27-30 - *And when the seven days were almost ended, the Jews which were of Asia, when they saw him in the temple, stirred up all the people, and laid hands on him, Crying out, Men of Israel, help: This is the man, that teacheth all men every* *where against the people, and the law, and this place: and further brought Greeks also into the temple, and hath polluted this holy place. (For they had seen before with him in the city Trophimus an Ephesian, whom they supposed that Paul had brought into the temple.) And all the city was moved, and the people ran together: and they took Paul, and drew him out of the temple: and forthwith the doors were shut.*

The *Nazarite vow* lasted eight days **(Numbers 6:10)**, and on the seventh day of the purification rites, there were Jews from Asia who started trouble. These were some of the Jews who had followed Paul on his journeys always stirring up riots. They had come to Jerusalem to keep the *Feast of Passover* and decided to stay unto the *Feast of Pentecost*.

"when they saw him in the temple, stirred up all the people, and laid hands on him, Crying out, Men of Israel, help: This is the man, that teacheth all men every where against the people, and the law, and this place" – When the Jews from Asia saw Paul in the temple, they began to stir up the people and Cry out! They were accusing Paul of *teaching all men everywhere against the Jews*. Again, Paul was teaching that people could only receive righteousness through the Lord Jesus Christ, not by keeping the Jewish Law. This was a false claim against Paul.

"and further brought Greeks also into the temple, and hath polluted this holy place. (For they had seen before with him in the city Trophimus an Ephesian, whom they supposed that Paul had brought into the temple.)" – They were accusing Paul of *teaching against the temple in Jerusalem*. They saw the Gentile, *Trophimus, an Ephesian*, walking with Paul in the

streets of Jerusalem and assumed that he had * brought him into the Jewish Temple. These hateful Jews were probably from Ephesus in Asia Minor.

(Gentiles were allowed in the outer Court of the Gentiles, but were not allowed in the inner Court of the Women, also called the Court of Israel. Gentiles who entered into the inner courts would be executed, even a Roman. There was an inscription at the entrance to the inner court that read: "No alien may enter within the barrier and wall around the Temple. Whoever is caught is alone responsible for the death which follows.")

"And all the city was moved, and the people ran together: and they took Paul, and drew him out of the temple: and forthwith the doors were shut." - The false news was spread so quickly and so violently that the entire *city of Jerusalem was moved*. The people dragged Paul from the inner court of the Temple to the outer court and *shut the doors*. Their intent was to bring Paul to a location where he could be executed quickly. Man's blood could not be shed in the inner court of the Temple.

ROMAN SOLDIERS RESCUE PAUL

Acts 21:31-36 - *And as they went about to kill him, tidings came unto the chief captain of the band, that all Jerusalem was in an uproar. Who immediately took soldiers and centurions, and ran down unto them: and when they saw the chief captain and the soldiers, they left beating of Paul. Then the chief captain came near, and took him, and commanded him to be bound with two chains; and demanded who* *he was, and what he had done. And some cried one thing, some another, among the multitude: and when he could not know the certainty for the tumult, he commanded him to be carried into the castle. And when he came upon the stairs, so it was, that he was borne of the soldiers for the violence of the people. For the multitude of the people followed after, crying, Away with him.*

What a thought! God had called the Jewish apostle Paul to carry the glorious gospel of Jesus the Messiah into the Roman world, and now many of the Jews were trying to *kill him* in the holy city of Jerusalem. There were *informers* who came and told what was happening to the ★ *chief captain of the band of the Roman soldiers*. The *chief captain* would have been in command of 600-1,000 troops. The Roman chief captain was stationed in the northwest corner of the Temple compound at the ★ *Antonio Fortress*. There was a stairwell leading directly down to the outer court where they were trying to kill Paul.

- ★ *(According to Acts 23:26, this chief captain was Claudius Lysias.)*
- ★ *(The Antonio Fortress was built by Herod the Great (37-1BC) and named after Mark Antony. It is also possibly the place where Jesus stood before Pontius Pilate in* **John 19:13.**)

"Who immediately took soldiers and centurions, and ran down unto them: and when they saw the chief captain and the soldiers, they left beating of Paul" - The Romans had no concern for Paul. They were concerned about keeping public order. They took Paul prisoner to remove the cause of the riot.

The Jews were afraid of the Romans, and when they saw the garrison of soldiers coming, *they stopped beating Paul.*

"Then the chief captain came near, and took him, and commanded him to be bound with two chains; and demanded who he was, and what he had done." – Did Paul remember the prophecy of Agabus in **Acts 21:11**? *Two chains* meant that Paul would have been handcuffed to a soldier on both sides. This was normally the way the Romans treated criminals, but they *demanded to find out just who Paul was and what he had done.*

"And some cried one thing, some another, among the multitude: and when he could not know the certainty for the tumult, he commanded him to be carried into the castle." – The people themselves were confused as to why they were causing the riot. When the captain of the soldiers could not make any *certainty* with the various accusations of the Jews, *he commanded Paul to be brought to the castle, or the Antonio Fortress.*

"And when he came upon the stairs, so it was, that he was borne of the soldiers for the violence of the people. For the multitude of the people followed after, crying, Away with him." – When the *soldiers* and Paul reached the *stairs* that led into the Antonio Fortress, they had to *lift up Paul* and carry him because the mob was so great. Some of the mob that was following began to cry out, ★ *Away with him*, or *Kill him*! Since the Roman soldiers had rescued Paul, he was now a prisoner of Rome. This incident began his five–year Roman imprisonment.

★ *(These same words were shouted at the trial of Jesus in* **Luke 23:18** *and* **John 19:15**.*)*

Paul Given Permission to Speak

Acts 21:37-40 - *And as Paul was to be led into the castle, he said unto the chief captain, May I speak unto thee? Who said, Canst thou speak Greek? Art not thou that Egyptian, which before these days madest an uproar, and leddest out into the wilderness four thousand men that were murderers? But Paul said, I am a man which am a Jew of Tarsus, a city in Cilicia, a citizen of no mean city: and, I beseech thee, suffer me to speak unto the people. And when he had given him licence, Paul stood on the stairs, and beckoned with the hand unto the people. And when there was made a great silence, he spake unto them in the Hebrew tongue, saying,*

When Paul spoke to the Roman captain, he spoke in the *Greek* language. Strangely enough, when the Roman soldier heard Paul speak fluent Greek, it led him to mistakenly identify Paul as an * *Egyptian* terrorist that attacked Jerusalem between the years of 52-58AD.

* *("There was an Egyptian false prophet that did the Jews more mischief than the former; for he was a cheat, and pretended to be a prophet also, and got together thirty thousand men that were deluded by him; these he led round about from the wilderness to the mount which was called the Mount of Olives. He was ready to break into Jerusalem by force from that place; and if he could but once conquer the Roman garrison and the people, he intended to rule them by the assistance of those guards of his that were to break into the city with him. About this time, someone came out of Egypt to Jerusalem, claiming to be a prophet.*

He advised the crowd to go along with him to the Mount of Olives, as it was called, which lay over against the city, and at the distance of a kilometer. He added that he would show them from hence how the walls of Jerusalem would fall down at his command, and he promised them that he would procure them an entrance into the city through those collapsed walls. Now when Felix was informed of these things, he ordered his soldiers to take their weapons, and came against them with a great number of horsemen and footmen from Jerusalem, and attacked the Egyptian and the people that were with him. He slew four hundred of them, and took two hundred alive. The Egyptian himself escaped out of the fight, but did not appear any more. And again the robbers stirred up the people to make war with the Romans, and said they ought not to obey them at all; and when any persons would not comply with them, they set fire to their villages, and plundered them." **Flavius Josephus Jewish War 2.259-263 and Jewish Antiquities 20.169-171; Acts of the apostles 21.38)**

"But Paul said, I am a man which am a Jew of Tarsus, a city in Cilicia, a citizen of no mean city: and, I beseech thee, suffer me to speak unto the people." – Paul told the captain that he was a citizen of *Tarsus*, not a suspected terrorist from Egypt. He was a Jew with a Roman citizenship from a *very significant city*. By the way Paul politely requested to speak and the fact that he was a Roman citizen, the Roman allowed Paul to speak.

"And when he had given him licence, Paul stood on the stairs, and beckoned with the hand unto the people. And when there was made a great silence, he spake unto them in the Hebrew tongue, saying," – Paul was granted permission and stood on the stairs and motioned to the crowd by shaking his hand downward. This was an ancient method of gaining the attention of what someone had to say. It's interesting that Paul spoke to the Jewish mob in the ★ *Hebrew* language.

★ *(While this truth has been brought out previously, it is an important truth that is overlooked by many Bible colleges today. Paul wrote his epistles in the Greek language, which was the common language of the Roman Empire, in order to <u>communicate</u> the gospel. The Greek language was the result of Hellenization that was brought into the known world by the pagan, Alexander the Great. (356-323BC) When Paul spoke to the religious Jews in Israel, he used the sacred Hebrew tongue. This was the pure language of the Old Testament* **(Zephaniah 3:9)** *and the language of Jesus* **(Acts 26:14).** *The Greek language was the communicative language, while the Hebrew is the language of thought of the Holy Bible. For example: When studying the Life and Ministry of Christ, it can only be properly interpreted and connected to the Old Testament by the Hebrew understanding.)*

CHAPTER TWENTY-TWO

Paul's Sermon to the Jerusalem Mob

Acts 22:1-2 - *Men, brethren, and fathers, hear ye my defence which I make now unto you. (And when they heard that he spake in the Hebrew tongue to them, they kept the more silence: and he saith,)*

Paul begins by using the same phrase that Stephen used in **Acts 7:2**: *Men, brethren, and fathers.* This address reminded the mob that Paul was a fellow Jew, and he was asking them to listen to his *defense* of the actions of his previous life. There was a hush that fell on the crowd when they heard Paul speak in their mother tongue, *Hebrew.*

Paul Tells Them of His Jewish Background

Acts 22:3 - *I am verily a man which am a Jew, born in Tarsus, a city in Cilicia, yet brought up in this city at the feet of Gamaliel, and taught according to the perfect manner of the law of the fathers, and was zealous toward God, as ye all are this day.*

Before Paul was converted as a follower of Jesus of Nazareth, the Jewish Messiah, he wanted them to know that he was a practicing *Jew and very zealous toward the law of their fathers.* Though he was *born in Tarsus, a city in Cilicia, he was brought up in Jerusalem and was taught by sitting at the feet of the rabbi Gamaliel.* Becoming a follower of Jesus did not erase his Jewishness. Paul wanted them to know that he had been guilty of the same kind of ★ misplaced zeal as they. He had to choose his words wisely because this was the same mob that wanted to kill him.

★ *(This reminds us of what Paul said in* **Philippians 3:5-7**: *"Circumcised the eighth day, of the stock of Israel, of the tribe of Benjamin, an Hebrew of the Hebrews; as touching the law, a Pharisee; Concerning zeal, persecuting the church; touching the righteousness which is in the law, blameless. But what things were gain to me, those I counted loss for Christ.")*

PAUL'S CONFESSION OF PERSECUTING CHRISTIANS

Acts 22:4-5 - And I persecuted this way unto the death, binding and delivering into prisons both men and women. As also the high priest doth bear me witness, and all the estate of the elders: from whom also I received letters unto the brethren, and went to Damascus, to bring them which were there bound unto Jerusalem, for to be punished.

Paul admitted that he was guilty of persecuting *this Way* unto the death. He would later describe his ignorance and sin as making him feel like the chief of sinners. **(I Timothy 1:13-**

15) *Paul had received letters from Caiaphas, the high priest, to go outside of the land to Damascus, and bring the fellow believer in Christ to Jerusalem to be punished.* His point was that he wasn't going to Damascus to preach the gospel, he was going to persecute the Jewish Christians. Paul wanted the mob to know that he could relate to them, and he understood why they had started a riot against him.

Paul Describes His Supernatural Conversion

Acts 22:6-11 - *And it came to pass, that, as I made my journey, and was come nigh unto Damascus about noon, suddenly there shone from heaven a great light round about me. And I fell unto the ground, and heard a voice saying unto me, Saul, Saul, why persecutest thou me? And I answered, Who art thou, Lord? And he said unto me, I am Jesus of Nazareth, whom thou persecutest. And they that were with me saw indeed the light, and were afraid; but they heard not the voice of him that spake to me. And I said, What shall I do, Lord? And the Lord said unto me, Arise, and go into Damascus; and there it shall be told thee of all things which are appointed for thee to do. And when I could not see for the glory of that light, being led by the hand of them that were with me, I came into Damascus.*

Paul's conversion is given three times in the book of Acts: **Acts 9, Acts 22,** and **Acts 26.** To put it simply, Paul was saying to the crowd that he was just like them until *a heavenly* *light shined down upon him on his way to Damascus.* The heavenly light was brighter than the noonday sun. The reason the light was so great was because it was the *Shechinah glory of God.*

"And I fell unto the ground, and heard a voice saying unto me, Saul, Saul, why persecutest thou me? And I answered, Who art thou, Lord? And he said unto me, I am Jesus of Nazareth, whom thou persecutest" - Falling to the ground was a biblical response when someone was confronted with the presence of God. Notice carefully that Saul's name was called out twice for *persecuting Jesus Himself,* not the believers in Jesus.

"And they that were with me saw indeed the light, and were afraid; but they heard not the voice of him that spake to me." - Those who were traveling with Paul saw the light, but they did not hear the voice that spoke with him. **Acts 9:7** states that they were conscious of a noise, but they could not make out what Jesus said to Paul.

"And I said, What shall I do, Lord? And the Lord said unto me, Arise, and go into Damascus; and there it shall be told thee of all things which are appointed for thee to do. And when I could not see for the glory of that light, being led by the hand of them that were with me, I came into Damascus." - The glorious light that shined from heaven and the powerful voice of the Lord Jesus Christ caused Paul to submit, *What shall I do,*
★ *Lord?* Paul's mission to Damascus was forever changed, and Jesus would let him know what he wanted him to do once Paul arrived. Paul had an additional problem. The light from heaven made him blind, and his companions would lead him by the hand into Damascus.

★ *(There is much debate over the centuries about Paul using the word "Lord" here. Did he know that Jesus was God at this point? The answer is found in the original word here, "Kyrios," which is the Greek equivalent for the Hebrew "Jehovah." This is a major point that should not go unnoticed. Paul was speaking to a monotheistic Jewish crowd who only believed in one God. Now Paul is saying to them that Jesus and God are the same person.)*

PAUL DESCRIBES HIS EXPERIENCE IN DAMASCUS

Acts 22:12-16 - And one Ananias, a devout man according to the law, having a good report of all the Jews which dwelt there, Came unto me, and stood, and said unto me, Brother Saul, receive thy sight. And the same hour I looked up upon him. And he said, The God of our fathers hath chosen thee, that thou shouldest know his will, and see that Just One, and shouldest hear the voice of his mouth. For thou shalt be his witness unto all men of what thou hast seen and heard. And now why tarriest thou? arise, and be baptized, and wash away thy sins, calling on the name of the Lord.

The Lord had the *devout* ★ Ananias ready to meet Paul and give him back his sight. He then witnessed to Paul to have faith in Jesus as the Messiah. Notice that the disciple Ananias did not criticize or condemn Paul for what he had done, but gave him encouraging news. *The God of our fathers hath chosen thee.* As Paul was looking upon Ananias, he was told that he would know God's will, and that it was ordained for Paul to see and to hear *the Just One, Jesus the Messiah.* What Paul had experienced was not just for his own salvation, he would be *witness unto all men what he had seen and heard.*

* (There is an underground structure in Damascus today that is believed to be the home of Ananias. He was martyred in Eleutheropolis, about 50 miles southwest of Jerusalem. There is a tomb of Ananias in the Zoravor Church in Armenia.)

"arise, and be baptized, and wash away thy sins, calling on the name of the Lord." - The book of Acts is again a transitional book where much false doctrine has originated. Because of the many doctrines of water baptism in different denominational churches, this verse has been used to try to prove that the Bible teaches baptismal regeneration. The Bible is clear that salvation is by grace through faith. **(John 3:16-17, Ephesians 2:8-9)** In the original Greek, a correct way to translate this phrase is, *"Rise up, get yourself baptized, and have your sins washed away by calling on his name."*

It also helps to connect this verse to **Acts 2:38**. We Gentiles need to understand that the Jewish understanding of water baptism was that once one heard the message of Christ, one was to get up and be identified with Him immediately. Paul's sins had been washed away through his faith in Jesus as Israel's Messiah before he was water baptized, but the baptism would be the outward sign of his true conversion. Paul was also separating himself from the unbelieving Jews, who would suffer the destruction of Jerusalem in 70AD.

The phrase *on the name of the Lord* has caused much debate as well. Paul probably called on the Hebrew *name of Yeshua* because he had just seen the glory of the risen Savior and heard

His voice on the Damascus Road. Some churches teach that one must be baptized in *Jesus* name, or in the name of the *Lord Jesus Christ,* or *the Father, the Son, and the Holy Spirit* as Jesus taught in **Matthew 28:19.** This author prefers to use the words that Jesus Himself said. The true meaning of Paul's water baptism was that he should align his life and thoughts around the Person of Jesus. He must be identified with His authority. *The name of* is a Hebrew idiom for everything that Jesus did and everything He claimed to be.

PAUL'S VISION FROM JESUS

> **Acts 22:17-18 -** *And it came to pass, that, when I was come again to Jerusalem, even while I prayed in the temple, I was in a trance; And saw him saying unto me, Make haste, and get thee quickly out of Jerusalem: for they will not receive thy testimony concerning me.*

Paul is still addressing the Jewish mob with some new information that had not been previously recorded by Luke. Paul was inspired to mention this vision now out of necessity. After his conversion in Damascus, *Paul came again to Jerusalem. While he was praying in the temple, he fell into a trance and saw Jesus.* Paul was given a sense of urgency by Jesus to leave Jerusalem because the Jews would not receive his testimony. This is the incident that occurred in **Acts 9:29-30.**

Paul's Answer to Jesus

Acts 22:19-21 - *And I said, Lord, they know that I imprisoned and beat in every synagogue them that believed on thee: And when the blood of thy martyr Stephen was shed, I also was standing by, and consenting unto his death, and kept the raiment of them that slew him. And he said unto me, Depart: for I will send thee far hence unto the Gentiles.*

Paul is telling the crowd here that he tried to argue somewhat with the Lord's command. He thought that because the Jewish people knew that he had persecuted the Jewish Christians, they would listen to him. It's interesting that Paul mentions again that he was there at the killing of *Stephen* and *kept the raiment* that he wore. Paul was trying to explain to Jesus why he should stay in Jerusalem.

"And he said unto me, Depart: for I will send thee far hence unto the Gentiles." - Paul would depart and travel northward to Tarsus where he would stay for ten years until he was sought out by Barnabas to go to Antioch **(Acts 11:25-26)** Paul is telling the mob that he was sent to preach the gospel *unto the Gentiles*, which meant that he would travel much of the Roman world. He wanted them to know that he could not disobey the command he had received from the Lord. It wasn't Paul's idea. He wanted to go to Jerusalem, but this wasn't God's plan for his life.

The Mob's Response

> **Acts 22:22-23** - *And they gave him audience unto this word, and then lifted up their voices, and said, Away with such a fellow from the earth: for it is not fit that he should live. And as they cried out, and cast off their clothes, and threw dust into the air,*

There was a specific word in Paul's address to the Jewish audience that triggered a fast response, *Gentiles*! Their issue was twofold:

* **The Gentiles (Romans) were the oppressors of the Jews**
* **Paul's way of converting Gentiles did not mandate circumcision**

The Jewish mob gave three absolute actions:

* **Paul should be killed**
* **They cast off their clothes**
* **They threw * dust up in the air**

* *(Throwing dust up in the air over their heads is a custom that goes all the way back to the pyramid texts in the Egyptian culture. Writings were found dating from 2278BC where they would throw dust up in the air at someone's funeral. The Hebrew people may have borrowed this culture while they were in slavery in Egypt.* **(Job 2:12, Joshua 7:6)** *This helps to connect the imagery with the intent of the Jewish mob. They were giving a picture of wanting Paul dead and already having his funeral.)*

PAUL IS ARRESTED

Acts 22:24 - *The chief captain commanded him to be brought into the castle, and bade that he should be examined by scourging; that he might know wherefore they cried so against him.*

Paul was brought as a prisoner into the Antonio fortress, and this began his five years of bondage. The *chief captain* <u>intended</u> to interrogate Paul by the terrible use of a *Roman scourge*, but he really didn't know what was going on since he only spoke Latin and Greek, while Paul had been speaking in Hebrew. The *Roman scourge*, called a *flagellum*, had no limits on the number of lashes given, many times ending in death, while the Jewish law had a limit of 40 lashes.

PAUL SPEAKS TO THE ROMAN CENTURION

Acts 22:25-27 - *And as they bound him with thongs, Paul said unto the centurion that stood by, Is it lawful for you to scourge a man that is a Roman, and uncondemned? When the centurion heard that, he went and told the chief captain, saying, Take heed what thou doest: for this man is a Roman. Then the chief captain came, and said unto him, Tell me, art thou a Roman? He said, Yea.*

When they *bound Paul with leather thongs* to a post ready to scourge him, he issued a protest to the *centurion*. Paul knew the Roman law was about to be violated by not having a trial and that Paul was a Roman citizen. When the centurion went to the chief captain he said, *"What are you at the point of doing? This man is a Roman."* The *chief captain* came and asked Paul, *art thou a Roman?* Paul simply answered, *"Yea."*

PAUL IS QUESTIONED ABOUT HIS CITIZENSHIP

Acts 22:28-29 - *And the chief captain answered, With a great sum obtained I this freedom. And Paul said, But I was free born. Then straightway they departed from him which should have examined him: and the chief captain also was afraid, after he knew that he was a Roman, and because he had bound him.*

The *chief captain* had given a large sum of money to become a Roman citizen, and Paul claims that he was ★ *free born*. Instead of examining Paul, they became afraid after they found out they had *bound up a Roman citizen* and were ready to scourge him.

★ *(It was very rare and unusual that an intelligent, religious Jew, who was raised under the Jewish Law, would also be a free born Roman citizen. It is believed that Paul's parents or grandparents were once slaves of Rome, and after many years of obedience to their owners, were made free under Roman law. Children of the once slaves to Rome were born free. Thus Paul was born a free Roman citizen. They would have attended the Synagogue of the Libertines.* **(Acts 6:9)** *We can view this as one of the reasons why God chose the Jewish and Roman citizen Paul to carry the gospel to the Gentiles.)*

The Captain Gives Paul to the Jewish Council

Acts 22:30 - *On the morrow, because he would have known the certainty wherefore he was accused of the Jews, he loosed him from his bands, and commanded the chief priests and all their council to appear, and brought Paul down, and set him before them.*

The Jewish council convened *on the morrow*. The chief captain wanted to know why Paul was being *accused*. Paul probably felt as though he was getting a second chance by being *loosed from his bands*. The Roman chief captain did three things:

* *He loosed the bands of Paul*
* *He ordered the Jewish leaders to assemble*
* *He set Paul down before the Jewish leaders*

This was not a trial, but to see if there was a cause for a trial. The Jewish council was made up of Sadducees and Pharisees. God's general plan had been revealed to Paul in **Acts 9:15-16**, but Paul didn't know how it would all play out. As Paul was sitting before the Sanhedrin, he had total trust that God was working out His plan for his life.

CHAPTER TWENTY-THREE

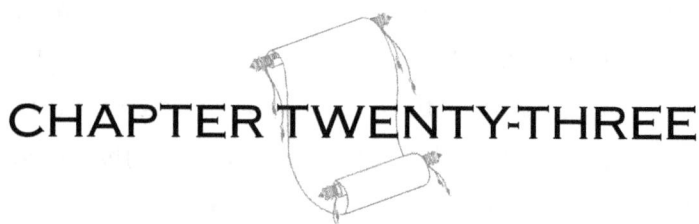

PAUL'S DEFENSE BEFORE THE SANHEDRIN

Acts 23:1-2 - *And Paul, earnestly beholding the council, said, Men and brethren, I have lived in all good conscience before God until this day. And the high priest* ★ *Ananias commanded them that stood by him to smite him on the mouth.*

Paul is looking at his defense as another great opportunity to preach Christ to his fellow Jewish *brethren*. It has been rightfully said that when talking to others, always look them in the eye. Try to imagine the earnestness in the eyes of Paul as he *beheld the council*. Paul had *lived before God in all good conscience*. Even when he was persecuting the church, he thought he was doing the right thing. For the high priest Ananias to *command them to smite Paul on the mouth* was not only against Jewish law, but it was also the action taken against Jesus in **John 18:22-23.** It was written in Jewish writings, *"He who strikes the cheek of one Israelite, strikes as it were the glory of God."*

★ *(This high priest was called Ananias, the son of Nebedeus. He held the office from 42-58AD. Ananias was appointed by Herod*

Chalcis, the grandson of Herod the Great. He was known to be hot-tempered, profane, greedy, and pro-Roman. Being deposed in 59AD, he was eventually assassinated by the Zealots in 66 AD.)

PAUL'S RESPONSE TO THE SMITING OF HIS FACE

Acts 23:3-5 - *Then said Paul unto him, God shall smite thee, thou whited wall: for sittest thou to judge me after the law, and commandest me to be smitten contrary to the law? And they that stood by said, Revilest thou God's high priest? Then said Paul, I wist not, brethren, that he was the high priest: for it is written, Thou shalt not speak evil of the ruler of thy people.*

Paul's prediction that *God would smite the high priest* was fulfilled in the way he died in 66AD. Paul calling him *a whited wall* was parallel to Jesus referring to the Pharisees as *whited sepulchers* in **Matthew 23:27.** Ananias was supposed to be there to uphold the Jewish law, and yet he had already broken the law by having Paul smitten on the face. **(Deut.25:1-2)**

"And they that stood by said, Revilest thou God's high priest?" - The office of the high priest always required respect, even if the man himself did not. In this case, Ananias did not deserve any respect, but it was the office that people were to respect.

"Then said Paul, I wist not, brethren, that he was the high priest: for it is written, Thou shalt not speak evil of the ruler of thy people." - Why did Paul not recognize Ananias as the high priest?

* *The office of the high priest had changed hands several times since Paul had been away*
* *Because they were not meeting in the usual place, but in the Antonio Fortress, Ananias may not have been wearing his usual high priestly garments*
* *Paul may have been using sarcasm since he didn't think the high priest would act in such a profane manner*

Paul agreed that it was written, *"Thou shalt not speak evil of the ruler of the people."* **(Exodus 22:28)**

Paul Uses Clever Strategy

Acts 23:6 – *But when Paul perceived that the one part were Sadducees, and the other Pharisees, he cried out in the council, Men and brethren, I am a Pharisee, the son of a Pharisee: of the hope and resurrection of the dead I am called in question.*

Since Paul knew that the Sanhedrin was made up of Sadducees and Pharisees, he decided to use the principle of *divide and conquer*. He made a loud proclamation, *"Men and brethren, I am a Pharisee, the son of a Pharisee: of the hope and resurrection of the dead I am called in question."* Paul not only was raised to become a Pharisee, he still followed the basic tenets of Pharisaism, such as the *resurrection of the dead*. Paul knew that the Sadducees did not believe in *a* resurrection, but the Pharisees did. He was specifically referring to *the* resurrection of Jesus of Nazareth, the Son of God. Paul was stricken down on the road to Damascus by the risen Christ, and he was more than convinced that Jesus was Israel's Messiah. He knew this subject would divide the Sanhedrin.

THE COUNCIL IS DIVIDED

> **Acts 23:7-10 - *And when he had so said, there arose a dissension between the Pharisees and the Sadducees: and the multitude was divided. For the Sadducees say that there is no resurrection, neither angel, nor spirit: but the Pharisees confess both. And there arose a great cry: and the scribes that were of the Pharisees' part arose, and strove, saying, We find no evil in this man: but if a spirit or an angel hath spoken to him, let us not fight against God. And when there arose a great dissension, the chief captain, fearing lest Paul should have been pulled in pieces of them, commanded the soldiers to go down, and to take him by force from among them, and to bring him into the castle.***

The Sadducees denied the possibility of the *resurrection* and also the existence of *angels or spirits*. The Pharisees, on the other hand, believed in all three. **(Matthew 22:23-33)**

"And there arose a great cry: and the scribes that were of the Pharisees' part arose, and strove, saying, We find no evil in this man: but if a spirit or an angel hath spoken to him, let us not fight against God" - The *scribes* were part of the Pharisees who spent their lives copying down the Holy Scriptures. They were called *sopherim* in Hebrew, which meant that they were copyists of the written Word and held a lot of authority when

it came to making religious decisions. Since they could find no fault in Paul, they were even suggesting that an *angel or a spirit* may have spoken to him. If Paul had received a special revelation, they would be *fighting against God*.

"And when there arose a great dissension, the chief captain, fearing lest Paul should have been pulled in pieces of them, commanded the soldiers to go down, and to take him by force from among them, and to bring him into the castle." - The division among the Sadducees, Pharisees, and the scribes was so violent that the *chief captain* commanded the soldiers to walk down the steps and bring Paul into the fortress. While Paul's opportunity was not successful, God used a Roman officer to rescue Paul.

Jesus Stands by Paul

Acts 23:11 - *And the night following the Lord stood by him, and said, Be of good cheer, Paul: for as thou hast testified of me in Jerusalem, so must thou bear witness also at Rome.*

Paul may have been having a miserable night trying to sleep thinking about how he failed. Paul, being human, was worried about what was next and how God was going to work through him now? Jesus stepped in to give Paul the assurance that He was with him and to bring comfort in his hour of darkness. Notice the three things that Jesus told Paul:

* *Be of good cheer*
* *Paul was in God's will for testifying about Him in Jerusalem*

★ *Paul must also bear witness of Him in Rome*

It's better to be in a jail cell with Jesus than to be a free man without Jesus. Paul was where God wanted him to be even though his circumstances were not good. He would be protected until his job was finished in Rome. We are reminded of Jesus speaking the same words, *"Be of good cheer,"* when the disciples were in a storm out on the Sea of Galilee. **(Matthew 14:27)**

THE CONSPIRACY TO KILL PAUL

Acts 23:12-15 - *And when it was day, certain of the Jews banded together, and bound themselves under a curse, saying that they would neither eat nor drink till they had killed Paul. And they were more than forty which had made this conspiracy. And they came to the chief priests and elders, and said, We have bound ourselves under a great curse, that we will eat nothing until we have slain Paul. Now therefore ye with the council signify to the chief captain that he bring him down unto you to morrow, as though ye would inquire something more perfectly concerning him: and we, or ever he come near, are ready to kill him.*

This *conspiracy from 40 men* happened the very next day after Jesus appeared to Paul. These evil men even took an oath that they would *neither eat nor drink till they had killed Paul*. This is called the ★ curse of *cherem* in Hebrew and is found in several places in the Old Testament. **(Lev.26:21, Deut.7:26, Joshua 6:17, Malachi 4:6)**

(It seems that this group of men were what was called dagger-men, possibly even Zealots. This curse or oath they took could be loosed from an individual by going to one of the religious sages. There was a clause in their traditions that said, "if by not eating he sins against his own life." It just goes to show how evil these 40 men were by lying about taking a pretended vow in order to kill Paul. Paul would live nine more years until he reached Rome, and he would not die from Jewish hands, but by the Romans.)

"Now therefore ye with the council signify to the chief captain that he bring him down unto you to morrow, as though ye would inquire something more perfectly concerning him: and we, or ever he come near, are ready to kill him." – These 40 men wanted to involve the Sanhedrin with their plot. They wanted the Sanhedrin to ask the Roman *chief captain* to bring Paul down to them in a pretense that they wanted to ask Paul something else. While Paul was on his way, they would assassinate him.

Paul's Nephew Warns the Roman Commander

Acts 23:16-22 - *And when Paul's sister's son heard of their lying in wait, he went and entered into the castle, and told Paul. Then Paul called one of the centurions unto him, and said, Bring this young man unto the chief captain: for he hath a certain thing to tell him. So he took him, and brought him to the chief captain, and said, Paul the prisoner called me unto him, and prayed me to bring this young man unto thee, who hath something to say unto thee. Then the chief captain took him by the hand, and went with* *him aside privately, and asked him, What is that thou hast to tell me? And he said, The Jews have agreed to desire thee that thou wouldest bring down Paul to morrow into the council, as though they would inquire somewhat of him more perfectly. But do not thou yield unto them: for there lie in wait for him of them more than forty men, which have bound themselves with an oath, that they will neither eat nor drink till they have killed him: and now are they ready, looking for a promise from thee. So the chief captain then let the young man depart, and charged him, See thou tell no man that thou hast shewed these things to me.*

  This is a part of the life and ministry of the apostle Paul that goes unnoticed. God had to protect Paul in order for him to go to Rome. He uses the Romans, and here he uses *Paul's* ⋆ *sister's son*. It's likely that Paul may have stayed with his sister in Jerusalem in times past, and Paul's nephew was very much aware of what was going on with his uncle. Paul's nephew was either present during the ambush by the Jews, or he had been told about what was going on. He went into the Antonio Fortress and told Paul about the 40 men who were lying in wait to kill him. *Paul told the centurion to go and tell the chief captain about this young man who had something important to tell him.* Once again, we see God's hand orchestrating the events and using a *Roman centurion* to bring Paul's nephew to the *chief captain*. Isn't it amazing!

  ⋆ *(While Paul mentions several of his relatives in* **Romans 16**, *we do not know who his sister was. The bravery that the nephew* *showed by going to the Roman chief captain proved his love for his uncle. We do not know for sure, but since Paul and his sister were both born from the Tribe of Benjamin (***Philippians 3:5***), and the action they took to rescue Paul, it stands to reason that his sister and son were believers in Christ.)*

This is the first time that Paul is referred to as a *prisoner*. Notice these three titles for Paul:

* *Paul the persecutor*
* *Paul the apostle*
* *Paul the prisoner*

Paul's nephew using the word *Jews* is not referring to the Jews in general, but to the corrupt Jewish leaders. The young man was able to give the *chief captain* advice about the 40 conspirators who had taken an oath to assassinate Paul. The Holy Spirit used the words of Paul's nephew to touch the heart of the *chief captain*. He let the young man go and told him not to tell anyone what he had spoken to him.

Paul Escapes to Caesarea with Full Military Escort

> **Acts 23:23-24 - *And he called unto him two centurions, saying, Make ready two hundred soldiers to go to Caesarea, and horsemen threescore and ten, and spearmen two hundred, at the third hour of the night; And provide them beasts, that they may set Paul on, and bring him safe unto Felix the governor.***

Paul had made a large impact for Christ in the Roman world and caused a large riot against himself in Jerusalem. When the Roman chief captain saw the uprising that Paul caused with the Sanhedrin, he was very cautious about his welfare. We must remember that the Roman officers had to answer to Caesar about keeping peace in their own territories. If they could not keep peace, they were not considered worthy enough to hold office.

Altogether there were 470 Roman soldiers appointed to take Paul between the hours of 9 and 10 pm. They were ordered to put Paul on a donkey or a horse on his way to Caesarea, about 55 miles northwest. The ultimate purpose was to *bring Paul safe unto* ⋆ *Felix the governor.*

⋆ *(His name was Marcus Antonius Felix, and he was 12th procurator, and the 4th procurator of Judea from 52-60AD. Pontius Pilate was the procurator during the time of Jesus. Felix was a cruel and very immoral man. A lot of these names that are mentioned in the book of Acts have strong connections to other famous people. For example: Felix' first wife was the granddaughter of Cleopatra and Antony. While he was in office, he fell in love with Drusilla, the daughter of Herod Agrippa I. Drusilla was the sister of Herod Agrippa II. Felix was known for giving bribes to get his evil desires accomplished. He was guilty of assassinating Jonathan the high priest for criticizing his misrule. He was extremely corrupt and lustful. It was before this man that Paul was brought.)*

THE LETTER FROM CLAUDIUS LYSIAS UNTO FELIX

Acts 23:25-30 - *And he wrote a letter after this manner: Claudius Lysias unto the most excellent governor Felix sendeth greeting. This man was taken of the Jews, and should have been killed of them: then came I with an army, and rescued him, having*

understood that he was a Roman. And when I would have known the cause wherefore they accused him, I brought him forth into their council: Whom I perceived to be accused of questions of their law, but to have nothing laid to his charge worthy of death or of bonds. And when it was told me how that the Jews laid wait for the man, I sent straightway to thee, and gave commandment to his accusers also to say before thee what they had against him. Farewell.

Once again we have the name of the chief captain in Jerusalem, *Claudius Lysias*. Notice that he begins by calling Felix *"most excellent."* This is the way Luke addressed Theophilus in **Acts 1:1**. The reason he writes a letter to Felix is to let him know that he *rescued Paul* from the Jewish leaders because he was a *Roman citizen*. While the Jews accused Paul of breaking their law, *Claudius* could find nothing worthy of death. Luke is careful when writing to let us and the readers of the first century know that Paul and the early Christians were repeatedly innocent in respect to the Roman law. Claudius was not fully truthful in his letter. He didn't tell Felix about Paul being bound and waiting to be scourged because he had already broken Roman law by mistreating Paul.

"and gave commandment to his accusers also to say before thee what they had against him. Farewell." - Felix was to wait for Paul's accusers to go up to Caesarea and spell out their charges against Paul. Claudius' plans were to wait until Paul was safely out of Jerusalem before telling the Sanhedrin that they would have to travel to Caesarea and explain their accusations against Paul to Felix.

Paul Departs Jerusalem to Caesarea

Acts 23:31-33 - *Then the soldiers, as it was commanded them, took Paul, and brought him by night to Antipatris. On the morrow they left the horsemen to go with him, and returned to the castle: Who, when they came to Caesarea and delivered the epistle to the governor, presented Paul also before him.*

The first leg of the journey led from Jerusalem to *Antipatris,* about 35 miles. In the second leg of the journey, only the 70 horsemen continued on with Paul. The other 400 soldiers were there to protect Paul during the most dangerous part of the journey. After they were out of the mountains of Jerusalem, they entered into the flat coastal plain. The 400 soldiers returned to the Antonio Fortress in Jerusalem, and the Roman cavalry escorted Paul the rest of the way and *presented the letter and the apostle Paul to Felix the governor.*

* (Antipatris is the Greek name of the Old Testament city of Aphek. It is mentioned several times in the Bible, but the most famous was the battle where the Philistines defeated the Israelites. In **I Samuel 4:1-11***, over 30,000 Israelites were slain, and the two sons of Eli, Hophni and Phinehas, also were killed.)*

Paul Awaits Trial

Acts 23:34-35 - *And when the governor had read the letter, he asked of what province he was. And when he understood that he was of Cilicia; I will hear*

thee, said he, when thine accusers are also come. And he commanded him to be kept in Herod's judgment hall.

The reason Felix *asked Paul what province he was from* was because there were imperial provinces that were under the direct authority of Caesar, and there were senatorial provinces that were under the authority of the Senate. Felix could only function under the latter, and *Cilicia* fell into his jurisdiction. *Paul was temporarily held in* ★ *Herod's palace in Caesarea until the Jews came from Jerusalem to accuse him.*

★ *(This was a Praetorium that was built by Herod the Great. The same name was given to the governor's palace in Jerusalem.* **(Mark 15:16)** *This would be the first time that the apostle Paul would speak to someone at this level of authority. This would also begin the fulfillment of the promise that Jesus made to Paul in* **Acts 9:15,** *that he would bear the name of Jesus to kings.)*

CHAPTER TWENTY-FOUR

Paul Accused by the Jews Before Felix

Acts 24:1 - *And after five days Ananias the high priest descended with the elders, and with a certain orator named Tertullus, who informed the governor against Paul.*

The Jews were so serious about convicting Paul that they didn't send the entire body of the Sanhedrin to Caesarea, only *Ananias the high priest with the elders.* They had hired a lawyer named *Tertullus,* derived from *Tertius,* meaning *"liar or impostor." Tertullus,* a legal advocate, understood Roman law and could speak Latin or Greek. It is not known whether he was a Hellenized Jew or a Gentile, but most likely he was a Gentile who could communicate better with the Roman governor Felix. Their accusations against Paul before Felix started *five days* after Paul had arrived.

Tertullus Tries Flattery Toward Felix

Acts 24:2-4 - And when he was called forth, Tertullus began to accuse him, saying, Seeing that by thee we enjoy great quietness, and that very worthy deeds are done unto this nation by thy providence, We accept it always, and in all places, most noble Felix, with all thankfulness. Notwithstanding, that I be not further tedious unto thee, I pray thee that thou wouldest hear us of thy clemency a few words.

Tertullus, the hired lawyer, tried flattering Felix by using several lies:

* *Seeing that by thee we enjoy great quietness*
* *Worthy deeds are done unto this nation by thy providence*
* *Most noble Felix, with all thankfulness*
* *That I be not further tedious unto thee* (or to hinder thee)
* *I pray thee that thou wouldest hear us of thy clemency a few words*

Tertullus was making it sound as if Felix was doing them a favor by hearing their accusation.

Paul's Accusers State Their Charge

Acts 24:5-6 - For we have found this man a pestilent fellow, and a mover of sedition among all the Jews throughout the world, and a ringleader of the sect of the Nazarenes: Who also hath gone about to profane the temple: whom we took, and would have judged according to our law.

Tertullus gives four indictments against Paul:

* ★ ***Paul was a pestilent fellow*** *(public pest)*
* ★ ***Paul was a mover of sedition*** *(riots)* ***among all the Jews***
* ★ ***Paul was a ringleader of the sect of the Nazarenes***
* ★ ***Paul profaned the temple in Jerusalem***

Notice that the Christian faith was considered a *sect* within Judaism, but still an enemy of religious Jews. Here the word *Nazarenes* is plural for all ★ *Christians*. Up until this point, the word *Nazarene* was singular referring to *Jesus of Nazareth*.

★ *(As previously mentioned, the Hebrew word in Israel today for "Christian" is "Notzri," which comes from the followers of Jesus of Nazareth.)*

Also notice that if Paul had profaned the Temple in Jerusalem, the Romans would have had no right in this case. *Tertullus* says that *Paul we took, and would have judged according to our law. Tertullus* was a typical hired lawyer who was crafty with his wording.

TERTULLUS CONCLUDES HIS ACCUSATION

Acts 24:7-9 - *But the chief captain Lysias came upon us, and with great violence took him away out of our hands, Commanding his accusers to come unto thee: by examining of whom thyself mayest take knowledge of all these things, whereof we accuse him. And the Jews also assented, saying that these things were so.*

The Roman chief captain, *Lysias,* is given a good light in the previous chapter, but here the lawyer paints him in a bad light. The lawyer, the high priest, and the elders assented to what had been said, but they gave no outside evidence. Their only hope was that Paul would incriminate himself under the examination of Felix.

Paul's Defense

Acts 24:10-13 - *Then Paul, after that the governor had beckoned unto him to speak, answered, Forasmuch as I know that thou hast been of many years a judge unto this nation, I do the more cheerfully answer for myself: Because that thou mayest understand, that there are yet but twelve days since I went up to Jerusalem for to worship. And they neither found me in the temple disputing with any man, neither raising up the people, neither in the synagogues, nor in the city: Neither can they prove the things whereof they now accuse me.*

Felix gave the nod for Paul to give an answer. Paul used no flattery toward Felix, but instead told him that he could *cheerfully answer for himself*. Paul reminded Felix that he had been a judge for many years, seven to be exact, and by now he knew the Jewish law.

Felix could easily verify that it had been only 12 *days* since Paul went up to Jerusalem. Paul was implying that in such a short period of time, he could not have started a revolt. His purpose was to worship at the Temple during the Feast of Pentecost. He was not a public pest that Tertullus had accused him of being.

"And they neither found me in the temple disputing with any man, neither raising up the people, neither in the synagogues, nor in the city:" - Paul was innocent of the charges that were punishable under Roman law. *Paul said that he did not dispute with any man in the Temple in Jerusalem, nor had he stirred up the people in the synagogues or the city.*

"Neither can they prove the things whereof they now accuse me." - It was only the words of the lawyer and the Jewish leaders, and they couldn't prove anything they had accused Paul of doing.

Paul Explains His Ministry

Acts 24:14-21 - *But this I confess unto thee, that after the way which they call heresy, so worship I the God of my fathers, believing all things which are written in the law and in the prophets: And have hope toward God, which they themselves also allow, that there shall be a resurrection of the dead, both of the just and unjust. And herein do I exercise myself, to have always a conscience void to offence toward God, and toward men. Now after many years I came to bring alms to my nation, and offerings. Whereupon certain Jews from Asia found me purified in the temple, neither with multitude, nor with tumult. Who ought to have been here before thee, and object, if they had ought against me. Or else let these same here say, if they have found any evil doing in me, while I stood before the council, Except it be for this one voice, that I cried standing among them,*

Touching the resurrection of the dead I am called in question by you this day.

Paul says that the Jews are calling the *sect of the Way as heresy*. He states that he *worshipped the God of his fathers, believing all things which are written in the law and in the prophets*. There was nothing in Roman law that forbade Paul's Jewish faith. Paul is saying that his faith is more than just a sect within Judaism. He was living in the fulfillment of what had been written in the Jewish law. He believed there would be a ⋆ *resurrection of the just and the unjust*. Paul told the governor Felix that he went to great pains to keep his *conscience clear toward God and men*. We must remember that the Holy Spirit was accompanying Paul as he spoke.

⋆ *(The resurrection of the just is the first resurrection.* **Daniel 12:2, Luke 14:14, John 5:29, Rev.20:4-6.** *The resurrection of the unjust is the second resurrection.* **John 5:29, Rev.20:12-13***)*

"Now after many years I came to bring alms to my nation, and offerings." - Paul *brought offerings to his own nation* from the churches he had started along his journeys. Why would he be causing trouble with his own people that he loved? This statement shows that the Jewish Christians throughout the Roman Empire did not show themselves at odds with the nation of Israel.

"Whereupon certain Jews from Asia found me purified in the temple, neither with multitude, nor with tumult. Who ought to have been here before thee, and object, if they had ought against me." - "The real instigators are not even here to accuse me," Paul said. Paul was in the process of being *purified in the Temple* and giving the offerings when the riot began. There was no crowd there at the time, and he was alone. He didn't bring any Gentile into the Temple compound. There were no eyewitnesses there to give any evidence against Paul.

"Or else let these same here say, if they have found any evil doing in me, while I stood before the council," - Paul is presenting a challenge. The Jews who were standing there with their hired lawyer were supposed to disclose what crime he had committed when he stood before them at the council. **(Acts 22:30-23:10)**

"Except it be for this one voice, that I cried standing among them, Touching the resurrection of the dead I am called in question by you this day." - More specifically, it was the resurrection of Jesus Christ for which he was on trial. There really was a resurrection because Jesus rose from the dead. This proved that he was the Messiah of Israel. Paul was guilty of being a follower of Jesus the Nazarene, but this was not a crime under Roman law.

FELIX AVOIDS MAKING A DECISION

Acts 24:22-23 - *And when Felix heard these things, having more perfect knowledge of that way, he deferred them, and said, When Lysias the chief captain shall come down, I will know the uttermost of your matter. And he commanded a centurion to keep Paul, and to let him have liberty, and that he should forbid none of his acquaintance to minister or come unto him.*

Felix had *more knowledge of the new faith called the Way* than the lawyer or the Jewish leaders. Felix adjourned the trial without making any decision. The governor used a delay tactic by saying, *"When Lysias the chief captain shall come down, I will know the uttermost of your matter." Lysias* was not needed to determine the outcome of this trial; furthermore, he already knew that Paul was not guilty.

Felix ordered *the centurion to keep Paul, but he gave him liberty* to have his relatives or fellow believers in Caesarea to visit him. There was a church already established in Caesarea. **(Acts 18:22)**

Felix Becomes Afraid

Acts 24:24-25 - *And after certain days, when Felix came with his wife Drusilla, which was a Jewess, he sent for Paul, and heard him concerning the faith in Christ. And as he reasoned of righteousness, temperance, and judgment to come, Felix trembled, and answered, Go thy way for this time; when I have a convenient season, I will call for thee.*

The Jewish accusers had returned to Jerusalem. Felix wanted his third wife *Drusilla, a Jewess*, to hear Paul. Maybe it was because he wanted his young, beautiful wife to hear Paul's testimony or because he wanted her advice. Paul gave them a clear presentation of the gospel that caused Felix to *tremble*. Notice the three things that was in Paul's message:

* *Paul reasoned of righteousness*
* *Paul talked about self-control*

* *Paul expounded on the judgment to come*

This is a powerful passage of scripture because it shows that Paul was neither ashamed nor afraid of Felix the governor. Felix would have to live the rest of his life knowing his sinful state and how he needed Christ as his Savior. Paul knew the sinful life that Felix had lived, and he didn't try to avoid the situation.

"Felix trembled, and answered, Go thy way for this time; when I have a convenient season, I will call for thee." - The message of the righteousness of Christ always makes some people feel very uncomfortable. The message of how sinful people are makes some people very nervous. The message of the judgment that is to come made *Felix tremble*. His response shows that he was under conviction, but he was not willing to turn from his sin. Felix decided to put things off until *he had a more convenient season;* but nevertheless, he rejected Paul's message.

THE GREED OF FELIX REVEALED

Acts 24:26-27 - *He hoped also that money should have been given him of Paul, that he might loose him: wherefore he sent for him the oftener, and communed with him. But after two years Porcius Festus came into Felix' room: and Felix, willing to shew the Jews a pleasure, left Paul bound.*

The ulterior motive of Felix's greed was revealed. He was known for accepting bribes, and this showed that he had continued to fail in righteousness and self-control. Although he did call for Paul often to hear him, it was only a pretense. Paul never took his hint about bribery.

Two years had passed and Felix was succeeded by ★ *Porcius Festus.*

★ *(Felix was actually deposed by Nero in 59 or 60 AD. A fight broke out between Jews and Gentiles in Caesarea at the marketplace, and Felix sent Roman soldiers to kill many of the Jews. The Jewish people made a complaint against Felix to the emperor Nero, and Festus was appointed to replace him. Festus served as procurator until 62AD when he died in office.)*

"Felix, willing to shew the Jews a pleasure, left Paul bound." – It was the Jewish community who had filed the complaint against Felix, causing his recall to Rome. Felix did not want to antagonize the Jews any further by releasing Paul. He tried to win their favor by keeping Paul in chains.

CHAPTER TWENTY-FIVE

FESTUS KEEPS PAUL IN CAESAREA

Acts 25:1-5 - *Now when Festus was come into the province, after three days he ascended from Caesarea to Jerusalem. Then the high priest and the chief of the Jews informed him against Paul, and besought him, And desired favour against him, that he would send for him to Jerusalem, laying wait in the way to kill him. But Festus answered, that Paul should be kept at Caesarea, and that he himself would depart shortly thither. Let them therefore, said he, which among you are able, go down with me, and accuse this man, if there be any wickedness in him.*

The *province* of Judea was a section of the larger Roman province of Syria. Syria was under the Roman legate, while Judea was under the lesser jurisdiction of a procurator. Festus decided to *ascend up to Jerusalem from Caesarea just after three days of taking office.* Why? Even though Caesarea was the Roman capital of the province, Jerusalem was the religious capital, and the most important city to the Jews. Felix was a bad man, while Festus was a pagan. He was a more reasonable man than Felix.

"Then the high priest and the chief of the Jews informed him against Paul, and besought him, And desired favour against him, that he would send for him to Jerusalem, laying wait in the way to kill him." - The case against Paul was still on the minds of the chief religious leaders in Jerusalem, and they *informed Festus against Paul*. It's astounding how people can be so religious and be so much against the message of the Lord Jesus. It was that way during Paul's day, and it is still true today. The two years of imprisonment of Paul in Caesarea was actually a providential provision of protective custody against the murderous intentions of the Jewish religious leaders.

"And desired favour against him, that he would send for him to Jerusalem, laying wait in the way to kill him." - The implication was that Festus could build a good relationship with the religious leaders in Jerusalem by doing them a favor. They wanted Festus to transfer Paul from Caesarea to Jerusalem, but their ulterior motive was that they would try to assassinate Paul along the way. They knew that Paul would not be found guilty, and they wanted to ambush and murder him before the trial took place.

"But Festus answered, that Paul should be kept at Caesarea, and that he himself would depart shortly thither. Let them therefore, said he, which among you are able, go down with me, and accuse this man, if there be any wickedness in him." - God protects Paul again through a pagan ruler. Festus was willing to put Paul on trial again, but it would happen in Caesarea, not in Jerusalem. Since Festus had made the decision

not to transfer Paul to Jerusalem, he now challenges the higher religious authorities in Jerusalem to make the journey back to Caesarea and accuse Paul again to see if he had broken the Roman or Jewish law.

FESTUS RE-OPENS THE TRIAL IN CAESAREA

Acts 25:6-8 - *And when he had tarried among them more than ten days, he went down unto Caesarea; and the next day sitting on the judgment seat commanded Paul to be brought. And when he was come, the Jews which came down from Jerusalem stood round about, and laid many and grievous complaints against Paul, which they could not prove. While he answered for himself, Neither against the law of the Jews, neither against the temple, nor yet against Caesar, have I offended any thing at all.*

Festus spent *more than ten days* in Jerusalem, then he went west over 50 miles to Caesarea. The next day after he arrived, Festus took his seat on the *judgment seat, or the tribunal*. At this point, he *commanded Paul to be brought in.*

"*And when he was come, the Jews which came down from Jerusalem stood round about, and laid many and grievous complaints against Paul, which they could not prove.*" - The Sanhedrin leaders wanted Paul done away with so much that they were willing to make the journey to the Roman city of Caesarea. This time they had no lawyer to represent their case. They brought up many things against Paul with greater intensity. *But they could not prove any of them.* They kept up a constant barrage of accusations.

"While he answered for himself, Neither against the law of the Jews, neither against the temple, nor yet against Caesar, have I offended any thing at all." - Paul declared his innocence and gave three specific instances:

* *He had not violated any Jewish law*
* *He had committed no crime against the Temple*
* *He was not guilty of treason against Caesar*

PAUL APPEALS TO CAESAR

Acts 25:9-12 - *But Festus, willing to do the Jews a pleasure, answered Paul, and said, Wilt thou go up to Jerusalem, and there be judged of these things before me? Then said Paul, I stand at Caesar's judgment seat, where I ought to be judged: to the Jews have I done no wrong, as thou very well knowest. For if I be an offender, or have committed any thing worthy of death, I refuse not to die: but if there be none of these things whereof these accuse me, no man may deliver me unto them. I appeal unto Caesar. Then Festus, when he had conferred with the council, answered, Hast thou appealed unto Caesar? unto Caesar shalt thou go.*

Festus knew that it was good for his reputation to have a working relationship with the Jews in Jerusalem. Festus was very apprehensive about making a decision due to the fact that Paul was a Roman citizen. Did Festus know about the plot to kill Paul if he went to Jerusalem? We do not know. It is strange that a ruler would ask Paul *"Wilt thou go up to Jerusalem, and there be judged of these things before me?"* Festus was caving into the pressure from the religious Jews. He knew Paul was not guilty of breaking Roman law, so he intended to win over the Jews by making his suggestion. He was trying to avoid making a decision at all. Paul could easily see that if Festus was not willing to bring justice in the Roman city of Caesarea, then he would not stand up for truth in Jerusalem where the Jews were so much against Paul.

"Then said Paul, I stand at Caesar's judgment seat, where I ought to be judged: to the Jews have I done no wrong, as thou very well knowest. For if I be an offender, or have committed any thing worthy of death, I refuse not to die: but if there be none of these things whereof these accuse me, no man may deliver me unto them. I appeal unto Caesar." – Paul reminded Festus that the proper place for judgment was at Caesarea. This was the capital of the province, and even the city was named after Caesar. Festus was Caesar's representative in the trial, and he knew very well that Paul was innocent. This again shows how the procurators were mere puppets trying to appease Caesar and play their cards right in keeping peace in their appointed regions.

Paul is saying hypothetically that, *"If I am guilty, I am not afraid to die."* The second point concerns Paul's innocence. *"I have not broken any Jewish law so why would you deliver me back to them?"* Paul could see and feel that Festus was trying to kick the can down the road.

"I appeal unto Caesar." - Under Roman law, every citizen had the right to *appeal unto Caesar*. This took the case legally out of the hands of Festus. Festus was just a procurator in Judea compared to the mighty Caesar ★ *Nero* in Rome. Paul wasn't afraid to die, but what the Jews were trying to do to him was ridiculous, and he knew that he was innocent.

★ *(Nero was the fifth and last emperor of the Julio-Claudian dynasty. His served from 54AD until his suicide in 68AD. His first few years were peaceful, and Paul had no reason to fear Nero at this point. In his later years, Nero turned fierce against the Christians.)*

"Then Festus, when he had conferred with the council, answered, Hast thou appealed unto Caesar? unto Caesar shalt thou go." - Festus had his own advisers who were outside of the Jewish authorities. He had to obey Roman law and turn Paul over to Caesar, which was probably a relief to him. This would free Festus from giving Paul an acquittal or a guilty verdict and from turning him over to the Jews. Before Paul would go to Rome, he would have to stand before *King Agrippa II*.

KING AGRIPPA II & BERNICE

Acts 25:13-14 - *And after certain days king Agrippa and Bernice came unto Caesarea to salute Festus. And when they had been there many days, Festus declared Paul's cause unto the king, saying, There is a certain man left in bonds by Felix:*

Because Festus was the new procurator over Judea, ★ *king Agrippa and his wife Bernice* came to Caesarea to pay their respects. *Festus declared Paul's case unto the king*, outlining the problem that he really needed a specific charge against Paul before turning him over to Caesar in Rome. Festus told Agrippa that he inherited the prisoner Paul from Felix. This is interesting because *king Agrippa* was the brother of Drusilla, the wife of Felix.

* *(The Herodian Dynasty is complex, but it is also very important to study. This particular king Agrippa II was the great-grandson of Herod the Great, who killed the children when Jesus was born. King Agrippa II's grandfather beheaded John the Baptist. His father martyred James in* **Acts 12**. *Now Paul stands before the last man who would rule in the Herodian Dynasty. His wife Bernice is his sister. King Agrippa II ruled a small territory in northern Israel, but Caesar had given him the authority to rule over the Temple in Jerusalem and the Jewish high priest. Agrippa II knew a lot about Jewish law and while he had no jurisdiction in Caesarea, he might be able to give some advice to Festus. Agrippa II died childless sometime between 92-100AD.)*

FESTUS EXPLAINS THE CASE TO AGRIPPA

Acts 25:15-22 - *About whom, when I was at Jerusalem, the chief priests and the elders of the Jews informed me, desiring to have judgment against him. To whom I answered, It is not the manner of the Romans to deliver any man to die, before that he which is accused have the accusers face to face, and have licence to answer for himself concerning the crime laid against him. Therefore, when they were come hither, without any delay on the morrow I sat* *on the judgment seat, and commanded the man to be brought forth. Against whom when the accusers stood up, they brought none accusation of such things as I supposed: But had certain questions against him of their own superstition, and of one Jesus, which was dead, whom Paul affirmed to be alive. And because I doubted of such manner of questions, I asked him whether he would go to Jerusalem, and there be judged of these matters. But when Paul had appealed to be reserved unto the hearing of Augustus, I commanded him to be kept till I might send him to Caesar. Then Agrippa said unto Festus, I would also hear the man myself. To morrow, said he, thou shalt hear him.*

While some of this has been previously discussed, we will make a few comments here to summarize the text. Festus rehearses the trial to Agrippa. He is letting Agrippa know that he went through all of the Roman protocols and met with Paul in Caesarea and that the Jews didn't have any evidence of proof that Paul had done anything wrong. *Festus had supposed* that Paul the prisoner was guilty of some real crime, but much to his surprise he wasn't guilty of anything.

The real issue was their Jewish law and *superstition*, or *religion*, and *of one Jesus, which was dead, whom Paul affirmed to be alive.* The bottom line of the entire issue was that Paul preached about the death and resurrection of *Jesus,* and the Jewish leaders thought it was blasphemy. They were trying to find something to claim against Paul by lying or adding traditions to their law. This was not a crime under Roman law since the message of *Jesus* was considered a sect within lawful Judaism. Festus, not knowing Jewish law, was hoping that Agrippa could help him sort it out.

"But when Paul had appealed to be reserved unto the hearing of Augustus, I commanded him to be kept till I might send him to Caesar." - There are two different titles for Caesar in this one verse, but we are referring to the same person. The Latin title *Augustus* is the English translation of the Greek, *Sebastou*, meaning *Emperor*. The title really means *"one who is worthy to be worshipped."* The title name dates back to 27BC with Octavian. Festus kept Paul in prison until it was time to send him to *Caesar* in Rome.

"Then Agrippa said unto Festus, I would also hear the man myself. To morrow, said he, thou shalt hear him." - This would be the third time that Paul would have the opportunity to present his message to a Gentile ruler. (**Felix, Festus,** and now **Agrippa**)

THE GREAT PUBLIC SPECTACLE

> **Acts 25:23 -** *And on the morrow, when Agrippa was come, and Bernice, with great pomp, and was entered into the place of hearing, with the chief captains, and principal men of the city, at Festus' commandment Paul was brought forth.*

The hearing was an excuse for a great public spectacle. Not only were *Agrippa, Bernice, and Festus* there, but also the *Roman officers* and ★ *principal men of the city* of Caesarea. *The place of hearing, akroaterion,* was the term for *auditorium*. It was the time and place for *Festus* to look as if he were the man of authority bringing in the prisoner Paul. While they all thought that Paul was the lesser important figure, Paul had the authority of Almighty God with him. Wow!

(The words for "principal men of the city," kat exochen, is only found here in the New Testament, and it is not in the original Greek. It was found in inscriptions from the first century. These were very important Gentile leaders in the Caesarea.)

FESTUS MAKES THE OPENING STATEMENT

Acts 25:24-27 - *And Festus said, King Agrippa, and all men which are here present with us, ye see this man, about whom all the multitude of the Jews have dealt with me, both at Jerusalem, and also here, crying that he ought not to live any longer. But when I found that he had committed nothing worthy of death, and that he himself hath appealed to Augustus, I have determined to send him. Of whom I have no certain thing to write unto my lord. Wherefore I have brought him forth before you, and specially before thee, O king Agrippa, that, after examination had, I might have somewhat to write. For it seemeth to me unreasonable to send a prisoner, and not withal to signify the crimes laid against him.*

Festus tells Agrippa that the Jews dealt with Paul in Jerusalem and Caesarea, *yelling that he ought not to live any longer.* It was important for Luke to write that Festus told Agrippa that he clearly understood and believed that Paul was innocent. Notice that Festus calls Caesar *"my lord."* Festus could not send Paul to Caesar without a letter to specify the charges against him. Festus is passing the difficult job of finding an innocent man guilty before Agrippa. He was hoping that after Agrippa's *examination,* or *anakriseos,* which means *"preliminary investigation,"* that he would have something legitimate to put in his letter to Caesar. The whole purpose of this big spectacle of bringing Paul before Agrippa was to remove Festus from this predicament.

CHAPTER TWENTY-SIX

> ### Paul's Introduction Before Agrippa

Acts 26:1-3 - *Then Agrippa said unto Paul, Thou art permitted to speak for thyself. Then Paul stretched forth the hand, and answered for himself: I think myself happy, king Agrippa, because I shall answer for myself this day before thee touching all the things whereof I am accused of the Jews: Especially because I know thee to be expert in all customs and questions which are among the Jews: wherefore I beseech thee to hear me patiently.*

Paul speaking before *King Agrippa* is the most detailed of his defenses, and also a partial fulfillment of **Acts 9:15.** Think about Paul being in chains and still *stretching forth his hand.* All that Paul had been through from the Damascus Road experience, his missionary journeys, being mocked, his beatings, and finally his imprisonment, Paul could still say, *"I think myself blessed."* He knew that he was where God wanted him to be, and he could see what Jesus Christ had told him was coming to pass.

Paul felt privileged to be able to *answer for himself* because according to the first-century historian Flavius Josephus, Agrippa was very knowledgeable about Judaism and *their customs and questions.*

PAUL'S EARLY LIFE AS A PHARISEE

Acts 26:4-5 - *My manner of life from my youth, which was at the first among mine own nation at Jerusalem, know all the Jews; Which knew me from the beginning, if they would testify, that after the most straitest sect of our religion ★ I lived a Pharisee.*

★ *(To be a Pharisee, one had to have a wife. Since Paul was single in* **I Cor.7:7-9***, it is believed by most Hebrew scholars that his wife deserted him when he became a follower of Christ. This was common in the first century and even today among the unbelieving, religious Jews.)*

Not only was Paul a faithful religious Jew, *he was known among the Jews as living the most strictest sect of the Pharisees.* He was well known by the religious Jews in Tarsus and in Jerusalem. Agrippa was familiar with the everyday lifestyle of a Pharisee. It is quite remarkable how our Lord Jesus condemned the Pharisees in **Matthew 23**, and then divinely call one of them to became one of the greatest Christians who ever lived.

PAUL QUESTIONS AGRIPPA

Acts 26:6-8 - *And now I stand and am judged for the hope of the promise made of God, unto our fathers:*

> ***Unto which promise our twelve tribes, instantly serving God day and night, hope to come. For which hope's sake, king Agrippa, I am accused of the Jews. Why should it be thought a thing incredible with you, that God should raise the dead?***

And now points to a sharp contrast between his early life and his present state. Paul says that he is being judged for the *Messianic hope of the promise made of God unto our fathers. This promise was to the twelve tribes of Israel* because there are no "ten lost tribes of Israel." Notice that the Jewish Luke mentions, *"day and night,"* while a Gentile author would have said *"night and day."* To a religious Jew in Paul's time, the day begins at sundown, not midnight. There are several important reasons why Paul is being accused:

* **The Jewish Messianic hope**
* **The promise made of God to the Jewish forefathers**
* **The twelve tribes of Israel**
* **The resurrection hope**

"Why should it be thought a thing incredible with you, that God should raise the dead?" - The word *you* in this context is plural and means that Paul probably turned to address the general audience there. Since God is the Creator of everything, and since nothing is impossible with the Almighty God, *why would they think it's incredible that God should raise the dead?* God did raise Jesus from the dead, and He was the fulfillment of the Messianic hope of the Jewish people.

Paul Was Once a Persecutor of the Church

Acts 26:9-11 - *I verily thought with myself, that I ought to do many things contrary to the name of Jesus of Nazareth. Which thing I also did in Jerusalem: and many of the saints did I shut up in prison, having received authority from the chief priests; and when they were put to death, * I gave my voice against them. And I punished them oft in every synagogue, and compelled them to blaspheme; and being exceedingly mad against them, I persecuted them even unto strange cities.*

Paul tells Agrippa and the audience that before he was converted, he believed that he *must* persecute the followers of Jesus. *He not only shut up many believers in prison, but also gave his voice to put many to death.* Paul thought he was doing the right thing.

* *('I gave my voice' was done by dropping a black pebble stone. This was one of the Jewish methods in ancient times of casting lots by using stones of different colors.* **Revelation 2:17***)*

The early Jewish Christians still met *in the synagogues, and Paul searched out the believers in order to get them to blaspheme Jesus as their Messiah.* This statement also means that Paul was unsuccessful is stopping the believers in Jesus. This weighed heavy on Paul's conscience the rest of his life. His zeal in persecuting the church was misguided despite his religious fervor.

For I am the least of the apostles, that am not meet to be called an apostle, because I persecuted the church of God. **I Corinthians 15:9**

This is a faithful saying, and worthy of all acceptation, that Christ Jesus came into the world to save sinners; of whom I am chief. **I Timothy 1:15**

JESUS CHRIST REVEALS HIMSELF TO PAUL

Acts 26:12-15 - *Whereupon as I went to Damascus with authority and commission from the chief priests, At midday, O king, I saw in the way a light from heaven, above the brightness of the sun, shining round about me and them which journeyed with me. And when we were all fallen to the earth, I heard a voice speaking unto me, and saying in the Hebrew tongue, Saul, Saul, why persecutest thou me? it is hard for thee to kick against the pricks. And I said, Who art thou, Lord? And he said, I am Jesus whom thou persecutest.*

Paul now gives his fullest account of his Damascus Road experience, his life, and his world. The very same *chief priests who gave him the authority and commission* to persecute the church are the ones who are accusing Paul.

"O king, I saw in the way a light from heaven, above the brightness of the sun, shining round about me and them which journeyed with me." - Paul tells Agrippa that *he saw a light from heaven that shined brighter than the sun, that caused he and those with* *him to fall to the ground.* It took the *Shechinah* glory of God to show Paul that he was wrong.

"I heard a voice speaking unto me, and saying in the Hebrew tongue, Saul, Saul, why persecutest thou me? it is hard for thee to kick against the pricks." - Not only did Paul see the glory of God from heaven, he heard the voice of Jesus the Messiah speaking in the *Hebrew tongue*. Since Paul was probably speaking to Agrippa in Greek, he mentions here the true language of Jesus that spoke to him. When Paul was persecuting the Christians, he was also *persecuting Jesus. It was hard for Paul to go against God's will and keep fighting his own conscience.* Paul even started a conversation with *Jesus* by saying, *"Who art thou Lord?"* The response came back from heaven, *"I am Jesus whom thou persecutest."* Paul immediately understood that Jesus was not in the grave. He was alive, and He was in heaven as the King of Glory.

Jesus Gives Paul the Commission

Acts 26:16-18 - *But rise, and stand upon thy feet: for I have appeared unto thee for this purpose, to make thee a minister and a witness both of these things which thou hast seen, and of those things in the which I will appear unto thee; Delivering thee from the people, and from the Gentiles, unto whom now I send thee, To open their eyes, and to turn them from darkness to light, and from the power of Satan unto God, that they may receive forgiveness of sins, and inheritance among them which are sanctified by faith that is in me.*

Jesus commanded *Sha'ul*, who became *Paul*, *to stand upon his feet* because it was time for him to *stand up and take a stand*. Jesus had commissioned him to *go somewhere and to become a minister and a witness*. The chief priests had ordered him to persecute the church, and now Jesus Christ commissions him to promote the church. Paul would not create the message, but would experience it and be a witness to the message. Jesus promised Paul there would be five results:

* ***Paul would be delivered from the people***
* ***The Gentiles would turn from darkness to light***
* ***The Gentiles would be set free from the power of Satan***
* ***The Gentiles would receive forgiveness of sins***
* ***The Gentiles would receive an inheritance being sanctified by faith in Jesus***

This message that Paul was commissioned to preach was also an invitation to the Gentile king Agrippa and those who were in the auditorium. The Holy Spirit must have been felt throughout the entire place when Paul was speaking.

Paul Was Obedient to the Call

Acts 26:19-20 - *Whereupon, O king Agrippa, I was not disobedient unto the heavenly vision: But shewed first unto them of Damascus, and at Jerusalem, and throughout all the coasts of Judaea, and then to the Gentiles, that they should repent and turn to God, and do works meet for repentance.*

The call was so real and so strong from the heavenly Jesus that *Paul was not disobedient to the heavenly vision*. Paul was called to give the gospel to the *Jews first in Damascus, Jerusalem, throughout the coasts of Judea, and then to the Gentiles.* **(Romans 1:16)** The message of Paul to the Gentiles was twofold:

* *Repent of their sins and turn to the one true God*
* *To show forth works to prove they had repented*

PAUL SUMMARIZES HIS DEFENSE

Acts 26:21-23 - *For these causes the Jews caught me in the temple, and went about to kill me. Having therefore obtained help of God, I continue unto this day, witnessing both to small and great, saying none other things than those which the prophets and Moses did say should come: That Christ should suffer, and that he should be the first that should rise from the dead, and should shew light unto the people, and to the Gentiles.*

Paul clearly states the truth of the case. *With the help of God, he continued to preach the gospel to the small and great. His message was simply the fulfillment of what was written in the prophets and in the books of Moses.* What Paul said was an echo of what the risen Jesus had previously said to His disciples after the resurrection:

And he said unto them, These are the words which I spake unto you, while I was yet with you, that all things must be fulfilled, which were written in the law of Moses, and in the prophets, and in the psalms, concerning me. Then opened he their understanding, that they might understand the scriptures, And said unto them, Thus it is written, and thus it behooved Christ to suffer, and to rise from the dead the third day: And that repentance and remission of sins should be preached in his name among all nations, beginning at Jerusalem. **Luke 24:44-47**

The message of Jesus being a *Light to the Gentiles* connects us to many scriptures such as these:

I the Lord have called thee in righteousness, and will hold thine hand, and will keep thee, and give thee for a covenant of the people, for a light of the Gentiles. **Isaiah 42:6**

A light to lighten the Gentiles, and the glory of thy people Israel. **Luke 2:32**

For so hath the Lord commanded us, saying, I have set thee to be a light of the Gentiles, that thou shouldest be for salvation unto the ends of the earth. And when the Gentiles heard this, they were glad, and glorified the word of the Lord: and as many as were ordained to eternal life believed. **Acts 13:47-48**

The Response of Festus

Acts 26:24-26 - *And as he thus spake for himself, Festus said with a loud voice, Paul, thou art beside thyself; much learning doth make thee mad. But he said, I am not mad, most noble Festus; but speak forth the words of truth and soberness. For the king* *knoweth of these things, before whom also I speak freely: for I am persuaded that none of these things are hidden from him; for this thing was not done in a corner.*

The Roman governor Festus shouted out that Paul not only *was beside himself, he was raving mad*. Paul reminded Festus that he was *sober* and giving them *divine truth*. King Agrippa knew more about what Paul was saying than *Festus*. Festus didn't believe anything that Paul said and from his pure Roman worldview, it was all just Jewish superstition. The king knew about the Jewish world and what had been taking place; *it was not done in secret*. The death, burial, and resurrection of the Lord Jesus Christ were historical facts.

KING AGRIPPA IS ALMOST PERSUADED

Acts 26:27-29 - *King Agrippa, believest thou the prophets? I know that thou believest. Then Agrippa said unto Paul, Almost thou persuadest me to be a Christian. And Paul said, I would to God, that not only thou, but also all that hear me this day, were both almost, and altogether such as I am, except these bonds.*

Paul directly challenges Agrippa by saying *"Do you believe?"* Paul brought the conviction deeper by answering his own question; *"I know that thou believest."* ★ King Agrippa responded with one of the greatest pagan statements in the Holy Bible, *"Almost thou persuadest me to be a Christian."* The statement that Agrippa made could be interpreted in two ways:

* *Are you trying to persuade me to be a Christian?*
* *In such a short time, do you think I would be a Christian?*

* *(In the original Greek language Agrippa was not even close to becoming a Christian. The KJV is misleading here, and many ministers have taken this phrase out of context to preach a sermon. Agrippa was showing irony and not of interest. He was fearful of his wife, of Festus, and all of the dignitaries sitting around him. Agrippa wanted the praise of others, and no Jewish prisoner in chains was going to convince him to become a Christian is such a short time. The closest he ever came to becoming a follower of Christ was by simply stating the name "Christian.")*

"And Paul said, I would to God, that not only thou, but also all that hear me this day, were both almost, and altogether such as I am, except these bonds." – Paul gives Agrippa and the audience a courteous wish by stating that *he desired for them all to be followers of Christ like himself, but without the chains.* This shows that Paul was still in chains. What a dramatic picture Paul was giving to them! He was standing there physically in Roman chains, but spiritually he knew the freedom of Christ. Agrippa and Festus were rulers living in pomp and splendor, and yet they were in spiritual darkness.

AGRIPPA ADMITS PAUL'S INNOCENCE

Acts 26:30-32 - And when he had thus spoken, the king rose up, and the governor, and Bernice, and they that sat with them: And when they were gone aside, they talked between themselves, saying, This man doeth nothing worthy of death or of bonds. Then said

Agrippa unto Festus, This man might have been set at liberty, if he had not appealed unto Caesar.

When the king *rose up,* everyone else got up. While Agrippa rejected Paul's message of Christ, he did respect Paul's integrity. The verdict was *not guilty*! *Agrippa* and *Festus* thought that the innocent Paul, *who was not worthy of death or of bonds,* should *not have appealed unto Caesar.* They did not understand God's plan for Paul's life.

> ***After these things were ended, Paul purposed in the spirit, when he had passed through Macedonia and Achaia, to go to Jerusalem, saying, After I have been there, I must also see Rome. Acts 19:21***
>
> ***And the night following the Lord stood by him, and said, Be of good cheer, Paul: for as thou hast testified of me in Jerusalem, so must thou bear witness also at Rome. Acts 23:11***

CHAPTER TWENTY-SEVEN

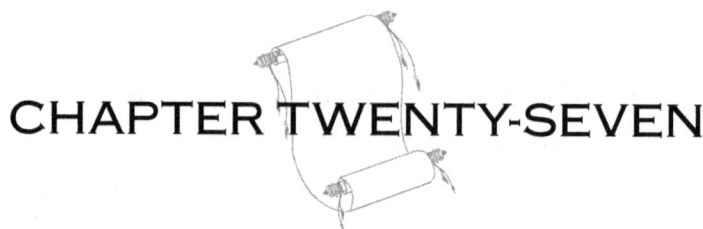

PAUL LEAVES CAESAREA FOR ROME

Acts 27:1-2 - *And when it was determined that we should sail into Italy, they delivered Paul and certain other prisoners unto one named Julius, a centurion of Augustus' band. And entering into a ship of Adramyttium, we launched, meaning to sail by the coasts of Asia; one Aristarchus, a Macedonian of Thessalonica, being with us.*

Paul's imprisonments in Jerusalem and Caesarea are over, and it is time for him to sail across the Mediterranean Sea to *Italy*. Notice here that Luke adds again the plural pronoun *we* to show that he was in the party. This is the first use of the plural pronoun since **Acts 21:17-18**. Apparently Luke was imprisoned with Paul in Caesarea, and of course we do know that Luke himself was an eyewitness to the events.

"they delivered Paul and certain other prisoners unto one named Julius, a centurion of Augustus' band." - Festus the governor gave the order for Paul to be transferred to Rome. We do not know the names of the *other prisoners* that are spoken here, but there were many *prisoners* who were sent to Rome under escort to be a part of the Roman sport arenas. *Julius* was a *centurion* who was a leader of one of five cohorts stationed in Caesarea. Luke wants us to know that he was a centurion of *Augustus' band*, which meant that Julius represented the imperial power of Rome, not just a senatorial cohort.

"And entering into a ship of Adramyttium, we launched, meaning to sail by the coasts of Asia; one Aristarchus, a Macedonian of Thessalonica, being with us." - The ship that carried Paul was from *Adramyttium*, which was a seaport town in the northwest side of Asia Minor between Troas and Pergamum. Julius probably embarked on the first merchant ship that was available hoping to find a larger vessel at one of the coastal ports along the way. It is interesting that one of the prisoners that is mentioned separately is *Aristarchus, a Macedonian of Thessalonica*. He is mentioned in **Acts 19:29, 20:4, Colossians 4:10,** and **Philemon 1:24.**

From Caesarea to Fair Havens

Acts 27:3-8 - *And the next day we touched at Sidon. And Julius courteously entreated Paul, and gave him liberty to go unto his friends to refresh himself. And when we had launched from thence, we sailed under Cyprus, because the winds were contrary. And when we had sailed over the sea of Cilicia and Pamphylia, we came to Myra, a city of Lycia. And there the centurion found a ship of Alexandria sailing into Italy; and he put us therein. And when we had sailed slowly many days, and scarce were come over against*

Cnidus, the wind not suffering us, we sailed under Crete, over against Salmone; And, hardly passing it, came unto a place which is called The fair havens; nigh whereunto was the city of Lasea.

Once again we find a Roman centurion being kind to Paul. The compassion and love of Paul was different from the other prisoners.

Their first stop was about 70 miles north to the town of *Sidon* on the western coastline of Israel. There were followers of Christ there, and the centurion gave Paul *the liberty* to visit his friends and refresh himself through fellowship.

"And when we had launched from thence, we sailed under Cyprus, because the winds were contrary. And when we had sailed over the sea of Cilicia and Pamphylia, we came to Myra, a city of Lycia." - This verse tells us that because of the northeastern winds of the Aegean Sea colliding with the southern winds on the Mediterranean Sea, they had to sail underneath or around the island of *Cyprus* and take the sheltered route along the southern coast of Asia Minor. No doubt Paul was thinking of his missionary journeys as they made their way to *Cilicia* and *Pamphylia* along the southern coast of Asia Minor. They came to *Myra, (Demre today)* a city of the province of *Lycia,* that is located on the southwestern coast where they would change ships.

"And there the centurion found a ship of Alexandria sailing into Italy; and he put us therein." - Myra was the primary port for the grain ship from *Alexandria*, Egypt, to *Italy*. (**vs.38**) According to some historians, the ship was 140 feet long and

36 feet wide with a large square mast. This was a much larger vessel that would carry them southwest.

"And when we had sailed slowly many days, and scarce were come over against Cnidus, the wind not suffering us, we sailed under Crete, over against Salmone; And, hardly passing it, came unto a place which is called The fair havens; nigh whereunto was the city of Lasea." - Because of this type vessel, they had to *sail slowly*. It took them several days to sail the 130-mile distance from *Myra to Cnidus*. They turned southward to the island of *Crete*. Because of strong winds, they had to sail to the eastern town of *Salmone* then travel along the southern coast of *Crete* to be protected from the winds. *Fair Havens,* which means *"good harbor,"* was a harbor near the city of *Lasea*. The little harbor was half exposed to the sea and would not provide them protection for very long, but at least for a time.

PAUL'S ADVICE TO THE CAPTAIN

Acts 27:9-10 - *Now when much time was spent, and when sailing was now dangerous, because the fast was now already past, Paul admonished them, And said unto them, Sirs, I perceive that this voyage will be with hurt and much damage, not only of the lading and ship, but also of our lives.*

After some considerable time had passed, the voyage had become *dangerous*. The Greek states, *"the voyage being already dangerous."* They had passed the date on the calendar when it was safe to put out to sea. It was very risky to sail between September 14 and November 11. After this date, all sailing ceased for the winter. Luke, being a Jew, writes that the *fast* was now already past without explaining the expression. The *fast* refers to the Jewish Feast of Yom Kippur, so this tells us they were sailing the later part of September or the first part of October. If this happened during the year 59AD as supposed, the feast would have fallen on October 5th. *Paul kept warning* them not to sail.

"And said unto them, Sirs, I perceive that this voyage will be with hurt and much damage, not only of the lading and ship, but also of our lives." - Paul knew the times and the seasons of the sea very well, and he tells them several things that are going to happen:

* *The voyage will be hurt and much damage*
* *The cargo will be lost*
* *The possible loss of their lives*

Paul's Advice was Overruled

Acts 27:11-13 - *Nevertheless the centurion believed the master and the owner of the ship, more than those things which were spoken by Paul. And because the haven was not commodious to winter in, the more part advised to depart thence also, if by any means they might attain to Phenice, and there to winter; which is an haven of Crete, and lieth toward the south west and north west. And when the south wind blew softly, supposing that they had obtained their purpose, loosing thence, they sailed close by Crete.*

It isn't a surprise that the centurion had more respect for the opinion of the chief sailor and *the owner of the ship* than

Paul's opinion. His decision he would later regret. Because *Fair Havens* was vulnerable to the winter winds and storms, it was not the ideal place to wait out the coming season. The crew advised the ship captain to sail about 34 miles around the southwestern side of Crete to *Phenice*.

"And when the south wind blew softly, supposing that they had obtained their purpose, loosing thence, they sailed close by Crete." - The dangerous north winds shifted for a while, and they felt the soft breeze that blew from the south up from the coast of Africa, about 180 miles away. They stayed close to the shoreline as they went around the southern part of *Crete*.

THE STORM

Acts 27:14-16 - *But not long after there arose against it a tempestuous wind, called Euroclydon. And when the ship was caught, and could not bear up into the wind, we let her drive. And running under a certain island which is called Clauda, we had much work to come by the boat:*

The south wind turned out to be misleading, and there arose a *tempestuous,* or the Greek, *typhonikos* wind. It describes a storm that causes a severe whirling motion of both the clouds and the sea and is where we get our English word, *typhoon*. The reason the storm was called, *Euroclydon*, or *Euraquilo*, is because it is a compound word of both Greek and Latin origin. The *"Euro"* means *"east wind"* and the *"aquilo"* means *"northeast."* This kind of storm was so destructive that ancient sailors felt helpless and just *let her drive*. The ship was looking the monster storm in the face, but the ship could not face it well enough to get to *Phenice* and was blown off course about 25 miles southwest of *Crete* to the small island of *Clauda*, which is really spelled *Cauda*. The little boat, or skiff, that was normally pulled behind the large vessel was now hoisted up and taken onboard, but *with much difficulty*.

Attempt to Save the Ship

> **Acts 27:17-19 -** *Which when they had taken up, they used helps, undergirding the ship; and, fearing lest they should fall into the quicksands, strake sail, and so were driven. And we being exceedingly tossed with a tempest, the next day they lightened the ship; And the third day we cast out with our own hands the tackling of the ship.*

They used cables to undergird the ship to secure the timbers of the hull. There was a real danger that the storm could destroy the main body of the vessel. They just went with the wind to avoid the shallow waters ahead in a place called the *Great Syrtis*, which was a gulf between Crete and Africa where there were treacherous *sandbanks*. In the attempt to save the ship, they threw over the cargo and the ship's furniture. Their situation was desperate!

The Hopelessness of the Crew

> **Acts 27:20 -** *And when neither sun nor stars in many days appeared, and no small tempest lay on us, all hope that we should be saved was then taken away.*

The *sun and the stars* were what the sailors followed when out on the open seas. *When they could not see them for the overcast skies for many days, they became hopeless.* It helps to keep in mind that this was a large vessel with a large crew of 276 people. (**vs.37**)

PAUL RECEIVES A VISION AND OFFERS COMFORT

Acts 27:21-26 - *But after long abstinence Paul stood forth in the midst of them, and said, Sirs, ye should have hearkened unto me, and not have loosed from Crete, and to have gained this harm and loss. And now I exhort you to be of good cheer: for there shall be no loss of any man's life among you, but of the ship. For there stood by me this night the angel of God, whose I am, and whom I serve, Saying, Fear not, Paul; thou must be brought before Caesar: and, lo, God hath given thee all them that sail with thee. Wherefore, sirs, be of good cheer: for I believe God, that it shall be even as it was told me. Howbeit we must be cast upon a certain island.*

The crew had not eaten for a long time because of the scarcity of food, and most likely what food they had was in very poor condition by now. Paul, by telling them that they should have listened to him was not being pious or judgmental, but rather setting the stage for them to listen to him now.

"And now I exhort you to be of good cheer: for there shall be no loss of any man's life among you, but of the ship." - What a blessing to be in the midst of a storm and to have someone who really knows the Lord! Paul had received a direct message from God that their lives would be saved, but the voyage would be a complete financial loss, and the vessel would be lost.

"For there stood by me this night the angel of God, whose I am, and whom I serve, Saying, Fear not, Paul; thou must be brought before Caesar: and, lo, God hath given thee all them that sail with thee" - Like all of those who belong to Christ, *Paul had an angel to stand by him.* The *angel* told Paul that he would not die because he was to *stand before Caesar,* who was Nero. God had granted Paul's prayer that the lives of all of the crewmembers would be spared. Paul loved them all! When we are in trouble, what a comfort it is to know that some of God's saints are praying for us! Wherever we are and whatever we may face, we can have the assurance that God knows where we are!

"Wherefore, sirs, be of good cheer: for I believe God, that it shall be even as it was told me. Howbeit we must be cast upon a certain island." - This author loves the phrase *"I believe God, that it shall be even as it was told me."* This is the kind of faith that every child of God needs to have during times of trials, doubt, and confusion. The good news was that in light of Paul's new revelation, they should take courage because they would survive. Try to imagine the expressions on the faces of the men onboard! The bad news was that the vessel would run aground on an island, and the ship would be wrecked. The name of the island would not be given until later.

Drawing Near to Land

Acts 27:27-29 - *But when the fourteenth night was come, as we were driven up and down in Adria, about* *midnight the shipmen deemed that they drew near to some country; And sounded, and found it twenty fathoms: and when they had gone a little further, they sounded again, and found it fifteen fathoms. Then fearing lest we should have fallen upon rocks, they cast four anchors out of the stern, and wished for the day.*

They had been blown around the Mediterranean Sea for two full weeks, being driven up and down in ★ *Adria*. At *midnight, the shipmen* probably heard the sound of the big rocks and breakers that told them they were nearing land. They knew if they ran too close to land, the rocks could wreck the ship.

★ *(Adria is not the Adriatic Sea that lies between Italy and Greece, as some scholars have supposed. It is the middle of the Mediterranean Sea between Sicily on the west, Crete on the east, Cyrene to the south, and Italy on the north. It basically describes the very central part of the sea.)*

"And sounded, and found it twenty fathoms: and when they had gone a little further, they sounded again, and found it fifteen fathoms." – In ancient times they would throw a line overboard that had a lead plummet attached to its end to determine the depth of the water. At the first sounding, the water underneath the ship was 120 feet. At the second sounding, the water was 90 feet.

"Then fearing lest we should have fallen upon rocks, they cast four anchors out of the stern, and wished for the day." – To keep from running into the boulders, they cast four anchors out of the stern to literally stop the ship. It's interesting that the original word for *"wished"* here is *"euchonto,"* and it means *"to pray."* They kept on praying for daylight to come.

Some Sailors Try to Escape the Ship

Acts 27:30-32 - *And as the shipmen were about to flee out of the ship, when they had let down the boat into the sea, under colour as though they would have cast anchors out of the foreship, Paul said to the centurion and to the soldiers, Except these abide in the ship, ye cannot be saved. Then the soldiers cut off the ropes of the boat, and let her fall off.*

These men were thinking only to save themselves at the expense of everyone else. They were pretending, or *under colour*, to use the little boat to cast anchors. They started to let the boat down into the water when Paul spoke up and told the *centurion and the soldiers, "Except these abide in the ship, ye cannot be saved."* The crew had experienced so much that by this time, they trusted Paul. *The soldiers cut off the ropes* from the little boat, and it drifted out of sight. The sailors could only be saved if they stayed on the ship. This principle is still applied today along our Christian journey. God has promised the end of our journey will be heaven, but we must keep serving Him to receive a reward. Many believers jump ship when troubles come, and they never enjoy the full blessings.

Paul Encourages the Crew to Eat

Acts 27:33-38 - *And while the day was coming on, Paul besought them all to take meat, saying, This day is the fourteenth day that ye have tarried and continued fasting, having taken nothing. Wherefore*

I pray you to take some meat: for this is for your health: for there shall not an hair fall from the head of any of you. And when he had thus spoken, he took bread, and gave thanks to God in presence of them all: and when he had broken it, he began to eat. Then were they all of good cheer, and they also took some meat. And we were in all in the ship two hundred threescore and sixteen souls. And when they had eaten enough, they lightened the ship, and cast out the wheat into the sea.

In the original wording, Paul was persistent in admonishing the crewmembers to eat. They had been *fasting for fourteen days,* and they needed to eat something for their physical salvation. *"For there shall not an hair fall from the head of any of you"* is a phrase that is used several times in the Holy Bible, and even by Jesus our Lord. **(I Sam.14:45, 2 Sam.14:11, I Kings 1:52, Luke 21:18)**

"And when he had thus spoken, he took bread, and gave thanks to God in presence of them all: and when he had broken it, he began to eat. Then were they all of good cheer, and they also took some meat." – Paul set the example himself *by taking bread and giving thanks to God in the presence of them all.* This was a Jewish practice, and the sailors aboard could feel the peace of God. What Paul did caused them to eat as well. As followers of Christ, we must always be sensitive to the fact that many people are watching us, and we need to be the example in our conduct and behavior, especially during times of trial.

"And we were in all in the ship two hundred threescore and sixteen souls. And when they had eaten enough, they lightened

the ship, and cast out the wheat into the sea." – Luke includes himself in the 276 aboard the ship. Having eaten enough to be satisfied, they *lightened the ship* even further by *casting the wheat into the sea*. The purpose was to raise the ship in the water so that it would run up farther on the beach.

THE SHIP RUNS AGROUND

Acts 27:39-41 - *And when it was day, they knew not the land: but they discovered a certain creek with a shore, into the which they were minded, if it were possible, to thrust in the ship. And when they had taken up the anchors, they committed themselves unto the sea, and loosed the rudder bands, and hoised up the mainsail to the wind, and made toward shore. And falling into a place where two seas met, they ran the ship aground; and the forepart stuck fast, and remained unmoveable, but the hinder part was broken with the violence of the waves.*

The sailors tried to recognize the land, but they could not see it well. They saw a *creek*, or bay, that might have enough water to *drive the ship into* to move them closer to the shore. They disconnected the ship from the *four anchors and let the ropes fall into the sea. They loosed the ropes from the rudders and raised up the mainsail to give them speed.* They *made toward shore*, or they began aiming the ship steadily toward the creek.

"*And falling into a place where two seas met, they ran the ship aground; and the forepart stuck fast, and remained unmoveable, but the hinder part was broken with the violence of the waves."* - There was a reef that created two strong opposing currents with deep water on each side of the reef. Unexpectedly, they *ran the ship into the ground and the front of the ship was stuck*. The *violence* of the breakwater *waves* was destroying *the hinder part of the ship*.

They All Escape to the Shore

Acts 27:42-44 - *And the soldiers' counsel was to kill the prisoners, lest any of them should swim out, and escape. But the centurion, willing to save Paul, kept them from their purpose; and commanded that they which could swim should cast themselves first into the sea, and get to land: And the rest, some on boards, and some on broken pieces of the ship. And so it came to pass, that they escaped all safe to land.*

The reason why the *soldiers* wanted to *kill the prisoners* was they knew if any of the prisoners escaped, the *soldiers* would be killed. It's a beautiful thing that God gave Paul favor in the eyes of the Roman *centurion*.

The centurion was *willing to save Paul* and stopped the soldiers from killing the prisoners. *He commanded that the ones who could swim to jump into the sea, and the ones who could not swim to float on broken boards, or other broken pieces of the ship.* The result was they all made it safely just as the angel had told Paul in **verses 22-23.**

CHAPTER TWENTY-EIGHT

LANDING ON THE ISLAND OF MALTA

Acts 28:1-2 - *And when they were escaped, then they knew that the island was called Melita. And the barbarous people shewed us no little kindness: for they kindled a fire, and received us every one, because of the present rain, and because of the cold.*

They were familiar with the island of ★ *Melita*, or *Malta*, but not from the side of the island they landed. Most all of the traffic came to the island from the other side.

★ *(Melita comes from the Phoenician language and it means "escape or refuge." Through the conquering nations of Greece and Rome, it was later named Malta. It is a part of a cluster of small islands that lie between Sicily and Africa. Today there is a place on the island called "St. Paul's Bay," or "Selmunett," and it is the largest town in the northern region.)*

The people that lived on the island in Paul's time were called *"barbarous people,"* not because they were savages, but because they didn't speak Latin or Greek. They probably spoke the Phoenician dialect. The people there showed *unusual kindness* to the new visitors. Even people who do not know Christ can sometimes show kindness because the stamp of God's creation is upon all men. They *kindled a fire and received everyone*. The weather was early winter, already getting *cold, and it was pouring rain*. The original Greek describes it as *the rain that stood upon them*.

Paul Bitten by a Viper

> **Acts 28:3-6 -** *And when Paul had gathered a bundle of sticks, and laid them on the fire, there came a viper out of the heat, and fastened on his hand. And when the barbarians saw the venomous beast hang on his hand, they said among themselves, No doubt this man is a murderer, whom, though he hath escaped the sea, yet vengeance suffereth not to live. And he shook off the beast into the fire, and felt no harm. Howbeit they looked when he should have swollen, or fallen down dead suddenly: but after they had looked a great while, and saw no harm come to him, they changed their minds, and said that he was a god.*

Paul, being the servant that he was, *gathered sticks to put on the fire*. In spite of the cold weather, the warm fire revived a *viper* enough that it ★ *fastened onto the hand of Paul*. The barbarians concluded that the reason why the *viper* bit Paul was *because he was a* ★ *murderer*. Though they knew that this species of viper was venomous, Paul *shook the serpent off into the fire and felt no harm*. After they looked at Paul for a time expecting him to die, *they changed their minds and said that he was a* ★ *god*.

★ *(Paul not dying by the viper is a fulfillment of* **Mark 16:18** *- "They shall take up serpents; and if they drink any deadly thing, it shall not hurt them; they shall lay hands on the sick, and they shall recover." We need to interpret the scriptures from a dispensational perspective and see a progression in the New Testament. Some have interpreted this verse in Mark's gospel to say that we are supposed to handle snakes today. Many have lost their lives to such ignorance. There are also strong traditions that say the preaching of Paul caused the serpent to try killing him, but the Lord took the venom away. It wasn't so much that nothing could stop Paul, but that nothing could stop God's promise from being fulfilled in Paul's life.)*

★ *(These island people believed that because Paul was a prisoner, he was a murderer. Even though he escaped from the storm on the sea, the pagan goddess for justice, "Dikee," would prevail.)*

★ *(Paul had been called "a god" back in* **Acts 14:11-12** *when he healed a lame man in Lystra.)*

Paul Heals the Father of Publius

Acts 28:7-10 - *In the same quarters were possessions of the chief man of the island, whose name was Publius; who received us, and lodged us three days courteously. And it came to pass, that the father of Publius lay sick of a fever and of a bloody flux: to whom Paul entered in, and prayed, and laid his hands on him, and healed him. So when this was done, others also, which had diseases in the island, came, and were healed: Who also honoured us with many honours; and when we departed, they laded us with such things as were necessary.*

In the neighborhood were lands that belonged to *Publius, the chief man of the island*. *Publius* was his Greek name showing that his nationality was Greek, but he may have represented Rome on the island. Notice that Luke uses the plural pronoun *us* twice in one verse. *Paul, Luke,* and *Aristarchus* were together for a short season of spiritual relief and encouragement.

"And it came to pass, that the father of Publius lay sick of a fever and of a bloody flux:" - This was an illness called *"Maltese Fever"* that was caused by a microorganism in the milk of Maltese goats. It was characterized by recurrent fever and dysentery. *Publius'* father had the disease that caused severe diarrhea with blood passing through his bowels.

"to whom Paul entered in, and prayed, and laid his hands on him, and healed him." - Once again Paul showed his apostolic authority by being able to heal this man. Normally this particular disease would last for months and could lead to physical death. When Paul *prayed and laid hands on him*, instantly the fever and dysentery were gone.

"So when this was done, others also, which had diseases in the island, came, and were healed: Who also honoured us with many honours; and when we departed, they laded us with such things as were necessary." - When God used Paul to heal *Publius'* father, the other people on the island who had diseases came to Paul. For the entire period they were on the island, people kept coming to Paul to be healed. Here we see Luke, a physician himself, **(Colossians 4:14)** recording the true miracles that were done by the apostle Paul. No doubt he was involved in caring for the people as well. Because the natives of the island were so thankful, they provided all that was needed for the remainder of their journey to Rome.

PAUL SETS SAIL FOR ROME

> **Acts 28:11-15** - *And after three months we departed in a ship of Alexandria, which had wintered in the isle, whose sign was Castor and Pollux. And landing at Syracuse, we tarried there three days. And from thence we fetched a compass, and came to Rhegium: and after one day the south wind blew, and we came the next day to Puteoli: Where we found brethren, and were desired to tarry with them seven days: and so we went toward Rome. And from thence, when the brethren heard of us, they came to meet us as far as Appii forum, and The three taverns: whom when Paul saw, he thanked God, and took courage.*

They spent three months on the island of Malta while waiting for the winter to end. This would have covered a period from November to February. Navigation opened up again, and Paul and his company set sail going northward to Rome.

"ship of Alexandria" - This was another grain freighter from *Alexandria* and possibly from the same fleet as in **Acts 27:6.**

"whose sign was Castor and Pollux." - In Roman mythology, *Castor and Pollux* were the twins born of Zeus and Leda. They were the patron gods of the sea mariners who they believed were responsible for the care of them through the storms at sea. Their images were often painted or carved on each side of the front of the ship. Isn't it astounding that one of the greatest Christians who ever lived, who would help to turn the world upside down for Christ, is being taken to Rome aboard a pagan ship. When God does not rule a situation, He overrules to accomplish His purpose.

"And landing at Syracuse, we tarried there three days." – Their first stop from Malta was 80 miles north to the eastern coast of Sicily to the town of *Syracuse*. Not only was it the capital of Sicily, it was one of the most beautiful cities in the ancient world. This could possibly be one of the reasons why they *tarried there three days.*

"And from thence we fetched a compass, and came to Rhegium: and after one day the south wind blew, and we came the next day to Puteoli: Where we found brethren, and were desired to tarry with them seven days: and so we went toward Rome." – They went from Syracuse 70 miles due north to *Rhegium*, which was on the very tip of the boot of Italy. They had a nice southern wind to blow that helped them to travel some 200 miles north on the western side of Italy to the city of *Puteoli*. It was located on the north shore of the Bay of Naples and was the main seaport of southern Italy for grain and the gateway to Rome. There was a church there, and Paul and Luke *found brethren* there. Apparently, the centurion had learned to trust Paul by now and allowed them *seven days* of fellowship before leaving for Rome, some 130 miles away.

"And from thence, when the brethren heard of us, they came to meet us as far as Appii forum, and The three taverns: whom when Paul saw, he thanked God, and took courage." –

The believers in Rome had received Paul's letter a few years before, so they probably felt as though they already knew him. The gospel had already reached Rome from the people who had been at the Feast of Pentecost in **Acts 2:10.** Since Rome was not a seaport city, they had to walk along the stone-paved roads to Rome. The Appian Way was one of the earliest military roads that started in 312BC. Paul had brethren to meet him about 40 miles southeast of Rome at the *Market of Appius,* or *Forum Appii*. The second meeting took place at *The three taverns,* or *Tres Tabernae,* that was approximately 30 miles southeast of Rome. These believers escorting Paul made a great impact on Paul; *he thanked God and took courage.*

Paul Arrives at Rome

> **Acts 28:16 -** *And when we came to Rome, the centurion delivered the prisoners to the captain of the guard: but Paul was suffered to dwell by himself with a soldier that kept him.*

It is possible that Julius *the centurion delivered the prisoners to the captain of the guard,* who was at that time *Burrus the Prefect of the Praetorian Guard.* He served in that position from 51-62AD.

The promise of Jesus was fulfilled; Paul made it to Rome. **(Acts 23:11)** Over 2,000 miles from his homeland of Israel, Paul would be one of the influential believers who would be instrumental in the gospel of Christ forever changing the course of history. Julius the centurion must have felt a huge relief to know that his prisoners had made it safely from Caesarea with much help from Paul. Paul was allowed to *dwell by himself* with a Roman guard who changed shift every few hours. Paul used this opportunity to witness to the Roman guards and others about the precious message of Jesus. Notice these words:

> *So that my bonds in Christ are manifest in all the palace, and in all other places.* **Philippians 1:13**

PAUL APPEALS TO THE JEWISH COMMUNITY

Acts 28:17-20 - *And it came to pass, that after three days Paul called the chief of the Jews together: and when they were come together, he said unto them, Men and brethren, though I have committed nothing against the people, or customs of our fathers, yet was I delivered prisoner from Jerusalem into the hands of the Romans. Who, when they had examined me, would have let me go, because there was no cause of death in me. But when the Jews spake against it, I was constrained to appeal unto Caesar; not that I had ought to accuse my nation of. For this cause therefore have I called for you, to see you, and to speak with you: because that for the hope of Israel I am bound with this chain.*

It took Paul only *three days* to have a meeting with the leader of the Jews in Rome. Paul continued to obey God's command to go to the Jew first. Being so far from his homeland, Paul still wanted them to know that they were *his brethren and he had not forsaken Israel.* He was not *accusing the nation of Israel* of anything. Paul summarizes that *he was not guilty of any crime under the Jewish law or under the Roman law, and yet, he was brought to Rome as a prisoner.* He wanted them to know that he was *bound with chains because of his faith in Jesus as Israel's Messiah, the hope of Israel.*

It would be only a few short years until Rome would level Jerusalem to the ground in 70AD, and the Jewish people would realize that Jesus was the fulfillment of the Old Testament promises to Israel.

THE JEWISH LEADERS RESPOND

Acts 28:21-22 - *And they said unto him, We neither received letters out of Judaea concerning thee, neither any of the brethren that came shewed or spake any harm of thee. But we desire to hear of thee what thou thinkest: for as concerning this sect, we know that every where it is spoken against.*

These Jewish leaders had heard of Paul, but *they had not received any letters from Judea accusing him.* This also shows that none of the Jewish leaders who hated Paul in Jerusalem had followed him to Rome. Even though they had heard negative reaction from the Messianic Jewish movement, *the sect called The Way, they wanted to hear what Paul thought.*

THE JEWISH COMMUNITY HEARS THE GOSPEL FROM PAUL

Acts 28:23-24 - *And when they had appointed him a day, there came many to him into his lodging; to whom he expounded and testified the kingdom of*

> *God, persuading them concerning Jesus, both out of the law of Moses, and out of the prophets, from morning till evening. And some believed the things which were spoken, and some believed not.*

The way the original wording reads here is that Paul went into detail expounding about *the kingdom of God.* Because he was speaking to a Jewish audience inside the place where he lodged, he explained why the physical kingdom of God was not established when Jesus came the first time. The kingdom was *spiritual* now, and God ruled in the hearts of those who embraced His Son Jesus. One day the kingdom of God will come *physically* when Jesus returns the second time. He took *the Law of Moses and the prophets* and showed them that Jesus had to be the Messiah of Israel. Paul preached *from morning till evening.* What a sermon that must have been! The message of the kingdom of God was never presented to unsaved Gentiles, but to unsaved and saved Jews.

"And some believed the things which were spoken, and some believed not." - No matter how clear the message of Christ is presented from the sacred scriptures, there will always be those who believe and those who do not believe. Concerning the Jews, we must remember that a *partial blindness* has been placed upon Israel until the fullness of the Gentiles be come in. **(Romans 11:25)**

Paul Explains the Rejection of the Gospel

> **Acts 28:25-27** - *And when they agreed not among themselves, they departed, after that Paul had spoken*

one word, Well spake the Holy Ghost by Esaias the prophet unto our fathers, Saying, Go unto this people, and say, Hearing ye shall hear, and shall not understand; and seeing ye shall see, and not perceive: For the heart of this people is waxed gross, and their ears are dull of hearing, and their eyes have they closed; lest they should see with their eyes, and hear with their ears, and understand with their heart, and should be converted, and I should heal them.

While Paul was certainly disappointed that some did not believe, he rejoiced in those who did. He gave the reason why some rejected the gospel. Paul referred to the time of Isaiah, the prophet that proved a *dual authorship* of the scriptures. The Divine Author was the Holy Spirit, and he used Isaiah to write these words down. What was true with Isaiah's generation was also true with Paul's generation.

This author finds this passage absolutely astounding. Paul is quoting a passage from **Isaiah 6:9-10,** and our Lord Jesus used the very same passage when referring to the unbelief in His day. This shows that God's Holy Word was written down centuries ago and still applies to people in every generation:

That the saying of Esaias the prophet might be fulfilled, which he spake, Lord, who hath believed our report? and to whom hath the arm of the Lord been revealed? Therefore they could not believe, because that Esaias said again, He hath blinded their eyes, and hardened their heart; that they should not see with their eyes, nor understand with their heart, and be converted, and I should heal them. These things said Esaias, when he saw his glory, and spake of him. **John 12:38-41**

Paul Will Take the Message to the Gentiles

Acts 28:28-29 - *Be it known therefore unto you, that the salvation of God is sent unto the Gentiles, and that they will hear it. And when he had said these words, the Jews departed, and had great reasoning among themselves.*

Because some of the Jews did not accept Christ did not make the gospel of ill effect. *God's salvation would be sent to the Gentiles.* When we preach the gospel of Christ today, we are a *savour of life* to those who receive Christ, and we are the *savour of death* to those who reject Him. **(2 Cor.2:16)**

God had not forfeited His covenants or His plan for Israel, but the unbelief of Israel would give the Gentiles a chance to hear the gospel. God's mysterious plan is greater than our minds can conceive. He knew when to send Jesus into the world so the gospel would be received by a remnant of Jews to start the church. The gospel would be rejected by the religious leaders of Israel and be sent to the Gentiles. **(Carefully study Romans 9-11)**

Paul Spends Two More Years in Rome

Acts 28:30-31 - *And Paul dwelt two whole years in his own hired house, and received all that came*

in unto him, Preaching the kingdom of God, and teaching those things which concern the Lord Jesus Christ, with all confidence, no man forbidding him.

There were many who heard the gospel of the *Lord Jesus Christ* from Paul during those two years. Paul was not hindered even though he was a prisoner; he was still given the freedom to live in *his own accommodations*. God did not waste Paul's time even during the time he was waiting to present his case before Nero. Paul wrote four of his epistles during these two years that have continued to influence the world: *Ephesians, Philippians, Colossians, and Philemon.* When it comes to the kingdom of God, may it be said of each one of us as followers of Jesus,

"and they continued."

EXTRA BIBLICAL RESOURCES OF PAUL & PETER

The book of Acts came to an end without telling us what really happened to the apostle Paul. While the works of historians and early Christian writers are not on the same level as the inspired Word of God, sometimes they can help us fill in some of the details and background without contradicting the sacred text. When we study the writings of such men as Clement, Tertullian, Irenaeus, Tacitus, Josephus, Eusebius, and Jerome, we find some interesting facts and dates.

Clement of Rome, who served as their first bishop from 88-99AD, wrote that Paul endured <u>two</u> imprisonments between 62-67AD, and that he was released by the Emperor Nero the first time. During this five-year interval, Paul wrote I Timothy and Titus. Paul was expecting to be released from his first imprisonment according to **Philippians 1:19, 25-26, 2:24, Philemon 22.** *At that time Demas was with him.* **(Philemon 24, Colossians 4:14)** *During the first imprisonment in Rome, Paul came in contact with Epaphras* **(Philemon 23),** *Onesimus* **(Philemon 10),** *and Epaphroditus who visited Paul and brought gifts to Philippi.* **(Philippians 4:18)**

There are a few events mentioned in the ministry of Paul that are <u>not</u> recorded in the book of Acts:

2 Timothy 4:20 - *Paul left Trophimus sick in Miletus.*
2 Timothy 4:13 - *Paul left his cloak, books, and parchment at Troas.*
2 Timothy 4:10 - *Paul was forsaken later by Demas.*
2 Timothy 4:6-8 - *Paul wrote that he was expecting to die.*
Titus 1:5 - *Paul ministered in Crete.*
Romans 15:24-28 - *Paul possibly went to Spain.*

It is believed that after about four to five years of travel, Paul was again arrested the second time in 67AD and taken back to Rome to face trial. It was during this second imprisonment that he wrote the book of 2 Timothy.

Clement of Rome, Dionysius of Corinth, Tertullian, Gaius, Origen, and Eusebius all wrote that Paul was martyred under the Emperor Nero. Since Paul was a Roman citizen, he was not crucified, but beheaded. The most satisfactory date for the death of Paul is the month of June in 67AD. Since Paul was born in the year 5AD, this would make him 62 when he died.

Christian friends took the body of Paul and buried him up the road to the second mile marker on the Ostian Way. It was during the fourth century that Paul's remains were moved into a marble sarcophagus and buried in the church's crypt that bears his name. The tombstone reads:

PAULO APOSTOLO MART (Latin for Paul Apostle Martyr)

The book of Acts focuses so much on the ministry of Peter and Paul. It is recorded by the Roman historian Tacitus that Simon Peter was martyred by the Emperor Nero during "the great persecution" in 64AD. Peter, being a Jew and not a Roman citizen as Paul, was crucified upside down in the month of October in 64AD. His tomb is supposedly under St. Peter's Basilica in Rome. His remains have not been confirmed. An ossuary was found in Jerusalem on the Mount of Olives in 1953 in a Jewish Christian cemetery with the inscription, "Simon the son of Jonah." It's possible that Peter's bones were brought back to Jerusalem, or it could be the bones of another person by the same name.

A NOTE FROM THE EDITORS

In this book, Carroll's commentary continues Luke's writings of the gospel from a Hebraic perspective. His research includes the history, political status, and economic affairs of the time period.

An important topic covered includes the first written history of the Christian church. The apostle Paul was a major player in the Christian movement to other parts of the world, starting with the Jews and then to the Gentiles, through travels as a Christian missionary. Traveling thousands of miles by sail was an arduous task, as well as the walking Paul did from city to city to spread the gospel. If every Christian was as committed to spreading the Word and saving the lost as much as Paul, what a different world we would be living in.

Carroll expounds upon an array of topics in this book, some of which include: the ascension of Jesus into heaven; choosing the disciple to replace Judas; the arrest of Peter and John in the Temple of Jerusalem; the sin of Ananias and Sapphira; the stoning of Stephen; Phillip's meeting with the enuch, which led to his baptism; Paul's conversion on the road to Damascus; Peter's contact with the Roman centurion, Cornelius; Paul's imprisonment in Rome.

In 2019, we had the pleasure of traveling with Carroll and Donna to Italy where we visited the prison in Rome where Paul was imprisoned.

Carroll has done a thorough research regarding events in the book of Acts, and this commentary will be an asset and a blessing to anyone yearning to have a more in-depth understanding of the Lord's gospel.

Virginia and Glenn Duggin
Editors